GUIDE TO LAW SCHOOLS IN CANADA

Please Note:

The McGill University Law School offers both Civil and Common Law Degrees, and should therefore be listed under both Civil and Common Law Sections in the Table of Contents. For information on both programs, please refer to page 90.

Guide to Law Schools in Canada

Catherine Purcell

ECW PRESS

1992

CANADIAN CATALOGUING IN PUBLICATION DATA

Purcell, Catherine
    Guide to law schools in Canada

ISBN 1-55022-160-4

1. Law education – Canada – Directories.
1. Title.

KE289.P87 1992   340'.071'171   C92-095192-9
KF266.P87 1992

Design and imaging by ECW Type & Art, Oakville, Ontario.
Printed and bound by Webcom, Toronto, Ontario.
Distributed by General Publishing Co. Limited, 30 Lesmill Road,
Don Mills, Ontario M3B 2T6.

Published by ECW PRESS, 1980 Queen Street East, 2nd floor, Toronto, Ontario M4L 1J2

CONTENTS

ACKNOWLEDGEMENTS

I would like to thank all the students who so willingly talked to someone they had never met and gave an hour of their time talking about their experiences. I appreciate their honest and open conversations. I would also like to thank the Deans, Chairs of Admissions Committee, and other administrative personnel for their co-operation and input.

From a personal standpoint, I would like to thank the people who encouraged me and believed in me — my parents; my good friends David Cannon and Elaine Bradley; and my Director Jim Kelly. Special thanks to my husband Michael who acted as my sounding board and spent hours working on the graphics for the book, and my children, Brendan and David, for their patience and understanding.

Introduction

The purpose of this book is to help people considering a Law degree to differentiate between schools and to answer common questions regarding the Law degree. The Law schools are not ranked. Instead, the emphasis is placed on what is unique about each one and where the school's strengths and weaknesses lie. Comparisons among the schools are made in the "Comparative Statistics on Canadian Law Schools" chapter, and special characteristics are highlighted in the "Unique Characteristics" chapter.

The dean of the law faculty (except for Université de Moncton), the chair of the admissions committee, and a minimum of eight students from each school were interviewed to gain a balanced perspective. A selection of quotations from the students interviewed is included in each university's chapter.

The dean was asked:

- what his/her vision of the program was
- what was unique about the program and its strengths and weaknesses
- how the law school was coping with increasing financial restraints.

The chair of the admissions committee was asked:

- to fill out a questionnaire and to release the Committee for Law Admissions Statistics Services and Innovations (CLASSI) statistics
- to describe the process of admission for the various categories of admission
- if an admissions formula was used, and how it was used
- to describe what misconceptions or myths they had encountered when talking to applicants.

The students were asked:

- what they felt the program's strengths were
- where they felt the program could improve
- what controversies, if any, were students or faculty involved in at the law school

- what advice they would give to students considering a law degree
- what it was like to live in the city as a student.

The following information is based on the interviews of the administration of each law school in Canada and over 160 student interviews. However, the following interpretations of the law programs are based on my opinion and students should conduct their own research which should include consulting university calendars, as the information is subject to change.

ABOUT THE STUDENTS INTERVIEWED

An effort was made to select students to represent the points of view of both men and women, minority groups, mature students, and those coming directly from a CEGEP or undergraduate studies. Students from first, second, and third years of the program were interviewed as well as two articling students. Please be advised that the names used to identify the students quoted are *not* their real names. Pseudonyms have been used to respect their anonymity. A few students were selected by the administration in accordance with the above mentioned criteria and the rest of the students were selected by the referral of a fellow student — someone they did not know well — in order to get as broad a sample as possible. Some students that were interviewed are not quoted at all at their request, but were used for background information.

The descriptions of the cities where law schools are located are a composite of the perceptions held by the students interviewed.

ABOUT THE STATISTICS

CLASSI statistics, which were released by each common law school, were used in the following chapters. Additional statistics for the common law schools, and all of the statistics for the civil law schools, were obtained directly from the law school. All statistics are based on the class of 1991-92, except for the tuition and application fees which are 1992-93 figures. The statistical profile of each school includes information ranging from the educational requirements to other related programs offered by that university. If a category does not appear, it is because the information was not available. The statistics have been provided to be used only as a guide.

Ten Myths Surrounding the Law Degree

1. A LAW DEGREE IS THE TICKET TO MONETARY SUCCESS

Money and power can be had by working for large corporate firms in downtown metropolitan areas such as Calgary, Montreal, Toronto, and Vancouver. However, relatively few students are given this opportunity since these firms traditionally hire only the top graduating students (see below under number seven for further information on the grading system).

For students entering private practice, it takes several years of hard work to establish a practice and make a salary in the $40,000 to $50,000 range. After completing at least two years of an undergraduate degree (for common law schools), three years of law school and up to one year of articling, plus bar exam expenses, many students have incurred substantial debt from student loans. A first-year lawyer can make anywhere from $20,000 to $50,000 depending on the size of the firm and the geographic location. There are many other professions where you could make more than this after five or six years.

Unemployment among graduating law students is also a factor. Articling positions are becoming harder to find. The legal profession is linked to the performance of the economy. For example, bankruptcy and family law are more in demand when the economy is on a downturn, whereas oil and gas law is at a low.

2. THE UNIVERSITY YOU GET YOUR UNDERGRADUATE DEGREE IN MAKES A DIFFERENCE

It is better to have good grades at any university than to have poor to average grades at what is perceived to be the best school. For students with very good grades and a good LSAT score, the university they attend is irrelevant. If you are applying under the regular admissions category at most universities, the admissions process is usually a mechanical exercise sometimes expedited by an admissions formula based primarily on grade point average (GPA) and the Law School Admissions Test (LSAT) score. The University of Windsor and The University of Calgary would be the biggest exceptions to this process.

However, if an applicant's grades and LSAT score are slightly below the average admissions criteria, then they fall into the "grey zone" where there is little differentiation between the applicants seeking to fill the last few places. Admissions personnel are human and they probably do have their preferences of universities based on the past performance of people admitted or impressions they have formed over the years. There is no way to know which schools they prefer so it is a waste of time trying to second guess this. Other factors can make as much of a difference in a close decision. An illegible form, a poorly thought-out personal statement, or poor references play a more important role.

3. GETTING INTO LAW SCHOOL IS THE HARDEST PART

This is true in the case of common law schools because they do their most stringent weeding out during the admissions process. The academic requirements are more demanding for the common law schools in that they require a minimum of two years of undergraduate study and most require three. The transition from undergraduate to law school will still be difficult since the context and way of learning is different and it takes time to adapt. However, the calibre of students is high and support systems, such as remedial tutoring and academic advising are more prevalent today than in the past. The attrition rate in common law schools is very low.

On the other hand, getting into law school is not the hardest part for most civil law schools; staying in the program is. The attrition rate from first to second year in civil law schools can sometimes be up to one-third of the incoming class. At least half of the student bodies in civil law schools, and sometimes significantly higher, come into law school directly from a CEGEP. Eighteen or nineteen is very young to start such an intensive program as law where maturity and discipline are required.

4. ALL OF THE COURSES LISTED IN THE CALENDAR WILL BE OFFERED

Think of the courses listed in law school calendars as potential offerings. Whether they are offered or not depends on many factors such as which professors are on sabbatical, the interest expressed by the students in a particular course, or, in the case of a moot course or a course involving a legal aid practicum, whether there are sufficient funds available. Furthermore, in upper years, even if the course is offered, sometimes students schedules are decided by lottery, balloting, or a selection process based on grades, or an interview.

Selecting a school based solely on the course offerings could be a disappointing exercise.

5. STUDENTS WILL CONTINUE TO GET THE SAME GOOD GRADES THEY ARE USED TO

The marking systems of law schools are based on the bell curve, making it impossible for more than a few students to get the good grades that were necessary for them to get into law school. This is very difficult for a lot of students to accept.

The method of evaluation is also radically different from undergraduate studies. With the exception of University of Calgary and Université Laval, law schools evaluate an entire course by a three-hour, one hundred per cent final. In first year, some law schools ease students into one hundred percent finals by giving mid-term exams which could be worth as little as twenty percent or up to forty percent depending on whether they do better or worse respectively on the final exam. In upper year seminar courses students may be evaluated on the basis of research papers or projects in place of, or in addition to, final exams. However, the majority of their grade will come from one source.

6. THE "L.A. LAW" IMAGE OF LAW IS REALITY

The media portrays the practice of law as being more thrilling than what it is. In reality, it is quite routine with only a few moments of excitement thrown in. Lawyers rarely deal with cosmic social issues. If you want to alter society, a law degree won't hurt, but it is not necessary.

L.A. Law, Matlock, and others portray lawyers in court the majority of time. In reality, approximately ten percent of a lawyer's time is spent in court. The objective of the law is to keep out of court. The adversarial process in the court room has a higher profile, but most of a lawyer's time is spent in the planning stages trying to avoid a fight.

In the movie Paper Chase, the media portrays law school as a cut-throat race to the finish, and L.A. Law romanticizes the practice of law. Neither view is true. Law school is a consuming experience followed by what can be an even more consuming profession. Take advantage of the breadth of opportunities an undergraduate degree provides you with. If you are tired of being in school and you are interested in pursuing another career first, do it. Law school will wait. In fact, the number of older students taking law as a second career is increasing. Come to law school when you are ready. The more, rather than the less experience you have, the more enriching the experience will be. There is no hurry to get on the treadmill so soon.

7. YOU CAN SPECIALIZE IN A CERTAIN AREA OF THE LAW, FOR EXAMPLE, CRIMINAL OR INTERNATIONAL LAW

Specializations in law school usually consist of only two or three courses. A law degree is a bachelor's degree with a mandate to give a good general education. You might be able to take one or two courses in an area but this is hardly a specialization. At some schools you can do a cluster of courses; for example, University of British Columbia has an Asian law cluster, McGill University has air and space law, and at Osgoode Hall Law School there are several criminal courses, but you actually specialize when you practise.

Many people come into law with a strong idea of what type of law they want to study, but they often change their mind many times during their three years of study.

Participating in a moot court (an appeal of a hypothetical case), or getting involved in legal aid and representing clients in traffic court can give you a good opportunity to decide if you want to be a litigator or a solicitor.

8. THERE IS A PRE-LAW PROGRAM

There is no such thing as a pre-law program at any undergraduate university in Canada. Law faculties encourage applicants to take any program that they are interested in. If you want to prepare, then develop your reading skills, read a wide variety of books, and perhaps take a course in logic where your analytical skills will be enhanced.

9. LAW SCHOOLS ARE HIGHLY COMPETITIVE WHERE STUDENTS CUT PAGES OUT OF BOOKS AND HIDE KEY RESOURCES

To the outside world, law schools are competitive, but to the students in the program, they are not. Natural competitiveness occurs as a result of the selection criteria used that puts so much emphasis on grades. In order to get into law school, students have to be overachievers and they are used to receiving A's. Law school then forces the students, all of whom are very bright, to compete among themselves by making only so many A's available on the bell curve. There are always a small number of students who are intensely competitive, but they are in the minority. Most law students form study groups and willingly share notes.

10. A LAW DEGREE IS A VERY PRACTICAL DEGREE THAT WILL GET ME A JOB

Law school does not purport to teach their students how to be lawyers. It is not a training school. Only a handful of courses deal with practical hands-on lawyering. However, of the law schools in Canada, there is a range of law schools that are more practical or more theoretical than others. For example, Université de Sherbooke and the University of Calgary might be considered two of the more practical law schools whereas the University of Alberta might be considered to have a more theoretical slant.

Not all graduates of law school practise law. Other possible career paths include legal research, legal librarianship, legal publishing, academic teaching, legal drafting, public legal education, and others. One can also practise law for the government and corporations as well as in private law firms.

Major Trends in Law

DIVERSITY

The student profile in law schools is gradually changing from one that was traditionally white, upper middle class to one that is more racially diverse. In part, this is a result of the proactive educating that young minority group law professors and communities have begun. They are trying to point out the need for the profession to be more representative of the people they serve. The Law School Admission Council is attempting to support this movement by serving as a vehicle for discussion at conferences and by helping to defray the costs of the Program of Legal Studies for Native People at the University of Saskatchewan. These efforts are being supplemented by the work of a group of Canadian law professors actively engaged in developing strategies and support programs to assist minority applicants and minority law students.

There is evidence that we are making advances in this area, although slowly. An increasing number of law schools are offering admission categories which target aboriginal people. The number of aboriginal law students is still small in relation to the aboriginal population, but it has improved significantly. In 1976, four aboriginal students graduated from law schools. In 1991, the total aboriginal law school alumni consisted of 163 graduates. An additional thirty aboriginal students may graduate in 1992. For additional information, please refer to the following chapter on *Aboriginal People and Legal Education*. Modest progress has been made with respect to access for other racial minorities, although with one or two exceptions, there are no special access programs as targeted for them as are the aboriginal programs.

Women were once a minority presence in law schools also. This too has changed to the point where women represent almost half the law student population and significantly higher than half in the French civil and common law programs. The next challenge is academia, where women are still a minority presence, and increasing the retention of women in the legal profession. Please refer to Graph 1 on *Percentage of Women in Tenured Faculty Positions by University as of 1991-92*, and to "Career Dissatisfaction of Women in the Legal Profession" in this chapter.

AN INTERDISCIPLINARY APPROACH
TO THE STUDY OF LAW

The study of law is becoming interdisciplinary. Faculties of Law are starting to take the approach of studying law in its social, historical, and economic context, rather than as an entity unto itself. The University of British Columbia, Dalhousie University, University of Saskatchewan, and University of Toronto are a few of the law faculties that have introduced an interdisciplinary "Bridge Program" into their curriculum. Topics such as history of law, economics of law, women and the law, and aboriginal law are some of the issues under discussion.

Faculties of Law are hiring more professors with cross appointments in Philosophy, Social Work, Economics, and Environmental Science. A few faculties are making it easier for law students to take courses outside of the faculty of law. In fact, at Université Laval, three credits outside of the faculty of law are a mandatory part of the curriculum.

GROWING CONTROVERSIES AMONG STUDENTS
AND FACULTY IN LAW SCHOOLS

Perhaps as a result of the increasing diversification of student bodies and a more theoretical study of the law which recognizes the impact of women, culture, history, and economics on the law, students are being forced to question how they perceive the role of the law. They are no longer a homogeneous group that is taught only the rules and process of the law. This has created controversies at all English common law schools in Canada around issues of gender, race, language, and politics. Older established faculty members who were educated in the more traditional concept of law are now having to adjust to a new style.

Transition for both students and faculty is often fraught with conflict to the point where, at some schools, students feel that it creates an atmosphere that takes away from their education. For this reason, the chapters on each law school include a section for students to talk about the controversies they believe to exist at their school. A section on the character of each school is also included.

Interestingly enough, there seem to be few controversies at French civil and common law schools. This may be attributed to the fact that minority groups are not present to the same extent in the French student bodies and therefore have not reached the critical mass that minorities are beginning to reach in the common law schools. The fact that the students are younger —

a good percentage coming directly from a CEGEP at eighteen or nineteen years of age — could also help to explain the lack of controversy. The younger students are more preoccupied with trying not to be weeded out during their first year of study than becoming involved with the more global issues, whereas in common law schools the attrition rate is low and the students are significantly older. Controversies over gender are not an issue in civil law programs, perhaps because the female students often outnumber the male. Whatever the reason, the French civil and common law schools have consistently high-spirited and friendly atmospheres not affected by controversies evident in English common law schools.

AN INTEGRATIVE APPROACH TO THE BAR EXAM, THE BAR ADMISSION COURSE, AND LAW SCHOOLS

There has been a movement towards a more co-ordinated and integrative approach to the selection of curriculums in law schools, bar admission courses, and the bar exams to avoid duplication and conflicts of purpose. The purpose of the law degree is to give students a broad overview of the law, and to develop in students analytical and critical reasoning. Many law school have over the years developed course offerings which have integrated analytical and practical education. Meanwhile, bar admission programs have more recently clarified their objectives and changed their instruction to emphasize practical hands-on lawyering skills, such as advocacy, interviewing, counselling, and negotiation.

It will be interesting to see how the clarification of the roles affects academic credit given for participation in course offerings with a substantial practical component, such as legal aid, moot court, and trial practice courses. These highly practical courses are very popular with the students, but are very costly to run. Dalhousie University's Legal Aid Clinic and Université de Montréal's mooting course are just two situations where the Faculties of Law are fighting to keep these opportunities available despite budget cutbacks. With the new trend towards reducing the duplication of material taught, the future of legal aid and mooting may be insecure.

CAREER DISSATISFACTION OF WOMEN IN THE LEGAL PROFESSION

According to a 1991 report by the Law Society of Upper Canada, *Transitions in the Ontario Legal Profession, a Survey of Lawyers Called to the Bar Between*

1975-90, there is a significant amount of dissatisfaction among women in the legal profession. One of the biggest complaints of female lawyers was the quality of life which resulted from the balancing of career and family responsibilities. The *Transitions* report states, "Respondents expressed growing concern over mounting hours of work, work-related stress, and the all-consuming nature of practising law." Similar studies, recently completed in Alberta and British Columbia, have found similar results and reached similar conclusions.

The percentage of men and women enrolled in law schools today is almost fifty/fifty, but flexible hours, alternative work arrangements, and special leaves are not yet widespread in the workforce. The *Transitions* report states that women are over-represented among departures from the practice of law. Women represent thirty percent of the past fifteen years of Bar admissions. However, they also represent thirty-seven percent of those no longer practising law.

According to the *Transitions* report, more women start their legal career working for the government compared to men (11% and 7% respectively), and they are also more likely to remain employed with the government. A smaller percentage of women than men enter the private practice of law (69% and 81% respectively), and they are more likely to depart from private practice due to general dissatisfaction.

Native People and Access to Legal Education

PREPARATORY ADMISSIONS PROGRAMS FOR ABORIGINAL PEOPLE

Native People are underrepresented in the legal profession and in an effort to change this an increasing number of law schools are offering admission categories targeting native people. A common requirement of these categories is the successful completion of one of three "pre-law" programs offered in Canada — the Pre-Law Program connected with the Indigenous Black and Micmac Program, Dalhousie University; the Native Law Centre at the University of Saskatchewan; and the Programme D'admission PreDroit En Français Pour Les Candidats Autochtones, Université d'Ottawa.

The Native Law Centre offers the Program of Legal Studies for Native People held at the College of Law, University of Saskatchewan. The program is eight weeks long and is held in the summer months. To be admitted to the program, applicants have to be of aboriginal descent and be either unconditionally or conditionally accepted at a law school upon successful completion of the course. In 1973 fourteen students were enrolled in the program and now seventy students are registered. The class of seventy is divided into four groups supported by a writing consultant, teaching assistant, and a faculty member. The Elders also participate in the program. The structure of the course used to simulate the law experience. Students took "Mini" versions of the law courses offered in the first year LL.B. program. In 1988 the curriculum was revised to offer only three courses for a longer period of time. There is also a skills-based approach where briefing, outlining, and exam preparation are reviewed.

The Native Law Centre has a library on law and native issues, and a publications section that publishes Canadian Native Law Research including all Canadian native law cases. The Native Law Centre also has a research component, but it has been minimal since the 1985 budget cutbacks. Elders participate in the program.

For more information on the Program of Legal Studies for Native People contact:

Director
Program of Legal Studies for Native People
141 Diefenbaker Centre
University of Saskatchewan
Saskatoon, Saskatchewan
S7N 0W0
(306) 966-6189

The Pre-Law Program at Dalhousie University is a one-month course which will be offered in August of each year. It is an intensive introduction to the Law School curriculum and academic skills emphasized in legal education. This Pre-Law is part of the Indigenous Black and Micmac (IBM) Program established in 1989 to attract applicants from the Indigenous Black and Micmac communities of Nova Scotia. Applicants to the IBM are required to have a degree or at least two years of undergraduate study.

For more information on the IBM Program and the Pre-Law Program contact:

Carol Aylward, Director
Law Programme for Indigenous Blacks and Micmacs
Dalhousie Law School
Halifax, Nova Scotia
B3H 4H9
(902) 494-3554

In 1990 the Université d'Ottawa established a Programme D'admission PreDroit En Français Pour Les Candidats Autochtones. It is the only French-speaking pre-law program in Canada. As is required in the IBM Program and the Program of Legal Studies for Native People, an unconditional or conditional acceptance from a law faculty is required. The seven-week program is offered in the summer, and presents an overview of the different areas of the law and the distinctions between the traditional Native law and the legal civil and common law systems.

For more information contact:

PreDroit En Français Pour Les Candidats Autochtones
Faculté de Droit
Civil Law Section
Université d'Ottawa
57 Louis Pasteur
Ottawa, Ontario
K1N 6N5
(613) 564-2254

Dalhousie University, Université d'Ottawa, and the University of Saskatchewan, as well as the University of Alberta, University of British Columbia, and the University of Manitoba also offer academic support for native students, such as tutoring and exam preparation. Please see the individual university chapters for more details.

A STATISTICAL SUMMARY OF NATIVE PEOPLE AND ACCESS TO LEGAL EDUCATION

According to the *Summary of Committee for Law Admissions, Statistics Services and Innovations (CLASSI) Statistics — 1991*, applications from aboriginal Canadians at common law schools increased to 335 from 311 in 1990 and 225 in 1989. This is an increase of 7.7% in the last year and a 48.9% increase since 1989. Since 1985 there has been an increase of 253.8% in the number of applications from aboriginal applicants. Even with this increase since 1985, however, applications from aboriginal persons represent only 1.1% of the total application pool.

The number of aboriginal students enrolled in first-year law increased to 84 in 1991 from 60 in 1990 and 50 in 1989. This is an increase of 40.0% in the last year and an increase of 350.0% over the 24 aboriginal students enrolled in 1985. Nevertheless, native students represent only 3.68% of the first-year law student population.

The following statistics for common law schools were compiled by Margaret Brown, University of Saskatchewan Native Law Centre, October 1991.

NATIVE LAW CENTRE ALUMNI WHO HAVE OBTAINED A LAW DEGREE: 163

Where the Law Degree Was Obtained

University of Alberta	6
University of British Columbia	51
University of Calgary	2
Dalhousie University	3
University of Manitoba	6
McGill University	4
Osgoode Hall, York University	21
University of Ottawa	5
Queen's University	22

University of Saskatchewan	18
University of Toronto	3
University of Western Ontario	6
University of Windsor	2
University of Victoria	14

NATIVE LAW CENTRE ALUMNI ATTENDING LAW SCHOOL IN 1991-92: 139

Law Schools Enrolled At

University of Alberta	8
University of British Columbia	31
University of Calgary	2
Dalhousie University	8
University of Manitoba	13
McGill University	3
University of New Brunswick	3
Osgoode Hall, York University	7
University of Ottawa	19
Queen's University	7
University of Saskatchewan	22
University of Toronto	7
University of Western Ontario	3
University of Windsor	4
University of Victoria	2

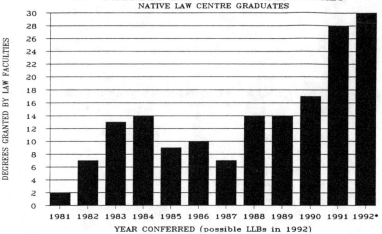

LAW DEGREES EARNED BY ABORIGINALS *
NATIVE LAW CENTRE GRADUATES

YEAR CONFERRED (possible LLBs in 1992)

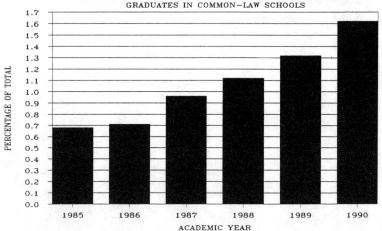

ENROLLMENT OF NATIVE LAW CENTRE *
GRADUATES IN COMMON-LAW SCHOOLS

ACADEMIC YEAR

* Graph based on data from "ABORIGINAL PEOPLES AND ACCESS TO LEGAL EDUCATION AND THE LEGAL PROFESSION: DATA AND TRENDS" created and compiled by Brian M. Mazer, Professor of Law, and M. Samantha G. Peeris, Law III, Faculty of Law, University of Windsor.

PROGRAM OF LEGAL STUDIES FOR NATIVE PEOPLE – 10 YEAR STATISTICS

Program Year	1982	1983	1984	1985	1986	1987	1988	1989	1990	1991	Total
Applications Received	55	58	61	68	67	74	101	82	112	114	792
Applications Accepted	30	31	34	34	35	42	62	50	65	79	462
Applicants who Registered in Program	30	28	29	34	30	36	58	43	53	64	405
Applicants who Withdrew from Program	(2)	(3)	(3)	(2)			(2)	(2)	(1)	(1)	(16)
Men/Women	18/12	18/10	17/12	17/17	19/11	17/19	33/25	19/24	25/28	34/30	217/188
Registered – Non-Status/Métis	23/7	18/10	20/14	17/17	15/15	24/12	43/15	33/10	36/16	52/12	280/123
– Inuit			1						1		2
No. of Students Recommended to Law School	21	13	17	24	18	23	34	31	40	55	276
No. of Students Who Enrolled in Law School	21	13	15	19	17	22	34	31	41	53	266
No. of Students in First Year Law		1		1					8	53	62
No. of Students in Second Year Law					1		3	10			47
No. of Students in Third Year Law						1	8	20	33		30
No. of Students Who Graduated from Law School	12	7	9	13	14	17	21				93
No. of students in program without any post-secondary academic work	4	1	3	4		2	2			4	18
No. of students in program with less than two years university work	2	5	8	1	2	8		3	6	1	42
No. of graduates without any post-secondary academic work			1	1							2
No. of graduates with less than two years university work	1	1	3	2		3	1				10

Compiled by M. Brown, University of Saskatchewan Native Law Centre – October, 1991

Consider This When
Choosing a Law School

THE SIZE OF THE LAW SCHOOL

The size of the incoming class in Canadian law schools ranges from a high of 335 to a low of approximately fifty. Université de Montréal has the largest class with Osgoode Hall Law School and Université Laval following close behind with 300 first-year students.

The smallest schools are Université de Moncton and Calgary with fifty and sixty-eight students respectively. For more detail please see the chapter on *Comparative Statistics of Canadian Law Schools*.

Size greatly affects the atmosphere of the school and the opportunities available. In a small student body, you get to know everyone in your year and probably a good percentage of the upper-year students as well. The class sizes are small. The atmosphere is reminiscent of high school, where both teachers and students know everything about you. This can be comforting or disconcerting depending on what you are looking for. A large school provides students with the option of anonymity. Large schools subdivide the first- year class into several smaller sections. You get to know the students in your section quite well but not all of the students in your year, let alone the program. Class sizes tend to be larger.

The larger the faculty the greater the opportunities available in terms of the diversity of courses offered, the variety of teaching styles, and the availability of combined programs (see chart 5 on *Other Related Programs*).

THE GEOGRAPHIC SETTING

The city the law school is located in will affect how much it is going to cost you to live for the next three years while you are doing your law degree. For example, Toronto and Vancouver have two of the highest costs of living in Canada, whereas Montreal and smaller centres in Quebec have the lowest cost of living in Canada and the least expensive tuition. Articling salaries are affected similarly by the size of the centre, although you do not have to article in the same city, or province, as the school you graduate from.

The atmosphere of the city often affects the personality of the law school and what area of law the Faculty of Law is known for. McGill University's Faculty of Law, located in cosmopolitan Montreal, has an international focus; the University of Ottawa, University of Victoria, and Université Laval's Faculties of Law are all strongly affected by the government functions of the city.

THE STUDENT PROFILE OF THE SCHOOL

The transition to law school can be very intense, exhausting, and a blow to the self-esteem. What kind of student mix would you like to have as your support group as you make your way through? Investigate if the student body leans towards younger students admitted directly from a CEGEP or an undergraduate program, or if there are a significant number of mature students. What percentage of the class are aboriginal students and other minority groups? The average age, percentage of mature students, aboriginal students, and other minorities are listed in each university chapter. Also see the chapter on *Aboriginal Students and a Legal Education*.

THE NATURE OF THE PROGRAM

The Faculty of Law at University of New Brunswick, and the University of Western Ontario offer the two most highly structured law programs in Canada, with relatively few opportunities to take electives in the second and third years of the program. The first-year curriculum is compulsory at all law schools, but the degree of structure varies greatly in the upper years. Osgoode Hall Law School has no required courses after first year. A structured program provides students with a general base or overview of many areas of the law. The less structured schools leave the choice up to you.

Law School Admission Test (LSAT) Format

The law school admission test (LSAT) is a half-day standardized test required for admission into all common law schools in Canada. Some law schools use a formula as part of their admissions process and an applicant's score is given a weight anywhere between twenty to sixty percent at these schools. Please refer to charts 1-4 in the chapter *Comparative Statistics on Canadian Law Schools*.

The test is made up of three different item types analytical reasoning, reading comprehension, logical reasoning, and variable items used to pretest new items and to pre-equate new test forms.

3 Item Types	5 Thirty-five Minute Sections
analytical reasoning	22-24 questions
reading comprehension	26-28 questions
logical reasoning (one format)	24-26 questions
logical reasoning (different format)	24-26 questions
experimental section	22-28 questions

The analytical reasoning items are the most quantitative measure. The candidate is required to use deductive reasoning in a systematic structure by way of scenarios. The reading comprehension items analyze and synthesize. The candidate will be required to analyze arguments, differentiate between two arguments, separate bias from argument, and draw inference from all studies. Lastly, the logical reasoning category is an interesting hybrid of the analytical and reading comprehension items which are shorter, stand-alone items that depend on analysis. The logical reasoning set of questions is a more informal logic set than the analytical and the reading comprehension. Different formats are used to test the same skills. This allows a candidate's skills to be brought out in spite of the structure of the test.

The writing sample is not scored by Law Services, but copies of the writing sample are sent to all law schools to which you apply.

The LSAT is designed to measure skills that are considered essential for success in law school: the reading and comprehension of complex texts with accuracy and insight, the organization and management of information and the ability to draw reasonable inferences from it, the ability to reason critically, and the analysis and evaluation of the reasoning and argument of others. The LSAT provides a standard measure of acquired verbal reading and reasoning skills that law schools can use in assessing applicants.

TO PREPARE

1. *Prepare*

- Review the current directions and sample items in the Information Book available from Law Services. The directions for each test type do not change from those given there. Do not waste time reading the directions during the test. You should already be familiar with them from your review of the Information Book.
- Practise the item types and learn how to draw the diagrams that you use in solving the questions. Simplify your diagrams by using a letter or symbol rather than writing the whole word in the diagram.
- Understand why the key is correct and why the distracters are incorrect when you are practising. Wrong answers are purposely chosen to define possible reasoning errors.
- Take one or more full-length tests under timed conditions to get a sense of how much time you can spend to get to the end.

2. *Pace Yourself*

- Answer every question. Some questions are very difficult and it is easy to get bogged down. When you don't completely know the answer, eliminate the ones you know are incorrect and then guess. If you want to check the questions you have guessed at after you are finished the test, mark them with an "x" in the margin of the test book and check them when you have finished, time allowing.
- Do not waste time on questions you cannot answer. Each question is worth the same amount so guess and keep going.
- Watch the time during the test.

3. *Minimize Test Stress*

- Allow enough time to get to the test site. Do not leave ten minutes before it starts if you know it takes ten minutes to get there. Leave time for traffic jams and parking.
- If you have never been to the test site before, investigate before the test. Find out how long it will take you to get there, what is the best route, and where you can park.

- Gather your materials that you need to write the test the night before. (This would include the correct HB type pencil, erasers, watch or clock, and ID.)
- Review and understand the test-day procedure; for example, you may be required to be fingerprinted, have to fill out forms etc.
- Remember, never take the test unprepared.

LSAT PREPARATION MATERIALS

The following preparation materials can be ordered from Law Services by using a form in the Information Book.

Prep Tests $7 each

Prep Test II	October 1991 LSAT
Prep Test III	December 1991 LSAT
Prep Test IV	February 1992 LSAT
Prep Test V	June 1992 LSAT
Prep Test VI	October 1992 LSAT

Each Prep Test is a real LSAT administered on the date indicated. You can practise as if you were taking an actual test by following the test-taking instructions and timing yourself. In addition to actual LSAT questions, each Prep Test contains an answer key, writing sample, and a score-conversion table.

The Official LSAT PrepKit $32

The PrepKit will help you maximize your mastery of the three LSAT question types. This boxed set of test preparation tools includes: an introductory booklet with instructions and general test preparation information; a complete practice test (The Official LSAT PrepTest Simulated Version), including a writing sample and answer key; and three workbooks that will lead you through practice exercises for each of the three question types — analytical reasoning, logical reasoning, and reasoning comprehension — with explanations and hints to help improve your skills.

The Official LSAT Workbooks $12 each

The analytical reasoning, logical reasoning, and reading comprehension workbooks that are included in the PrepKit are also sold separately. Each workbook is the perfect tool for anyone who needs focused practice on one or two question types.

The Official LSAT PrepBook $17

This publication provides additional practice opportunities for all three LSAT question types. It contains three hundred actual questions from previously administered LSATs along with an answer key.

GENERAL INQUIRIES

Law Services
Box 2400
661 Penn Street
Newtown, PA 18940-0977
U.S.A.

(215) 968-1001
8:30 am-8:00 pm (ET)
September–March
 8:30 am-4:45 pm (ET)
April–August

THE LAW SCHOOL ADMISSION TEST

The following test dates and deadlines were taken from the Information Book, Canadian Edition, put out by the Law School Admissions Services. Please consult the address below for up-to-date information.

DEADLINES FOR LSAT TEST APPLICATION				
Registration Type	Fall 1992	Winter 1992	Spring 1993	Summer 1993
Regular*	September 1	November 3	January 12	Early May
Late by mail*	September 2–11	November 4–13	January 13–22	Mid May,
Late by telephone	September 14–23	November 16–25	January 25 – February 3	Late May

* Law Services Order Forms postmarked on these dates must include the LSAT fee and late fee, if applicable.

LSAT TEST DATES				
	Fall 1992	Winter 1992	Spring 1993	Summer 1993
Regular	Saturday October 3	Saturday December 5	Saturday February 13	Mid June
Saturday Sabbath Observers	Monday October 5	Monday December 7	Tuesday February 16	
Score Report Mailed (approx.)	November 16	January 18, 1993	March 29	Late July

FEES

Application Fee	$81 Canadian + GST
Late Application Fee	$46 Canadian + GST

GENERAL ENQUIRIES

Law Services	(215) 968–1001
Box 2400	8:30am – 8:00pm (EST)
661 Penn Street	September – March
Newtown, PA 18940–977	8:30am – 4:45pm (EST)
USA	April – August

Improve Your Chances of Being Admitted

APPLY AS EARLY AS YOU CAN

Most law schools begin to make decisions on applicants' files as soon as they are complete. A file is considered complete when the application form has been filled out and signed, the application fee has been paid, and the LSAT (or the test d'admission en droit civil) score and official transcripts have been received. In addition, some schools require reference letters, personal statements, and medical documentation if illness has affected your performance.

If you are an average or slightly below average applicant, applying early is advisable. At the beginning of the admissions cycle the academic profile of the applicant pool is still unknown. The admissions committee has not had enough applications to be able to determine what the average grade point average (GPA) or Law School Admissions Test (LSAT) score is for that year so each file is assessed on a more individual basis. As the number of places become fewer, the admissions committees become progressively more selective.

APPLY TO ALL LAW SCHOOLS

Initially, applying to all law schools might seem too costly because the application fees add up (see Comparative Statistics charts 1-4 for application fees), and you may not want to move outside of your home province. However, the fact is that if you want to be a lawyer you must have a law degree. Would you give up your opportunity to be admitted to law school, the first step in your law career, because you only wanted to live in Ontario, or you wanted to save five hundred dollars in application fees? Limiting your choice of schools also limits your chances of acceptance. Think of the expense as a long-term investment in your future.

CUSTOMIZE YOUR APPLICATION FORMS

Most law school application forms ask for similar information, but filling them out generically is a mistake. Each school has its own mandate and the information you provide on the application form or personal statement should always be relevant to the criteria stated by the school. For example, evidence of significant community involvement would be relevant to the University of Windsor, the number of upper-year courses in your program would be of interest to the University of Western Ontario, an Acadian background should be mentioned when applying to Université de Moncton, or the fact that you have lived outside Canada or have travelled extensively might be of interest to McGill University. By reading the descriptions of the law schools, it should be clear what points should be stressed when applying to each school.

SELECTIVELY CHOOSE YOUR REFERENCES

References should be from people who know you well enough to offer specific examples as to why you are a good candidate. The best references support the mandate and admissions criteria of the law school you are applying to. Since law school is an academic program, at least one of your references should be from an academic who can attest to your intellectual ability, your ability to think critically and analytically, and your ability to express yourself logically both orally and in writing.

Do not assume everyone will give you a good reference. The admissions committee is expecting to see glowing reports since who you ask is something you have control over. Instead of asking someone if they would be your reference, you might say, "Do you think you could write me a *good* letter of reference?" Asking in this manner gives the referee an opportunity to decline if they are too busy or they really do not feel they know you well enough.

Educate the people you ask for references on what you think the admissions committee would be most interested in and then remind them of an instance when you showed evidence of this in their class. Providing them with a copy of your résumé, application form, and personal statement or cover letter will help them in their preparation. Writing reference letters is a very time-consuming process and taking the time to write a thank-you note in appreciation is a nice gesture. You never know if you might have to ask them for more letters of reference if you change your mind and apply to a different program, or apply again the next year.

FILL OUT APPLICATION FORMS CAREFULLY

Neatness counts when you are filling out law school application forms. Sometimes it helps to photocopy the application form first and do a draft. If you think of how many application forms the admissions committee has to read, you can imagine how frustrated they must become when the form is illegible, not complete, or there are spelling or grammatical errors. You are making a first impression and having a neat, complete application form with perfect spelling and grammar counts.

Pay attention to directions that specify how many words or lines a personal statement is restricted to. Part of the assessment is often how succinct and precise you can be.

APPLY UNDER AS MANY ADMISSIONS CATEGORIES AS YOU CAN

The most competitive category for admission is the regular category where you are applying directly after you have completed your university or CEGEP requirements and you have no extenuating circumstances. Other categories of admission such as mature, aboriginal, or special categories where illness, culture, or language have been a barrier are also available at most law schools.

Increase you chances of admission by investigating if you are eligible to apply under more than one admission category. Find out how each law school defines a mature student, since it is often different for each law school. Perhaps your ancestry allows you to apply under a minority classification. A priority of a number of law schools in Canada, and law school admission organizations, is to promote the diversification of the student bodies to ensure that they are more representative of the people they serve. (See the chapter on *Trends and Issues in Legal Education.*) Many students have a shaky beginning to their university careers due to illness or because they have selected a program that they are not suited to or are not interested in. Most law schools do take this into consideration. Some even allow these courses to be omitted from the calculation of the cumulative GPA. For further details see the chapters on the individual law schools under the admissions section.

BE PREPARED FOR THE INTERVIEW

A few law schools, such as Dalhousie University and the University of Manitoba will interview applicants as a further tool to help differentiate between applicants in the "grey zone," i.e. applicants that are not a clear reject nor accept. Evidence of good communication skills and critical reasoning will be looked for. An argument may even be provoked to see how you can think on your feet — be objective and rational. Law school can be a very consuming endeavour and so can the profession; therefore, interview panels will be looking for well-rounded and mature individuals that they feel will be able to succeed in the program and contribute to the class.

SUBMIT YOUR APPLICATION IN PERSON

Not many law schools grant interviews as part of their admissions process. However, delivering your application in person, taking a tour of the school, briefly talking to someone who is on the admissions committee can help the admissions officer put a face to the name on the application form. People make up the admissions committee and although the admissions process can seem quite mechanical, whenever there are people involved it is a subjective process. When it comes down to deciding who will be admitted to fill the last few places, admissions committees are usually choosing applicants out of the "grey zone," where qualifications are very similar. It is harder to say no to someone you have met than just a piece of paper.

REMEMBER THIS

Do not be intimidated by the high apply/accept ratios that are stated for the law schools that follow. A more realistic overall ratio is 4:1. Remember that the number one reason for being refused admission is because the candidate simply does not meet the minimum requirements. Also, many applicants have also applied to other graduate and professional schools as well to increase their options. Even if they are given an offer of admission they may not accept it because their first choice was really another program. Evidence of this is the number of offers listed beside the size of the incoming class on the statistics pages in the descriptions of the law schools.

COMMON LAW SCHOOLS

University of Alberta

■ **INQUIRIES**

Law Admissions
4th Floor, Law Centre
University of Alberta
Edmonton, Alberta
T6G 2H5
(403) 492-3067

ADMISSIONS INFORMATION

■ **APPLICATION DEADLINE DATE FOR ADMISSIONS**
1 February. This is a firm deadline date.

■ **REQUIRED TO SUBMIT**

Regular Applicants

- Two official copies of all post-secondary academic transcripts
- LSAT score report
- Résumé
- TOEFL score may be requested where English is a second language

Special Applicants (Mature and Aboriginal Applicants)

In addition to all of the above, reference letters are strongly recommended and a personal statement not exceeding two pages explaining why you want to study law.

■ **EDUCATION REQUIREMENT**
A minimum of two full years of academic work towards a degree at a university recognized by the University of Alberta.

- **AVERAGE GPA**

    7.7 (9 point system used) or 3.8 (4 point scale) or A- or 80-84% (range 6.7-8.8 or range 3.4-4.2)

- **AVERAGE LSAT**

    80th percentile
    The December test date is the last LSAT that can be written by applicants seeking admission in the following September.

- **RATIO OF APPLICANTS TO REGISTRATIONS**

    7.7 : 1

- **SIZE OF INCOMING CLASS**

    180   (348 offers given)

- **CAN YOU DEFER ACCEPTANCE**

    No. All documentation is kept on file for approximately three years.

- **APPLICATION FEE**

    $50

- **TUITION FEE**

    1992-93 fees for Canadian students will be approximately $2,100 and approximately $1,300 for books and materials.

CLASS PROFILE

- **AVERAGE AGE OF STUDENTS ENTERING THE PROGRAM**

    26

- **PERCENTAGE OF THE CLASS WHO ARE WOMEN**

    43%

- **PERCENTAGE OF WOMEN WHO ARE TENURED FACULTY**

    10.7% (Three women out of a faculty of 28 are tenured. In addition, there are 4 women who hold tenure-track appointments.)

- **PROFILE OF LL.B. POPULATIONS**

    (for all three years, 500 students)
    Minorities   stats are not collected
    Mature Students   7% (35 out of 500)

OTHER RELATED PROGRAMS

Master of Business Administration/LL.B., Master of Public Management/ LL.B., LL.M, Postgraduate Diploma in Law.

PART-TIME PROGRAM: The Faculty has approved a part-time program with an anticipated commencement date of September of 1993. A maximum of six places will be available in each year. To qualify for this program, students must be admitted through the normal admissions process for full-time students, and demonstrate to the satisfaction of the Admissions Committee special circumstances to justify part-time studies such as exceptional family obligations, personal or family health problems, physical or learning disability, employment commitments, financial hardship, or other personal disadvantages.

ADMISSIONS REQUIREMENTS

The application process for candidates applying for admission to the Faculty of Law under the Regular Admissions Category is quite straightforward. A candidate's grade point average (GPA) and Law School Admission Test (LSAT) score are the only two criteria used in the admissions process. These two numerical values are put into an equation where the GPA is given a weight of two-thirds and the LSAT score is weighted at one-third to arrive at a prediction indicator. The indicators are then ranked, filling the 180 positions from the top down. Although a résumé is used to provide an overview of the candidate, it is not given any weight in the process. Reference letters are not requested nor do they have any bearing on the decision if they are submitted.

At first glance, this process appears highly inflexible. However, a closer look reveals some room for flexibility. First, the GPA is calculated on an applicant's most recent sixty hours (two years) of their degree. This provides applicants with the opportunity to have their first-year grades deleted. The majority of law schools use a cumulative grade point average in their decision process unless a candidate has mitigating circumstances that have affected his or her academic performance. The Faculty of Law places emphasis on the grades themselves, and not how they have been derived. The admissions committee does not look at how many upper-year courses are taken, or the institution attended.

Every applicant is reviewed under the regular category initially. However, if an applicant is at least thirty years of age prior to the first day of September in the year they want to start law school, has a minimum of two years of university credits toward a degree, and significant non-academic achievements, they might qualify as a Mature Student under the Special Admissions

Category. A lower standard of academic achievement may be accepted in recognition of grade inflation. This category is not designed to accommodate recent university graduates whose academic records are not comparable to the standards expected of regular applicants and are seeking admission solely on the basis that they are now thirty years of age.

Aboriginal Applicants may also be reviewed under the Special Admissions Category. Lower GPA's and LSAT scores are acceptable. In addition to the criteria of GPA and LSAT scores, assessments of career or personal achievements and community involvement are done. Both mature and aboriginal applicants are strongly advised to submit reference letters and personal statements in support of their application.

In order to ensure that the admissions process is culturally relevant and sensitive to aboriginal people, the Admissions Committee requests information from each applicant that will assist in reaching a fair evaluation. Factors such as whether the first language spoken was an aboriginal language, whether you were raised in an isolated community, the financial and social circumstances of your family, educational experiences, and the degree to which you hold onto traditional culture and values are important considerations.

Historically, the Faculty has drawn most of its students from Alberta, the Northwest Territories, and the Yukon. However, recently the Faculty has begun to develop a national profile and this is reflected, in part, by the presence of a growing number of non-resident students. A permanent resident is defined as one who normally has resided in Alberta, the Northwest Territories, or the Yukon for one year immediately preceding the first day of September in the year admission is sought. For the 1991-92 academic year, thirty-nine per cent of the total offers made were extended to non-residents. Thirty-five of the 175 places in first year were taken by applicants who reside outside of the Province of Alberta.

CHARACTER OF THE SCHOOL

The atmosphere at the Faculty of Law is reminiscent of the movie *The Paper Chase* — quite formal and traditional. The Faculty has a long tradition, dating back to 1921, and the students attending the faculty of law are quite proud of their school.

The relationship between professors and students is a hierarchical one rather than one of equality. Professors' offices are found on the top floor of the building, which distances them from the students, reinforcing a sense of separation. In the opinion of some, there is a strong emphasis placed upon research and publishing.

The hierarchy that exists between faculty and students also exists among the students themselves. The first-year students are given the nickname "puppies." In second year they become known as "beagles," and ultimately they become the graduating class and are referred to as "eagles."

The school has a fairly structured, traditional curriculum. The first year is compulsory, as it is in all law schools. However, there are four required courses in second year and three in third year. Osgoode Hall Law School, University of British Columbia, and University of Toronto have less structured programs. University of New Brunswick probably has the highest number of mandatory courses.

A healthy competition is part of the atmosphere. All law schools are naturally competitive as admissions criteria self-select highly motivated and bright individuals. The competitiveness at Alberta is certainly not cut-throat but there is a seriousness there, especially in second year, the completion of which immediately precedes interviews for articling positions. The current economic downturn and the accompanying downsizing of some law firms probably contributes to the sense of uncertainty felt by some students.

First-year students are encouraged to participate in a mentor program in which new students are paired with upper-level students. In addition, each first-year student participates in the school's small group program. The basis for this program is the course in Constitutional Law and students study throughout the year in groups of approximately twenty. It is also in this course that students begin to develop their legal writing and research skills, and are expected to participate in a first-year moot exercise. Both the mentor and small group programs help first-year students to make the transition to law school and to form strong friendships. In addition, there is a very active Law Students Association which organizes a wide variety of social and sporting events and fund raising activities for various charitable causes during the year. Other student-organized activities include the Women's Law Forum, the Aboriginal Law Students Association, the *Cannons of Construction* (the Law School's student newspaper), the Film Society, the Wine Tasting Society, and Student Legal Services.

STRENGTHS OF THE PROGRAM

Areas of strength at the Faculty include Constitutional Law, Legal Theory, Health Law, and Environmental Law. Over the past few years the Faculty has placed an emphasis on a more interdisciplinary approach to the study of law. Individual faculty members have developed courses in co-operation with colleagues from other departments and faculties, including Political Science, Economics, and the School of Native Studies.

The Indigenous Law Program began in 1990, with funding from the Alberta Law Foundation. As well as actively recruiting Aboriginal applicants, the program provides an academic support program in the form of structured academic tutorials and skills training sessions. Curriculum development of aboriginal legal issues is a fundamental objective of the program. At present, the Faculty's course offerings include Native Law and First Nations Government (an interdisciplinary study of Aboriginal self-government), and Aboriginal Peoples and the Law. In addition, the program provides cross-cultural and Aboriginal awareness training to faculty, staff, and students to foster a better understanding between Aboriginal and non-Aboriginal societies. Approximately five percent of the first-year class is made up of aboriginal students.

Another area of recent expansion at the school is Environmental Law Studies, where the offerings include Environmental Law and Policy, and International Environmental Law. The presence of an interdisciplinary Centre of Environmental Studies at the University of Alberta facilitates teaching and research in this area.

The Institute of Law Research and Reform, founded in 1968; the International Ombudsman Institute, founded in 1978 and representing approximately twenty-five countries; the Health Law Institute founded in 1977; and the Centre for Constitutional Studies all enrich legal education at the Faculty of Law. Law students are permitted to take one three-credit course outside the Faculty as part of their degree. "Law schools are no longer islands unto themselves, and hence our increasing emphasis on interdisciplinary courses and approaches," comments Acting Dean, Ann McLellan.

There has been about a forty percent turnover of faculty over the past five years and this has served to revitalize the school, injecting a critical mass of young faculty with a strong commitment to teaching and research.

The Faculty of Law's library is the third largest in Canada and is supplemented by access to computer Quick Law (QL systems), which includes European and American data bases. Computer instruction is a compulsory component in the first year of the program with further training and funding available to upper-year and graduate students. The library houses a twenty-two station microcomputer lab facility funded by the Alberta Law Foundation. It provides students access to computer search services and the University mainframe computer.

The students at the Faculty of Law have done very well in international and national mooting competitions, most notably the Jessup Moot. (Please see the chapter on *Unique Characteristics* for recent standings.) Students interested in research and editing can take advantage of the well respected *Alberta Law Review* which was established in 1955 and is student-run. Credit may be given for students acting as editors.

WHERE THE PROGRAM COULD IMPROVE

Along with the formal nature of the school goes a fairly traditional and structured curriculum and a faculty which, until recently, could not be described as particularly innovative in either the development of course offerings or teaching methodologies. However, changes are taking place, including an expansion of the curriculum into areas such as Legal Theory, skills training, Environmental Law, Computers and the Law, and Health Law. There also appears to be a perception among some students that the administration could be more flexible and open to student concerns in areas such as course sectioning and meeting the needs of particular student groups, such as single parents.

The Faculty of Law has one of the highest student-faculty ratios of Canadian law schools at approximately 16:1. According to Ann McLellan the average student faculty ratio is approximately 14:1. Budget cutbacks have not helped to improve this situation over the past few years. For example, last year the Faculty gave up one tenure-track position to meet budget requirements and expects to lose another one in the academic year 1992-93.

Perhaps the biggest concern of the students interviewed was the marking scheme used by the Faculty of Law. A nine-point grading system is used by the Faculty and throughout the University of Alberta. There is a perception among the students that there is less differentiation of grades within this system compared to the four point system used by other schools. This, combined with the fact that all law schools bell their grades, only allowing for so many A's, may add to the competitive undertones at Alberta's Faculty of Law.

ON EDMONTON

The University of Alberta is the second largest English-speaking university in Canada. The campus is large and the architecture of the campus varies from modern high-rises to turn-of-the-century original buildings. This is reflective of the personality of Edmonton which is a little bit of the old and a lot of the new. Edmonton is a young city with a history starting around 1890.

The campus is situated on a cliff overlooking the North Saskatchewan River, and is surrounded by trees. Students are often seen biking or jogging for miles through the scenic river valley. Excellent sports facilities are available on campus with a large indoor running track and two swimming pools.

The North Saskatchewan River divides the city of Edmonton into north and south. University of Alberta's campus is across the bridge and about a fifteen-minute walk from downtown. Expansion of the Light Rail Transit

(LRT) to the south side of the city will link the campus more directly and quickly to downtown. One of the LRT stops will be located close to the Faculty of Law and will open in the fall of 1993. This should relieve the parking problem on-campus which is very frustrating at present.

Accommodations average around $500 for a two-bedroom apartment or $675 for a two-bedroom apartment in a high-rise. The HUB mall, one of the largest shopping centres in Canada, has residence accommodation where bachelor apartments are priced around $500. The HUB mall is connected to the Faculty of Law, which makes it very convenient during the cold winter months. In the HUB you also have access to health facilities, food stores, pubs, and the underground LRT. Another popular housing area for students is the market area downtown, about fifteen minutes from campus. It is advised to look early for accommodation near campus.

WHAT THE STUDENTS SAY
(Pseudonyms have replaced the following students' names)

Strengths of the Program

"It is a fairly tight-knit law school. We think of ourselves as independent of the rest of the University of Alberta. In first year there is a mentor program and there is a bond between the students. It is stressed that you should get involved. In fact, you could form your life around the law school and this really helps — especially if you are from out of town." Stanley LL.B. '93
"It is a fairly cohesive group. There is a pride connected to being at U of A's Law Faculty and we have law sweatshirts with U of A emblazoned on our chest." Stanley LL.B. '93
"All areas of the law are represented in the curriculum, but oil and gas is strong and there is a large constitutional course selection." Jessica LL.B. '92
"The program gives you a good backing for the practical aspects of law. . . . They have Student Legal Services which is very extensive, involving around 250." Justin LL.B. '93
"The library is extensive and this is very important from a student's perspective. Most of the professors were very accessible." Paolo, articling student
"The program forced you to learn to organize your time and to face the rigorous challenges without understanding what you were doing all the time, and having to learn to master it by yourself." Jay, articling student
"Marks are not stressed. Professors are constantly telling us that C's are fine and that you shouldn't expect A's in first year. Marks are given to us in sealed envelopes and it is your choice if you want to disclose them." Sue LL.B. '95

Where the Program Could Improve

"The Stanine marking system is definitely a weakness. The professors are curtailed in that they can only give out so many A's to fit the curve. This doesn't allow for more than one or two students in each class to rise to the top. There are definitely two standards in the way one is treated at the University of Alberta. If you have outstanding marks (top 10%), the faculty will do everything for you, but if your marks are mediocre (the rest), it is difficult to accomplish the same ends. All professors enjoy having bright students, but when one goes to law school one must have at least the perception or trappings of an egalitarian process." Jay, articling student

"First year is unnecessarily tough. They say look to your left and look to your right and one of these people will not be here when you graduate. The hierarchy doesn't help but it depends on the person. When you get into second and third year it is better." Jessica LL.B. '92

"There is a hierarchy in law school but it exists in the profession too. It doesn't bother me. If you play within the rules you will do fine." Paolo, articling student

"There is a hierarchical system built in [to the physical setting]. The professors do not have their offices on the same floor as the classes. All the faculty are on the fourth floor. The first-year students only get half lockers whereas the second- and third-year students get full lockers." Ronald LL.B. '94

"There is a feeling among the students that our evaluations of professors are not taken seriously. They are supposed to be given weight in tenure decisions, but those who aren't great professors are still pushed on to tenure track because they have published. The emphasis is more on an academic reputation rather than on teaching quality. More professors are interested mostly in their research." Stanley LL.B. '93

"The mooting program is not pushed. Only thirty-one people try out for twenty-eight spots. At the Eastern schools it is thought to be an honour to be on a mooting team." Stanley LL.B. '93

"Some argue that there are cliques. Eighty-five percent of students are from the province of Alberta and this can be a problem for people from out of province." Stanley LL.B. '93

"Jurisprudential or perspective courses [courses that take a more theoretical approach to the law and focus on why the law is how it is] is an area the faculty is trying to build on, but there has not been that much of it and it has not been stressed." Stanley LL.B. '93

"There are only two black students in all three years of the program. It's not a big faculty and therefore there is not a variety of different ethnic groups." Sue LL.B. '95

Controversies

"Gender issues are a great controversy and seem to occupy more and more faculty and student time each year. Many of the students commented that 'thought police' were everywhere. One had to be careful as to exactly what they said, as quite often it would be found later that someone had taken offence. It was the rule, as opposed to the exception, that when advertising posters of events on campus were posted in the faculty of law, they would often be objected to and ultimately redone or removed as a result of pressure." Jay, articling student

"The first year I was there it was more happy go lucky. The faculty participated in a lot of school events. In second year there were some instances with sexist posters and it got out of hand. The faculty stopped coming out to social events to show they would not support them. By third year the faculty participation wasn't there. There was a greater awareness of equality of rights." Paolo, articling student

"Over the past three years there has been controversy over the discussion of women's issues, but in my view it is a lot of hype over only a few instances. It's more of a lack of awareness over feminist issues." Jessica LL.B. '92

"The Laissez-Faire Legal Group started this year in reaction to feminist social ideas sneaking into teaching. They started their own group to show that there are other ways to solve problems rather than feminist or marxist philosophies. There is a conflict between left- and right-wing methodologies. Conflict exists between those who want to practise the law and those who are concerned with the more academic discussions of law." Stanley LL.B. '93

On Faculty

"A lot of practitioners give courses and this gives you more of a reality-based approach. The quality of the professors is very good too. We have some of the most respected profs in their field, for example, Lewis Klar who teaches Torts." Jessica LL.B. '92

"Alex Pringle is a very good teacher. He teaches criminal law and is a practitioner who has been to the Supreme Court. He is the perfect mix between practice and theory, with a clear idea of where courts cross the line between making the law and upholding it. The students respect him because of his command of the material, easy speaking style, and because he is a fair marker. On our midterm exams he took the time to make comments on them and meet with the students afterwards to discuss them." Ronald LL.B. '94

"Ronald Hopp teaches contracts and wills. As well as teaching he acts as an advisor for students involved with Student Legal Services. He uses the socratic method with a sense of humour and his knowledge of the subject matter is amazing." Justin LL.B. '93

"Moe Litman is a really outstanding but demanding professor. He teaches real property." Jay, articling student

"Len Pollack teaches family law and was a bencher for the law society. He is very good and well respected as well as being quite a character." Stanley LL.B. '93

Other Comments

"Young people seem to see only the big bucks myth in law school, which is seldom tempered by any form of reality. In Calgary, in excess of fifty per cent of the articling students are seeking forms of employment elsewhere after their year, largely as a result of the boom-bust economy. Many students will feel that they have already paid their dues in undergraduate studies by getting good grades to enter law school. They will soon discover that the demands of law school are far in excess of their undergraduate career, and even when this is successfully completed, prospects for finding a job are slim. Before deciding on becoming a lawyer, you should do your homework. This means checking out how much work there is in the area that you plan to practise and possibly the number of unemployed lawyers, as well as speaking with junior lawyers as to their career prospects." Jay, articling student

"Don't get hung up on marks. Marks are not the end all and be all. What is important is understanding the law. The Stanine system is used at U of A [a nine point system where four is a pass]. There is very little difference between a grade of six or seven and if this is going to cause you grief, you will be upset a lot." Paolo, articling student

"Don't form too solid an image of what law school will be like. I was more interested in criminal law and litigation and I pictured myself studying that all the time. I overlooked the other courses that I had to take and I found them really quite dull." Justin LL.B. '93

University of British Columbia

- **INQUIRIES**

    Administration
    Faculty of Law
    University of British Columbia
    1822 East Mall
    Vancouver, B.C.
    V6T 1Z1
    (604) 822-6303

ADMISSIONS INFORMATION

- **APPLICATION DEADLINE DATE FOR ADMISSIONS**

    1 February. Applications should be postmarked by this date.
    Late applications will not be considered.

- **REQUIRED TO SUBMIT**

    ### Regular Applicants

    - Official copies of all university academic transcripts
    - LSAT score report
    - Personal statement is optional

    ### Discretionary Applicant

    - All of the above plus a personal statement is required
    - Letters of reference
    - Biographical resume

- **EDUCATION REQUIREMENT**

    Three completed full years of academic work at a recognized university
    with a minimum overall standing of 65%. If a student is currently in

their third year, an offer would be conditional upon its successful completion with a minimum overall standing of 65%.

■ **AVERAGE GPA**

78% or B+ (range 70%-91%)
or 3.6 (range 2.7 – 4.3)

■ **AVERAGE LSAT**

83rd Percentile (range 37th – 99th percentile)
An LSAT score is considered valid for four years. Only valid LSAT scores are acceptable. Multiple LSAT scores based on the same scale are averaged.

■ **RATIO OF APPLICANTS TO REGISTRATIONS**

9.0 : 1 (the application rate for 1992-93 is 10 : 1)

■ **SIZE OF INCOMING CLASS**

240 (645 offers made)

■ **CAN YOU DEFER ACCEPTANCE**

No

■ **APPLICATION FEE**

$40 for applicants with B.C. transcripts
$50 for out of province transcripts

■ **TUITION FEE**

The 1992-93 tuition fee for Canadian citizens is $2,732. This includes students' interest fees.

CLASS PROFILE

■ **AVERAGE AGE OF STUDENTS ENTERING THE PROGRAM**

26 (older student body due to minimum of three years of university education admission requirement)

■ **PERCENTAGE OF THE CLASS WHO ARE WOMEN**

48%

■ **PERCENTAGE OF WOMEN WHO ARE TENURED FACULTY**

9% (4 out of 44 tenured faculty are women and an additional 4 women are tenure track)

■ PERCENTAGE OF THE CLASS WITH

two years or more after senior matriculation but no undergraduate degree	7%
a three-year degree	40%
a four-year degree	50%
a post-graduate degree	3%

■ PROFILE OF FIRST-YEAR LL.B. POPULATIONS

(out of 240)

14	Native Students
35 approximately	Visible Minorities

mature students (over 30 years old with a minimum of 2 years undergraduate or equivalent and LSAT with special circumstances)

OTHER RELATED PROGRAMS

UBC has one of the largest graduate level programs in Canada — Master of Laws, M.B.A./L.L.B., and a Doctoral program — S.J.D. is proposed for September 1992. A half-time program will be starting in September of 1992.

ADMISSIONS REQUIREMENTS

Regular applicants are required to submit their academic transcripts and LSAT scores and for the most part this is the only criterion which determines whether a regular applicant is admitted or not. Reference letters and interviews are discouraged and a personal statement is not required.

A formula is used in the admissions process in which a candidate's grade point average (GPA) and LSAT score are given an equal weight of fifty percent each. As a result, each candidate is assigned an index score which is rank ordered from the top down, filling the places in the regular admissions category. Prior to 1992, the weighting system was 60% GPA and 40% LSAT score. The administration changed the formula in April of 1992 to the present 50/50 formula which puts more emphasis on the LSAT score.

According to Jim MacIntyre, Chair of the Admissions Committee, the GPA is calculated only on undergraduate courses as they were thought to be most representative of an applicant's abilities. However, averages of master's level courses may be included in the calculation, as work required for a master's thesis is similar to the research done in a law office.

The calculation of the GPA is based on all academic years, but some tinkering does occur before the formula is applied. If aberrations exist on a transcript and they can be explained by reasons of health, family emergencies, bad choice of courses, or working part-time for example, they may be discounted. Information on these circumstances should be volunteered in a personal statement.

The last 50 of the 240 spaces are filled by applicants whose fate is not clear. Within this grey zone differentiation is difficult because many of the applicants have similar index scores. Therefore, the seemingly mechanical admissions process becomes more subjective considering, for example, the degree of difficulty of the courses taken during the applicant's program.

UBC's law school has a **Discretionary Category**, which includes mature students (age 30) with some work experience, Native students (approximately twelve to fifteen each year), and students with physical disabilities or other special circumstances such as membership in a disadvantaged goup. In this category, the LSAT and GPA are not controlling factors. UBC has an affirmative action program to encourage native students to apply to law school. A First Nations Law Director acts as support to Native students in all years. Generally, Native applicants in the discretionary category are required to attend the two month pre-law program offered by the University of Saskatchewan College of Law in the summer months.

CHARACTER OF THE SCHOOL

UBC's law school is not the same law school that it was three or four years ago. It has undergone dramatic change and revitalization in response to the issues that are at the forefront today, such as the study of law in a more integrative context, considering social and economic factors and diversification of the student body. Lynn Smith took over as Dean from Peter Burns in 1991 and with her came a strengthened emphasis on feminist legal studies and women and the law. The administration is currently conducting a search to fill an endowed chair in Women and the Law. Other pro-active steps have been the appointment of a First Nations Law Director to add support for the growing number of aboriginal students in the program, and a mandatory Perspectives course covering theoretical and interdisciplinary approaches to law has been established.

Comparative and integrative approaches to the law are highlighted by the Asian Legal studies, the International Centre for Criminal Law Reform, and Criminal Justice Policy, also offered in collaboration with Simon Fraser University.

"The faculty should continue with the emphasis of academic programs with theoretical and interdisciplinary strength. Students should not only have an understanding of legal doctrine and methodology but be able to put it in a framework where it fits in historically and philosophically in order to be thoughtful practitioners," comments Lynn Smith. There are few restrictions placed on students' choice of upper-year classes. Only two courses and a second-year moot are compulsory in second and third year, leaving plenty of opportunity for students to take theoretical and comparative courses.

STRENGTHS OF THE PROGRAM

Growing trade, financial, social and cultural links with Japan, China, Hong Kong, and Korea have resulted in a strong international trade law focus at UBC's faculty of law. Key faculty members in this area are Bob Paterson, who wrote the first Canadian textbook on the subject, and Pitman Potter, who specializes in relations with China and Taiwan. The legal systems of the countries involved are so radically different that the Centre for Asian Legal Studies was established at British Columbia's Faculty of Law to develop an area of expertise and understanding on the legal systems of their trade partners.

Japanese legal studies has been ongoing since 1980 at UBC supported by the Law Foundation of B.C. A comparative law course in Japanese law is offered annually as well as a specialized course or seminar in the area in most years. The law library's holdings in Japanese materials are extensive and provide an excellent resource for students wanting to do directed comparative research at the undergraduate or graduate level.

Faculty and graduate students take part in exchange programs with the law faculties of three Japanese national universities and a number of private universities. There have been eight visiting professors from Japan since 1980 at UBC's Faculty of Law. Exchange agreements for faculty and graduate students have also been made with the faculty of law at Peking University in China.

The Centre for Asian Studies, Japanese legal studies, and scholarly exchange opportunities with Japan and China have made UBC's Faculty of Law attractive to leading faculty members in the areas of corporate and international law. This richness in research affects students in the undergraduate law program by the introduction of courses in comparative international courses.

Another strength of UBC's Faculty of Law is their focus on feminist legal studies headed by the Dean — Lynn Smith. Pre-eminent scholars in this area are Christine Boyle and Isabel Grant, and an endowed chair in Women and the Law will be in place by 1992.

UBC's Faculty of Law is also committed to the Law and Computers Program in conjunction with IBM Canada. The purpose of the program is to explore the application of leading edge technology to the legal profession. IBM Canada has donated in excess of two million dollars worth of computing equipment and services to the University and additional funding was provided by the Law Foundation of British Columbia, the Social Sciences and Humanities Research Council of Canada, British Columbia's Ministry of the Attorney General, and the Federal Departments of Communications and Supply and Services. To the law student, this has resulted in credit courses available in Law and Computers, Legal Reasoning and Artificial Intelligence, Technology and the Law, and Industrial and Intellectual Property. Research opportunities at the master's and doctoral level are available in Expert Systems and other advanced systems in law.

The size of UBC's Faculty of Law makes it possible for the variety and diversity of its strengths. There are forty-four faculty members for seven hundred students. In 1990 four new faculty members were hired. They have had a revitalizing effect to the established faculty, bringing with them new approaches and methodologies. The faculty is supported by practitioners from the Vancouver area who offer specialized courses in their areas of expertise. Both faculty and practitioners coach students for mooting competitions. Participation in competitive moots is encouraged by the faculty and UBC law students have done very well. (See chapter on *Unique Characteristics*.)

WHERE THE PROGRAM COULD IMPROVE

Increasing links with the Pacific Rim, a focus on feminist legal studies, and a more integrative approach to the study of law in general have affected the atmosphere of the law school. What once might have been described as a relatively laidback law school, where the students were more concerned with getting the work done in order to get out and practise, has changed to a student body that is more aware of gender and racial issues and the under-pinnings of our legal system.

The atmosphere among the students seems to be tense and more competitive than some other schools. UBC's Faculty of Law is the second biggest common law school in Canada with 240 students making up the first-year class. Through the orientation program, and by putting students in groups of about sixty in their first year, students get to know the other people in their group quite well, but beyond this group there is a sense of isolation. This, plus the increasingly tight labour market for lawyers, might also add to the competition felt by the students.

The location of UBC's campus, although beautiful, is a drawback in terms of reasonable accommodation. The campus is in the middle of a very established and exclusive residential area. This makes nearby housing difficult to come by and also very expensive. There is no student housing "ghetto" close to the university and it is hard to identify where to look for accommodation. The cost of living in Vancouver is among the highest in Canada.

ON VANCOUVER

The University of British Columbia is built on the westernmost point of the city of Vancouver. From the university's campus the view is breathtaking. The campus spreads over a promontory surrounded by the Pacific Ocean and is overlooked by towering mountains. The parkland forest acts as a buffer between the campus and the residential area. The campus is approximately a half-hour bus ride from downtown. You can see the city of Vancouver from campus but you don't feel like you are in a big city until you go downtown.

Housing is expensive, with a one-bedroom basement apartment costing in the area of $600/month. Accommodation can also be difficult to find so you may be advised to start your hunt for accommodations in July. Graduate residences and a condominium complex are available on-campus, but they often have a waiting list. One student commented, "I don't recommend that people live in residence because it is so isolated on a campus that is spread out. The bus service is terrible after hours and there isn't even a nearby grocery store."

Vancouver is an outdoor person's dream with parks everywhere, beaches five minutes from campus, and skiing about forty-five. Not only does a year-round temperate climate permit full enjoyment of outdoor living, but it is indeed possible to ski in the morning, sail in the afternoon, and enjoy a concert in the evening of the same day. The pace of life in Vancouver is described as "laid back."

WHAT THE STUDENTS SAY

(Pseudonyms have replaced the following students' names)

Strengths of the Program

"In the last three or four years the faculty of law has started to address contemporary issues — feminism, poverty, racism, and there is a whole group of fairly young faculty members." Peter LL.B. '93

"I think because Vancouver is laid back, the law school isn't extremely competitive and there is quite a bit of sharing." Caroline LL.B. '92

"The type of people attracted to law schools are competitive by nature. It is very cloistered here at UBC and, therefore, there is a very tight faculty. The atmosphere is not overtly competitive but naturally competitive." Nelson LL.B. '92

"In first year you are in the same section with fifty or sixty other students all year. You make your friends in this group and they become your support group when you are going through final exam crisis or whatever. You don't get to meet students in other sections until second year." Jocelyn, articling student

"There is a good range of courses to choose from as well as a black letter and theoretical focus [courses that focus on the process and rules of the law as well as courses that focus on why the law is how it is], and legal political issues such as aboriginal, women's, and gay rights. Some professors are involved in First Nation studies and there are a large number of aboriginal students." Stephen LL.B. '93

"UBC does seem to recognize and work towards aboriginal issues. The administration in consultation with first nation students have appointed a Native Law Director who starts in July 1992." Cheryl LL.B. '94

"UBC prides itself on its Asian Pacific Studies because it is such an important aspect of the law in Vancouver." Stephen LL.B. '93

"A trademark of UBC is its strength in the constitutional area — especially focusing on the Charter." Lesley LL.B. '92

"The professors are quite approachable, even after hours, and the library is excellent." Stephen LL.B. '93

"Students can volunteer at the Law Student Legal Advice Clinic (LSLAC). It is a free legal advice clinic with fifteen clinics all over the city. There is a high number of students who participate in the clinics — especially in first year." Lesley LL.B. '92

"You are encouraged to go into competitive moots. It's a lot of work but it gives you confidence being in front of a group and trying to persuade them to accept your opinion. It is also an opportunity to get to know the professors." Stephen LL.B. '93

Where the Program Could Improve

"The trial advocacy course was difficult to get into and there were not that many very practically oriented courses. The ones that they had were in high demand." Jocelyn, articling student

"There are some practical courses but they have limited enrollment and are often at night." Caroline LL.B. '92

"The theme of the orientation program is that this is not the *Paper Chase* and that they are not weeding you out, but this law school still has an uncomfortably competitive atmosphere." Cathy LL.B. '94

"It is very competitive. Everyone was an A student before but in law school the marking is curved around seventy percent. Most students will end up with C's and B's . . . It is very ego bruising. I think it is unnecessary to set an arbitrary mark at seventy. It could be set at eighty and you could still differentiate or have more pass/fail courses so it would be less competitive. There is an attitude that you will get the job you want if you stand in the top quarter of the class. Below this you get what you can. There isn't much room in the top quarter. Also you need to be in the top quarter to get into a master of law program." Cathy LL.B. '94

"It is a very competitive environment driven by the bell curve. If you have a different point of view of how you go about life, it can be difficult. To Indians, sharing is very important." Cheryl LL.B. '94

"Graduate school is very collegial whereas in law school there is a hierarchy and first-year students especially are at the bottom of the ladder . . . It is a lot like high school. Lockers are in the basement, the bell rings, and homework assignments are on the board." Cathy LL.B. '94

Controversies

"Gender was a factor between the students themselves. In my first year I was surprised at how narrow minded the men were. It might have been that they had not interacted with women as equals yet like they would in the work world." Jocelyn, articling student

"Feminist issues are in the forefront of controversies. The whole idea of looking at the law from a white affluent male perspective is still prevalent but is changing in terms of the curriculum. The student body might be up to fifty percent female but it isn't reflected in the curriculum — not to the extent that it might be." Peter LL.B. '93

"There has been a change in the curriculum with the addition of a Perspectives course. This is a volatile subject area on all sides. People who are attracted to law are conservative. Some people say it is too much work and not necessary. The atmosphere is tense and angry but with time I am sure it will settle down." Lesley LL.B. '92

"UBC in general is apathetic. There are certain groups who are into issues like First Nation issues, but this doesn't spill over to the rest of the student body. Women's issues are big campus wide. In first year this is addressed in the Perspectives course which highlights areas that are not picked up in other courses, but there is no conflict." Stephen LL.B. '93

On Faculty

"Michael Jackson teaches criminal law and two or three Native law courses. He actively supports First Nation issues." Cheryl LL.B. '94

"Joel Bakan teaches constitutional law and is a very popular provocative professor." Lesley LL.B. '92

"Nitya Duclos teaches family law from a critical stance. She is challenging and creates a lot of discussion." Lesley LL.B. '92

Other Comments

"The law school is off by itself and you can feel a bit isolated. This is good in that you really get to know the law faculty and students, but it does separate you from the rest of the university." Jocelyn, articling student

"I had a really good time when I went to law school. It's a lot of work but you have to keep your perspective. Sometimes you can work like a dog and your grades might not reflect it. Decide what you want — to be in the top ten percent or have a balanced life. Law school doesn't represent the realities of practice. It is an academic exercise." Jocelyn, articling student

"You have to start working from day one because it's hard to do well if you don't. The hardest part is getting in. In terms of doing well you have to be disciplined and study regularly. It is important to do well to increase the choices available to you when you graduate." Peter LL.B. '93

"At times the school can seem a bit impersonal since it is large but the law faculty is like a school in amongst itself and there is more of a sense of community. It is difficult, however, to integrate because of the way the first-year program is set up in groups. You only know the people in your group best although in upper years you mix more since you have classes together. You only really get to know about sixty of the 240 students in the program." Caroline LL.B. '92

"When you are one out of 240 admitted each year you can find yourself a little lost." Nelson LL.B. '92

"Initially, I thought I would practise with a big law firm but that idea is becoming less attractive. I am more interested in public advocacy, legal aid, and crown work. There are lots of things you can do with a law degree without going into a courtroom everyday." Cathy LL.B. '94

University of Calgary

- **INQUIRIES**

  Admissions Office
  Faculty of Law
  University of Calgary
  Calgary, Alberta
  T2N 1N4
  (403) 220-7222

ADMISSIONS INFORMATION

- **APPLICATION DEADLINE DATE FOR ADMISSIONS**

  1 February
  This is a firm deadline and there are no exceptions. All supporting documentation must be compete by 1 May.

- **REQUIRED TO SUBMIT**
  - Official copies of all university academic transcripts
  - LSAT score report
  - Three letters of reference (two of these should be academic references).

- **EDUCATION REQUIREMENT**

  Completion of two full years, or the equivalent of two full years of study leading to a degree. Students who are applying after two years of study must have completed their two years by 1 January of the year in which they apply.

- **AVERAGE GPA**

  3.26 based on eleven band system or B+
  (Range 1.75 -3.96)

- **AVERAGE LSAT**

    76th percentile
    (Range 15th − 100th)
    Applicants should write the LSAT prior to 1 January.

- **RATIO OF APPLICANTS TO REGISTRATIONS**

    17.4 : 1

- **SIZE OF INCOMING CLASS**

    66 (131 offers were given)

- **CAN YOU DEFER ACCEPTANCE**

    No
    Applicants' files are kept for three years. If you wish to reapply you must submit a new application, one more letter of reference, and any new pertinent information. This will be added to your file.

- **APPLICATION FEE**

    $45

- **TUITION FEE**

    The 1992-93 tuition fee (not including books or other fees) is approximately $2500 for Canadian or landed immigrant status students and $5000 for non-exempt foreign students.

CLASS PROFILE

- **AVERAGE AGE OF STUDENTS ENTERING THE PROGRAM**
    28

- **PERCENTAGE OF THE CLASS WHO ARE WOMEN**
    64%

- **PERCENTAGE OF WOMEN WHO ARE TENURED FACULTY**

    35% (6 women are in tenured positions out of 17 faculty)

- **PERCENTAGE OF THE CLASS WITH:**

two years or more of an undergraduate degree	7%
a three-year degree	87%
a four-year degree	n/a
a post-graduate degree	6%

■ **PROFILE OF LL.B. POPULATIONS**

Native Students (class of 1991-1992	0%
Visible Minorities	n/a
Mature Students	n/a

■ **OTHER RELATED PROGRAMS**

A Master of Law was established in 1989 and focusses on Natural Resources, Energy, and Environmental Law.
No half-time program exists yet at Calgary's Faculty of Law.

ADMISSIONS REQUIREMENTS

There is no formula used in the admissions process at Calgary's Faculty of Law. Each applicant's file is read carefully by two committee members. Seven people make up the admissions committee with four faculty members, one student member (elected by the students), a judge or lawyer from the community, and an alumni of the Faculty of Law. Independently of each other, the two randomly selected committee members rank each file with an explanation of why they assigned that rank. If the two rankings are different, the file is read a third time by someone who does not know that the file has already been reviewed. The two (or three) scores are then averaged and the decision to admit is based on this value.

Several factors are taken into consideration by the committee when a file is evaluated. The first is evidence of intellectual ability. The grade point average (GPA) and the Law School Admissions Test (LSAT) score form the basis of this category; however, other factors are taken into consideration. C. Levy, Chair of the Admissions Committee, describes an example of another indicator of intellectual ability: "We had a candidate with a GPA of 1.75 obtained twelve years ago, and an LSAT score of 37, [close to the eightieth percentile], but in only twelve years they had been steadily promoted from the position of secretary to vice president of a large corporation. People can prove they have the intellectual ability in other ways, but if we are not satisfied that a candidate can handle it intellectually, they are rejected." Academic performance in a master's program is taken under consideration separately from the undergraduate degree and it is an advantage if it was done reasonably well.

Maturity is also taken into consideration. Calgary's Faculty of Law has the highest average age of students in any law school in Canada. Maturity is determined by commitment to voluntary activities. This particularly applies to people in the work force as it shows an ability to juggle many responsibilities. This same ability to juggle responsibilities will be required in law school.

A contribution to society is considered an important factor in the admissions process. The statement of purpose should describe what type of contribution the applicant has already made. "We are looking for someone who has already proven themself — someone who is not just taking an income out of society but putting something back in," comments C. Levy. When describing volunteer work, applicants are advised to select the most important ones and explain specifically their role or contribution. A general list of volunteer activities is not as effective.

Communication skills, which are of paramount importance to a lawyer, are evaluated by a candidate's statement of purpose and the written score of the LSAT. These samples of a candidates's writing abilities, one under time pressure and the other not, are painstakingly reviewed. Oral communication skills are evaluated by an applicant's references.

Applications from Aboriginal Canadians who do not meet the GPA and LSAT score standards listed above are encouraged to take the Program of Legal Studies for Native People offered each summer by the College of Law, University of Saskatchewan (see chapter on *Native Canadians and Legal Education*). Upon successful completion of the program, admission is normally granted.

There are only two admission categories at Calgary's Faculty of Law — the Regular Category described above and the Aboriginal Canadian Category. There is no mature student category because mature students are already admitted under the existing categories. Also, at Calgary's Faculty of Law, all candidates must have completed at least two full years of university education.

CHARACTER OF THE SCHOOL

Calgary's Faculty of Law is the youngest English-speaking common law school in Canada, and it has chosen another young law school, Windsor, as its mentor. The founding dean of Calgary's Faculty of Law, John McLaren, was one of the early deans at Windsor's Law School. As a result, they have a common bond — an emphasis on access to a legal education. Like Windsor, Calgary's Faculty of Law goes through each candidate's file reviewing applicants as people rather than as quantitative scores. Both schools look for candidates who have given back to the community and have an older student body than other law schools in Canada.

Calgary's Faculty of Law is the smallest English-speaking law school in Canada. With a first year class of only sixty-eight, the atmosphere is intimate, and the nature of the program is very practical and hands-on. There is a strong emphasis on lawyering skills, including oratory ability, writing, interviewing and counselling clients, and a practicum component.

STRENGTHS OF THE PROGRAM

Calgary's Faculty of Law is one of the leaders in the area of Natural Resources. Its strength comes from its location in Calgary, the heartland of Canada's oil and gas production, and the Institute of Natural Resources housed in the Faculty of Law. Building on this, the Faculty established a master of law program in natural resources in 1989. Students in the LL.B. program benefit from the Institute of Natural Resources through the guest speakers, specialized courses that are developed in this area, and the opportunity to be hired in the summer as research assistants.

Generally, the professors at Calgary's Faculty of Law have a strong interest in the impact of law on real people. There is a core group of professors forming a community of committed faculty who actively organize conferences and seek knowledge in the fields of feminist issues and critical theory. Supporting this is the Institute of Family Law established in the Faculty. In Dean Sheilah Martin's words, "Calgary's Faculty of Law is an exciting place to be where we believe you can use law to make a difference."

On a continuum of practical versus theoretical, Calgary's Law School is definitely on the practical side focusing on the skills one will need as a lawyer. "We undertake an academic treatment of the law and place law in a socio-economic context, but we go beyond that to emphasize the practical skills, such as advocacy and written work," comments Martin.

In the first year of the program, students are required to participate in three moots. In the first month of law school students are on their feet in a mock court setting, getting the feel of what it is like to be a lawyer. Some of these exercises are not graded, making it a comfortable environment to learn from the experience. Students have the opportunity and are encouraged to participate in national and international mooting competitions and have done very well. (See the chapter on *Unique Characteristics*.)

Also in first year, there is a one-week "block week," that is set aside and speakers and sessions are held on legal ethics. In second year "block week" focusses on how to interview and counsel clients and how to negotiate. In the second term of the third year, students are required to take a practicum, which is heavily weighted as the equivalent of three courses, in either Oil and Gas Law, Business Law, Criminal Law, or Family Law.

The atmosphere at Calgary's Faculty of Law is fondly referred to by the students as "warm and fuzzy." The small class size, one of the best student/faculty ratios in Canada, and the Faculty's system of grading contribute to this. Performance is not evaluated by one hundred percent finals, as is the norm at most other law schools in Canada. Evaluation is more commonly determined by a combination of assignments and exams. Moreover, students cannot be asked to leave at Christmas due to failing grades. If students are having difficulty, they are put in tutoring groups to receive additional help. Christmas grades are seen as an early warning system so that individuals can be identified and helped. "There is an understanding here that law takes time and not everyone gets it in the first three months of class," states Sheilah Martin.

WHERE THE PROGRAM COULD IMPROVE

Some of Calgary's Faculty of Law's strengths can also be seen as weaknesses depending on the kind of experience sought. If an applicant wants to specialize, the small faculty limits the selection and diversity of courses offered. The basic courses are available but there is not much of an opportunity to get a selection of advanced courses or a variety of teaching styles from which to choose, compared to what UBC's, Osgoode Hall's, or Toronto's Faculty of Law could offer.

The small size of the program also provides a very tight-knit group which may be good for applicants used to a smaller school. On the other hand, if an applicant is used to a large school, they might miss the anonymity and feel that the atmosphere is a bit intrusive. This might be especially felt by minority groups, since both the student population and that of the city is predominantly white.

Calgary's Faculty of Law is the smallest faculty at the university and this makes across-the-board budget cutbacks, which they have been experiencing for some time, even harder to cope with. As a result, the professors are forced to work harder, to publish more, and yet try to maintain their commitment to teaching.

As noted in the strengths section, grades are based on both assignments and exams. This is a positive factor, especially in first year, when students are making the transition to law school, but overall this method can make it more difficult to obtain good grades. For example, once you know what is expected of you, it may be easier to do well on a one hundred percent final than to consistently do well on three assignments and an exam. Law firms in the Calgary area are aware of the lower grades given by Calgary's Faculty of Law and take this into consideration when they are hiring. However, if a student is applying to firms in Eastern Canada, the Calgary candidate may not look as strong when compared to candidates from other schools that have had the opportunity to get better grades. The faculty is aware of this and has a letter prepared that explains the grading system.

ON CALGARY

The Faculty of Law, the Research Institute on Law and the Family, the Institute of Natural Resources, and the law library are currently housed in one-and-a-half floors of the biology building. The lay-out of the current building is not well-suited to the law faculties' purposes in terms of mooting. This will be rectified in September 1994 when the Professional Faculties Building will be completed and the Faculty of Law moves into their wing.

Calgary's Faculty of Law is primarily a commuter campus. The older student body is generally involved with their family or life outside of the faculty and therefore social life on campus is quiet. The University of Calgary's campus is located well outside of the downtown core, but by light rail transit it only takes ten or fifteen minutes to go downtown. This helps to alleviate the expense of parking. Accommodation is relatively reasonable compared to other major cities in Canada, with a one-bedroom apartment costing in the neighbourhood of $450/month.

The weather in Calgary is cold in the winter but it is frequently broken by incredible warm spells caused by the Chinook winds. To avid skiers and hikers, perhaps the biggest advantage to living in Calgary is that the mountains are only an hour away.

WHAT THE STUDENTS SAY

(Pseudonyms have replaced the following students' names)

The Strengths of the Program

"There is a strong emphasis on social responsibility. The professors bring it up in all the courses and make us think beyond the principle of the case." Hazel LL.B. '93

"U of C places a lot of emphasis on procedural law. Any kind of practice you can get in speaking in front of people is excellent and so far in first year we have had three moots." Gael LL.B. '94

"U of C's Faculty of Law is world-renowned for Natural Resources Law. We have advanced courses in Environmental Law, Oil and Gas Law, and Natural Resources in addition to a Master of Law in Natural Resources." Hazel LL.B. '93

"It [Calgary's Faculty of Law] is very friendly and informal and not competitive in a cut-throat way. Co-operation is actively fostered. It is often referred to as the "warm and fuzzy" law school where the students are more conservative than the faculty." Hazel LL.B. '93

"People are very supportive and you can talk to upper year students if you need help with any problems. The law library is very good and the atmosphere is co-operative and internally supportive throughout all classes." Tom LL.B. '94

"The faculty-to-student ratio is very good. The first-year class of sixty-five to seventy is broken down to thirty or thirty-five so you get personal contact with professors, and you are able to ask questions in a small group." Leonard, articling student

"If you are interested in being a litigator, U of C has a very strong mooting program. Owen Saunders and others are faculty advisors for the Jessup moot team and they are very good. U of C has done consistently well in the Jessup and we were the Canadian champions in 1991-92. We also have a one-week trial advocacy course in third year and the bar association in Alberta offers the same course for $1900. We get it included in our tuition." Leonard, articling student

"There are lots of activities such as bowling parties, Christmas parties for the kids, men's and women's hockey teams, and a softball tournament. The Professors take part too." Will LL.B. '93

"I represented the student body on the admissions committee. I was elected and it is a paid position over the summer. Marks are a factor in the decision, but we would rather look at the whole person. Volunteer and work experience play a big part. Our average age is twenty-eight and it isn't uncommon for a person to know two languages and sometimes three or four. Once you get in, it is structured to succeed, not fail. If you are in trouble at Christmas you have the option of tutoring at no extra cost. We are looking for a well-rounded person as opposed to someone with a high GPA and LSAT score but no personality." Will, LL.B. '93

"It is a non-traditional school in terms of its admissions process and curriculum. In terms of admission, they don't just factor in the GPA and LSAT score. They place a lot of emphasis on life experience. I know people who have been CFL football players; I am from a journalism background; there are M.B.A.'s and nurses. The students aren't just straight out of undergraduate and therefore you get a lot of interesting backgrounds. The curriculum has a fair amount of emphasis on legal writing and advocacy skills starting in first year. A fair amount of our grades in first year come from writing and mooting assignments. U of C has done very well in mooting, especially in national competitions like the Jessup. Credit should be given to the faculty advisors." Jeffrey LL.B. '92

"The newness of the school is a strength since the professors are fairly young and not as traditional as in the more established schools." Jeffrey LL.B. '92

"I took the Criminal Law practicum and rode around in a patrol car, spent two weeks with a defense attorney, and had the opportunity to prosecute some traffic offenses in traffic court. Seminars and discussions were also part of the practicum. It was a good experience." Jeffrey LL.B. '92

Where the Program Could Improve

"The small size of the school limits you to the number of upper-year courses you can take, but there are directed research opportunities." Will LL.B. '93
"I am constantly surprised by purchases of reading materials throughout the year that we were not informed about at the beginning of the year. It could affect course selection and financial planning." Tom LL.B. '94
"I didn't think it would be as humbling as it is. Most of us had GPAs of 3.0 at least, and it's hard to adjust to lower grades." Gael LL.B. '94
"Get used to C's. The school is called U of C and they really mean it. The vast majority of marks handed out are C's. A C means you are competent, B's are very special and A's are gold plated. The average in most years is B-. This is hard for people to deal with after performing well in previous degrees. It is also annoying when we are compared with other law schools, but Calgary law firms are aware of the way we are marked." Hazel LL.B. '93
"There should be some stimulus for the professors to be more interested in teaching and place more of an emphasis on teaching as their primary responsibility, and less on their pet projects outside the school." Francis LL.B. '92

Controversies

"Gender and social policy issues come up a lot. Some students would rather have a narrow black letter approach than a contextual approach. In a business association course, half the course was spent on discussing greater corporate responsibility. Some liked it and some hated it. The first-year class is two-thirds women. There is no backlash, only good-natured feminist jokes. It is a small school and over half the student body are women, so we don't feel that we have to be represented by a special interest group. " Hazel LL.B. '93
"The professors get a lot of speakers on feminist issues. There should be a whole range of speakers. Feminism shouldn't be the only area." Leonard, articling student

On Faculty

"The faculty is very good and I appreciate the fact that many are involved outside the classroom and this gives a practical aura to their teachings. There is a strong relationship with the school and practising lawyers in the city, and they have been supervising the moots." Tom LL.B. '94

"Nigel Banks teaches Property. He explains things well and encourages class participation. Any time you have a question he is more than willing to talk about it." Gael LL.B. '94 [Nigel Banks has won teaching awards university wide. He was nominated by the students.]

"Richard Devlin teaches Contracts and Business Associations. He is a very demanding professor but outstanding." Jeffrey LL.B. '92

"Sheilah Martin teaches Torts and Women and the Law. She recently got her doctorate and she is an excellent speaker and teacher." Leonard, articling student

"Nick Rafferty teaches Contracts and Conflicts of Law. He is extremely committed to teaching, he is witty, and his lectures are very interesting. He gives excellent evaluations and feedback on exams and he is generally a best friend to the students." Jeffrey LL.B. '92

"Ann Stalker teaches Criminal Law and Criminal Procedure. She is organized, prepared, accessible, and presents her material in a clear fashion." Francis LL.B. '92

Other Comments

"I have been surprised by how human this law school is. At Calgary you know everyone in the faculty and it is a great experience, but don't come to U of C unless you want to think of the big picture." Hazel LL.B. '93

"For aboriginal students, U of C has had a less than ideal image but in reality this isn't the case, I have had no problems as an aboriginal student." Will LL.B. '93

"In order to be successful in law school you have to be organized to get through it. Don't plan on a life for the next few years." Francis LL.B. '92

Dalhousie University

- **INQUIRIES**
  Dalhousie Law School
  Weldon Law Building
  6061 University Avenue
  Halifax, N.S.
  B3H 4H9
  (902) 494-2068

ADMISSIONS INFORMATION

- **APPLICATION DEADLINE DATE FOR ADMISSIONS**
  28 February

- **REQUIRED TO SUBMIT**
  - Official copies of all university academic transcripts
  - LSAT score report
  - Application form
  - Application fee
  - Personal statement
  - Two reference letters
  - (Medical statement from physician or psychiatrists etc. where applicants allege that some medical condition has adversely affected their previous performance)

- **EDUCATION REQUIREMENT**
  - Three full years of academic work at a recognized university after a junior matriculation (i.e. Nova Scotia Grade XI or equivalent) *or*
  - Two full years of academic work at a recognized university after senior matriculation (i.e. Nova Scotia Grade XII or equivalent). Normally this means that the candidate is within one year of receiving a degree.

- **AVERAGE GPA**

  3.3 or 74.7% or B+

- **AVERAGE LSAT**

  81st percentile (the February writing of the LSAT is the last writing which will allow an applicant to be considered). LSAT scores will be averaged if the test has been written more than once.

- **RATIO OF APPLICANTS TO REGISTRATIONS**

  13.7 : 1

- **SIZE OF INCOMING CLASS**

  156

- **CAN YOU DEFER ACCEPTANCE**

  Some one-year deferrals are granted.

- **APPLICATION FEE**

  $25

- **TUITION FEE**

  The 1992-93 tuition fee is $3,063 for Canadian students.

CLASS PROFILE

- **AVERAGE AGE OF STUDENTS ENTERING THE PROGRAM**

  25

- **PERCENTAGE OF THE CLASS WHO ARE WOMEN**

  48%

- **PERCENTAGE OF WOMEN WHO ARE TENURED FACULTY**

  18% (five of 28 faculty members are women who have tenure)

- **PERCENTAGE OF THE CLASS WITH:**

two years or more of an undergraduate degree	6%
a three-year degree	81%
a four-year degree	11%
a post-graduate degree	2%

- **PROFILE OF LL.B. POPULATIONS**

Native students	4 (3%)

Students admitted under special category   33 (21%)
Mature students   5 (3%)
Mature student is defined as someone who is twenty-six years old and has a minimum of five years work experience and who does not have the minimum two years of university education. Many of Dalhousie's students in the general admissions category are mature (ie. older) students.

OTHER RELATED PROGRAMS

Master of Laws, Master of Business Administration/LL.B., Master of Public Administration/LL.B., LL.B/ Master of Library Science, J.S.D.
PART-TIME PROGRAM: The same entrance requirements and application deadline dates as the full-time program apply for the part-time program. In addition, applicants must demonstrate that full-time attendance would be a hardship. Only the first year has to be done half-time. There is more flexibility after first year when the rest of the program can be completed on a part-time basis, taking up to seven years to complete the degree requirements. All first year courses are taken during the day. Very few courses are offered during the evening.

ADMISSIONS REQUIREMENTS

A formula is used as part of the admissions process at Dalhousie's Faculty of Law. An applicant's academic average is given a weight of sixty percent and the LSAT a weight of forty percent. The result is that each candidate has a composite score and the scores are rank-ordered. A student's entire transcript is used in the calculation of the academic average and the courses are closely scrutinized. An emphasis is placed on the academic average in an applicant's two most recent years if that average is better than the cumulative average.

The process is not as mechanical as it may seem. The personal statement and references are taken seriously in the decision-making process. Although the academic average and the LSAT scores have the most weight, community service and what a student has to offer the law school is the next most influential factor. When reading personal statements Vaughan Black, Chairperson of the Admissions Committee, states that they want applicants who "want to go to law school beyond helping themselves. You say you want to help everybody but what have you done in the past?"

The admissions process is taken very seriously. Candidates with marginal composite scores are interviewed to get a full picture of their qualifications.

Between 200 and 250 students are interviewed each year. Admissions personnel travel across Canada interviewing students.

Likely candidates in the mature student category are interviewed to ascertain if they have the analytical skills they need to succeed in law school. During the interview, an argument might be provoked to assess the candidate's ability to logically defend their stand. Well qualified applicants who may only have two years of their undergraduate degree completed may be interviewed to assess their maturity.

The majority of applicants fall within Dalhousie's general admissions category. There are six categories: aboriginal, disadvantaged, general, mature, the Program for Indigenous Blacks and Micmacs, and special status.

The admissions formula is only used to admit students who fall in the general category. The academic performance and LSAT criteria take on a lesser role in the decision-making process for other categories. Aboriginal students whose academic background does not meet the admission standards are eligible to apply for admission to the faculty of law upon successful completion of the Program of Legal Studies for Native People at the University of Saskatchewan, College of Law.

Students who feel that racial, social, or economic background places them at a disadvantage to general applicants may receive special consideration. Personal statements should explain the circumstances and how they have affected their studies.

Mature students may or may not have the educational requirements for admission, but they must be twenty-six and have a minimum of five years work experience.

Dalhousie's Faculty of Law is committed to increasing the representation of Indigenous Blacks and Micmacs in the student body and faculty. Dalhousie has two Blacks and one First Nation full-time faculty members. This is the highest representation of faculty in these minority groups of any law school in Canada. There are fewer than five aboriginal professors in Canada.

The Program for Indigenous Blacks and Micmacs (IBM) was established in 1989. Applicants in this category must submit the same material and meet the same basic educational requirements as other applicants. In addition, candidates may be required to enrol in the one month Pre-Law program that takes place in August. The course is an intensive introduction to the Law School curriculum with an emphasis on the academic skills required in legal education. The performance throughout the course is part of the evaluation process for admission. Upon acceptance into the Faculty of Law, tutorial support and counselling is available. The administration projects that twelve students (seven Indigenous Blacks and five Micmacs) will be enrolled in the IBM Program each year for the next three years.

CHARACTER OF THE SCHOOL

Dalhousie's Faculty of Law has set a new course. Leaving behind a traditional outlook, it is moving toward a more diverse student body and a more integrative approach to the study of law. What used to be a white upper middle class student body is starting to change with the help of a pro-active admissions process. Indigenous Blacks and Micmacs, mature students, and students who are not just the academic elite are added to the mix.

A shift in the priorities of the Law School has accompanied the transition to diversity. In the past, Dalhousie focused on a good grounding in the fundamental areas of the law which make up many of the components of corporate commercial law. Dalhousie's law school has incorporated into this base feminist legal issues and a few critical theory courses. Current concerns are represented in environmental and marine law.

Students are slightly restricted in their opportunities to explore other areas of the law due to the number of required courses. Like all law schools, first year is entirely compulsory. However, in second year at Dalhousie you also have two compulsory courses plus a major research paper. In third year there is only one required course and a major research paper. Dalhousie's Faculty of Law is less structured than University of the Western Ontario or the University of New Brunswick, but more structured than Osgoode Hall's Law School, which has no required courses after first year.

Dalhousie's Law School has not lost its traditional spirit of camaraderie. The changes in the make-up of the student body and the focus of the school have resulted in some flare-ups among the students, but on the whole there is a mutual respect among the students and faculty. Teaching seems to be a priority among the faculty and the open door policy of access is respected. The faculty actively attend student functions in an atmosphere of equity. Thursday afternoons at the Domus Legis Society, nicknamed the "Dome" (a type of fraternity house located near the law building), is a ritual where faculty often mix informally with the students. Dalhousie has probably one of the closest relationship between faculty and students — with the University of Alberta on the other side of the continuum — representing more of the relationship depicted in the movie "The Paper Chase."

STRENGTHS OF THE PROGRAM

Dalhousie's Faculty of Law offers a solid basic program with strengths in the areas of Maritime and Environmental Law, and emphasis on Law of the Sea. Ocean studies is an area of interest for Dalhousie University in general, and the law school contributes significantly in this area. The Maritime and Environmental Law Program now offers over a dozen courses in Maritime and Environmental Law and related areas. According to P. Girard, Acting Dean, "this is perhaps the largest concentration of courses in Canada." The Oceans Institute of Canada is established at Dalhousie University and attracts experts from many countries.

Dalhousie's Faculty of Law has achieved significant recognition for their strong feminist analysis of the law in terms of courses offered and scholarship. Constitutional and Public Law are also recognized areas of strength.

Three new faculty were hired in 1991-92, two faculty members in the Health Law Institute, and the Director of the Indigenous Blacks and Micmacs Program (IBM Program). The IBM Program offers a pre-law intensive preparation course for all IBM students before classes start in September. The Director also provides tutorials and ongoing support for native students. There are only two other programs like this in Canada — the Native Law Centre in Canada at the University of Saskatchewan, and the program for Francophone Civil Law Students at the University of Ottawa.

Two clinical opportunities are available for students. The criminal law clinic gives second- and third-year students a chance to get hands-on experience. It is an intensive session where students are assigned a judge, a crown counsel, or a defence lawyer, to observe and to participate in the criminal law work of that person. Students attend seminars on the topic and write a paper.

The Legal Aid Clinic at Dalhousie was formed in 1970, and it was the first major clinical legal aid training program of its type in Canada. The Clinic provides legal services to the low-income population of the Halifax-Dartmouth metropolitan area. Up to thirty students can spend a term at the Legal Aid Clinic in their third year.

In 1991-92, students established the student-run *Dalhousie Journal of Legal Studies*. Students also have an opportunity to become involved in the faculty run *Dalhousie Law Journal*, a respected legal periodical.

Dalhousie is a national Law School which attracts approximately fifty percent of students from outside the Maritimes. Many students from Ontario and other Western provinces are attracted to Dalhousie to see the Eastern region of Canada.

WHERE THE PROGRAM COULD IMPROVE

The change in priorities and timing has resulted in a re-evaluation of the allocation of funds. The Business Law Immersion Term started in 1989 was not offered in the 1991-92 session because the professor who taught it was on sabbatical. The Business Law Immersion Term was an intensive program limited to twelve third-year students which took the participants through a simulation of the life of a typical small business corporation. However, with budget constraints the Business Law Immersion Term's future is uncertain. The immersion program offered a unique dimension to the program's corporate commercial focus.

Budget cutbacks every year for the last several years have forced the administration at Dalhousie's Faculty of Law to look for ways to cut costs yet again. Recently, the Legal Aid Clinic was the centre of a much heated debate. The Legal Aid Clinic offers sixteen students per term the opportunity to develop their skills and refine the processes and material they have learned in class in a real-life context. Some students argued that in times of constraint, the money could be spent to strengthen areas of the curriculum which were more central to the study of the law. Others countered that the Legal Aid Clinic was important not only as an experience for the students, but as a public service to the community.

The Legal Aid Clinic has survived for the time being. Students continue to get a practical legal education experience developing professional skills and refining their understanding of the rules and processes taught in a real life context. Cases in family, criminal, and administrative law make up most of the demand on the clinic.

From recent events concerning the Business Law Immersion Program and the Legal Aid Clinic, the trend is clear. Dalhousie's Faculty of Law has suffered from severe financial cutbacks, thereby forcing special programs that only serve the needs of relatively few students to be closely scrutinized.

ON HALIFAX

Halifax is a university town without equal in Canada. It is the home of six post-secondary institutions — Dalhousie University, King's College University, Mt. St. Vincent University, Nova Scotia School of Art and Design, St. Mary's University, and the Technical University of Nova Scotia (TUNS). Dalhousie has a beautiful ivy-covered limestone campus within a twenty-minute walk of downtown and the waterfront.

Housing is not difficult to find and an average rent might be $350-$400 for three people sharing a house. Most students live close to the campus. Student housing is not concentrated into a ghetto area but is interspersed with residential areas.

The historical city is well treed and is quite colourful, with brightly painted clapboard houses. It is easy to get around on foot or by bike, making a car an unnecessary and expensive luxury as parking is expensive and hard to come by.

Halifax has the largest per capita black population in Canada. This factor, combined with the weak economy of the Maritimes, causes an underlying racial tension in certain areas of the city. Generally speaking, however, the atmosphere of Halifax is very friendly and operates at a slower maritime pace.

WHAT THE STUDENTS SAY

(Pseudonyms have replaced the following students' names)

The Strengths of the Program

"They [the administration] are very positive about being a national law school. There are students from every province and you get different regional perspectives. Dalhousie also accepts civil law students and lawyers from Europe so that they can get common law accreditation in one year. This allows them to practise anywhere in Canada except Quebec. My classmates are now all over Canada." John, articling student

"The legal writing course in first year is very strong. They teach you how to write and do research. It is very intense — comprised of three assignments, including one long paper that is marked by second- and third-year students [and faculty]." Paul LL.B. '91

"Educationally, it is very good and the people are really nice. That competitive edge isn't there. There is no practice of hiding books. People are ready to give you notes and help you." Lillian LL.B. '92

"It is a laid-back school. Students learn to balance their lives and students are always encouraged to work together." Elizabeth LL.B. '92

"It is quite a friendly law school. The Domus Legis is a bar across the street from the law school. It is like a frat house. There are all kinds of signatures on the ceiling — some signed by Supreme Court Judges." Dave LL.B. '92

"There is a diversity of students. The [admissions] focus isn't so much on grades. They have disadvantaged groups, different socio-economic groups, and all of this gives a wide perspective of views." Eilene LL.B. '93

"The faculty are accessible and very open regarding the course material and other issues. The largest classes are about fifty to sixty students; some highly specialized classes may have only three or four. Only in one first-year class and one third-year class does the whole class of 156 take a class together." Ruth LL.B. '92

"The curriculum is strong in terms of constitutional and public law with an emphasis on public service." Alec LL.B. '93

"Dalhousie is a well-balanced school in terms of curriculum, but really excels in Maritime Law." Dave LL.B. '92

On Faculty

"Tom Cromwell taught me civil procedure. He has a high regard for students and puts a lot of effort into teaching. He deals with the material presented and tries to let you know what to keep an eye out for when practising." Alec LL.B. '93
"Bruce Wildsmith teaches constitutional law and administrative law. He is very straightforward and breaks down the material into manageable steps." Ruth LL.B. '92

Where the Program Could Improve

"The law faculty went overboard in trying to satisfy women's, blacks', and native students' interest groups. I sometimes felt like there was too much patting themselves on the back saying aren't we nice and forgetting that their main job was to turn out well-qualified lawyers and not social reform." John, articling student
"Some of the faculty aren't teaching in the areas of their competency. We evaluate faculty but don't get any feedback. They are hiring people who are specialists in only one area." Eilene LL.B. '93
"International law is not as strong as I thought. There are only three or four courses in it and it doesn't seem to have the same bent as its reputation." Lillian LL.B. '92
"They should improve the marking scheme. The school uses a C-bell curve which means that the average grade is C. This makes it difficult when we are interviewing for articling jobs because most other schools use a B-bell curve." David LL.B. '92

Controversies

"Given the resources, you could say that the school is trying to do too much. There is an attempt to cover a lot of areas — the Indigenous Black & Micmac Program, criminal clinics, excellent professors and courses — and funding is limited. I would personally like them to discontinue the legal aid clinic since we already have a criminal clinic and other legal aid clinics for the community. The legal aid clinic may not be the best way to distribute the resources." Alec LL.B. '93
"When I first came to Dalhousie, I didn't know what political correctness

was and I still don't like the term. Sometimes it makes me angry but we can still talk about it. Politically active groups are strong and it attracts people from Upper Canada. It has opened my eyes and made me more tolerant and understanding of gender issues. It has been a good experience for me although sometimes difficult. Generally, there is quite a degree of respect despite the differences of opinion. We are friendly to one another even when we disagree." Alec LL.B. '93

"Being in law school has raised my consciousness on a number of issues. A large portion of the student body is politically active. Their presence has made me more aware of gender, racial, and social issues. I feel this is beneficial to critical thinking. Controversy also has obvious disadvantages. For example, last year there was a controversy over the legal aid clinic. The legal aid debate polarized the student body and faculty. If you supported the legal aid clinic you were considered to be a socialist and if you did not support them you were a capitalist pig. When lines of communication break down completely as they did during the legal aid debate, it has a negative effect on everybody. This debate has now subsided, but controversies over gender, black letter, corporate versus other areas occasionally flare up in the classroom." Ruth LL.B. '92

"The biggest controversy involves gender. It isn't that divisive, but the main fallout is that the faculty hired people to be politically correct and these people could have had more experience. Their views are so one-sided that it's hard to have a conversation in their class." Dave LL.B. '92

"The majority of hiring is in public Law and aboriginal Law and some students want more of the traditional courses. The school is changing from a focus on international law to more of an environmental, human rights focus even though international law is still strong." Elizabeth LL.B. '92

Other Comments

"It is very intense in first year and the class becomes quite close. You do everything together, both socially and academically. Law school is your world." Paul LL.B. '91

University of Manitoba

- **INQUIRIES**
  Faculty of Law
  The University of Manitoba
  Robson Hall
  Winnipeg, Manitoba
  R3T 2N2
  (204) 474-9773

ADMISSIONS INFORMATION

- **APPLICATION DEADLINE DATE FOR ADMISSIONS**
  1 March

- **REQUIRED TO SUBMIT**

Academic Category

- Official copies of all university academic transcripts
- LSAT score report
- TOEFL score may be requested where English is a second language

Special Consideration Category (in addition to the above)

- Personal statement
- Résumé
- Names of three referees

- **EDUCATION REQUIREMENT**
  For Ordinary applicants: two full years of academic study in a degree program at a recognized university.
  For Mature applicants: at least one full year of academic study in a degree program at a recognized university.

- **AVERAGE GPA**

    3.7 or A- or 80% (range 3.1 – 4.0)

- **AVERAGE LSAT**

    85th percentile (range 45th – 99th percentile)

- **RATIO OF APPLICANTS TO REGISTRATIONS**

    10.9 : 1

- **SIZE OF INCOMING CLASS**

    95 plus up to 5 half-time positions

- **CAN YOU DEFER ACCEPTANCE**

    No

- **APPLICATION FEE**

    $40 for Canadians and permanent residents
    $50 for International students including those studying in Canada

- **TUITION FEE**

    The 1992-93 tuition fees are $2,650 plus $70.25 for Student Association
    and Student Union fees

CLASS PROFILE

- **AVERAGE AGE OF STUDENTS ENTERING THE PROGRAM**

    25

- **PERCENTAGE OF THE CLASS WHO ARE WOMEN**

    40% (in 1990-91 there were 47% women)

- **PERCENTAGE OF WOMEN WHO ARE TENURED FACULTY**

    16.5%

- **PERCENTAGE OF THE CLASS WITH:**

two years or more of an undergraduate degree	16%
a three-year degree	63%
a four-year degree	18%
a post-graduate degree	3%

- **PROFILE OF LL.B. POPULATIONS**

    Native Students   7%

| Visible Minorities | 3% |
| Mature Students | 9% |

OTHER RELATED PROGRAMS

LL.M. with an emphasis on aboriginal law and legal history. The degree is primarily research based with the hope that, where appropriate, a candidate will work in close co-operation with the Legal Research Institute of the University of Manitoba.

HALF-TIME PROGRAM: Three students were admitted into the half-time program in 1991-92, bringing the total half-time enrollment to fourteen. For the first two years, a half-time course load is required, but after the completion of first year, there is more flexibility in terms of course load. Students have six years to complete the program and classes are offered only during the day.

ADMISSIONS REQUIREMENTS

For Applicants Applying to the 1992-93 Law Program

Out of the ninety-five full-time positions at Manitoba's Faculty of Law, approximately eighty are filled with applicants applying for admission under the **Academic Category**. The only criteria used to determine whether an applicant will be admitted in this category is the LSAT score and cumulative average (grade point average — GPA). The admissions process is strictly a numerical exercise. An applicant's GPA and LSAT score is entered into a formula whereby both factors are given equal weights of fifty percent. An index score is computed.

Although all years of an undergraduate degree are taken into consideration when the GPA is calculated, lower grades can be discounted depending on how many courses have been completed at the undergraduate level. Ten courses are the minimum accepted for eligibility. A grade in one course can be dropped for each additional two full courses taken past the minimum of ten courses. For example, if a candidate has a four-year degree with a total of nineteen to twenty full courses, the admissions committee would omit the lowest five grades (thirty credit hours), when the overall GPA is calculated.

Within the academic admissions category, there is no formal opportunity to present additional information such as a personal statement, volunteer or work experience, or reference letters. Manitoba's Faculty of Law has one of the more mechanical processes of admission.

More flexibility in the selection process is available in the **Special Consideration Category**. Up to fifteen percent of applicants may be selected in this way. In contrast to the academic selection procedure, the special student application process is highly subjective. The objective of the program is to try to enrich the student body by increasing diversity. The committee looks into the applicant's motivation, obstacles that they may have had to overcome, evidence of leadership, and extra-curricular activities. More emphasis is placed on these factors than on the LSAT and GPA. However, a baseline LSAT score in at least the fiftieth percentile is required, or an average GPA of 3.00. Most of the applicants admitted in this category are older because significant achievements are looked for. The admissions committee is looking for applicants that can add to the mix of the student body.

The **Mature Student Category** is a category of eligibility to apply for admission. Applicants in this category have to be at least twenty-six years old, but more importantly, they must have less than five full credits, or the equivalence thereof, completed towards an undergraduate degree. Mature student applications are processed in either the Academic Consideration Category or the Special Consideration Category, depending on their circumstances.

For Applicants Applying to the 1993-94 Law Program

Significant changes have been made to the admissions process for applicants applying to the 1993-94 session. First, the names of the categories have been changed to more accurately reflect the basis on which the decision to admit is made. The academic category described above will be changed to the **Index Score Category** and the special consideration category will be renamed the **Individual Consideration Category**. Starting in the 1993-94 admissions cycle, the number of places reserved for the **Individual Consideration Category** will be increased from nine to fifteen.

Candidates applying under the **Index Score Category** should be aware that the weighting of the admissions formula will be changed to sixty/forty, with the most weight on the GPA score. The GPA will also be calculated differently. Before 1993, the process allowed grades in course(s) to be dropped after you had completed more than ten full courses. After 1993, no grades will be eliminated unless the applicant has completed a university degree. An applicant with a three-year degree will have their three lowest grades eliminated and a maximum of five grades will be eliminated if nineteen or more course credits are presented.

As of the 1993-94 admissions cycle, the admissions subcommittee will have the discretion to eliminate "stale dated" academic records, provided the candidate has a more current program that is at least two years in length (forty-eight credit hours). The committee would have to be convinced that the previous program was not indicative of the applicant's capabilities. Similarly, there is a possibility that false starts can be eliminated, provided the applicant transferred to a new faculty and has completed at least two years of work toward a new program. The decision to expunge a prior old academic record is not automatic. The applicant will have to request that their situation be reviewed.

The number of applications from out-of-province (predominantly Ontario) has dramatically increased by 147 percent since 1990. Applications from the province of Manitoba rose only slightly over 1990. The dramatic increase in out-of-province applications took place when the $75 non-refundable out-of-province application fee was replaced by one of $40, which was more in alignment to those of other schools.

Another reason for the increase in applications is the concerted outreach program targeting aboriginal students conducted by the Director of the Academic Support Program, Wendy Whitecloud. Eighteen Aboriginal students applied in 1991, compared to thirty-six in 1992, a one hundred percent increase. Seven aboriginal students were admitted for the 1991–92 academic year.

CHARACTER OF THE SCHOOL

The unimpressive eight-page information brochure which acts as the University of Manitoba's calendar, the very cut-and-dried admissions process that is followed, and an application form that is generic for all professional programs, gives the impression of a cold and distant law faculty. However, once admitted, you see a different picture. The faculty and administration are very student-centred, and the small numbers create a supportive academic community. Professors know their students by name and stand by their commitment to an open-door policy.

The students are bonded to each other by their commonality of purpose, but once classes are over, the majority of students leave campus and live their other lives. At least sixty percent of the student body come from Manitoba and the majority of these from Winnipeg. Manitoba's Faculty of Law could be described as a commuter school. The thirty percent of out-of-province students do not really get involved outside of the law faculty because most of them will be going back to Ontario and do not really feel they have much of a stake in either the law school or the city of Winnipeg. The students are very involved in their studies but are quite apathetic about concerns going on outside of the law school.

STRENGTHS OF THE PROGRAM

Manitoba's Faculty of Law has a strong practical focus and is one of the few Canadian law faculties which emphasizes the study of professional responsibility. Compulsory skill courses are an important part of the program. In first year a legal methods course is taken. In second year, courses on advocacy, counselling, interviewing, and negotiating are a mandatory part of the program, and in third year clinical courses in solicitors transactions, criminal law, family law, and administrative law are offered. Practitioners play a vital role throughout the skills courses. Second- and third-year students can volunteer with the Legal Aid Clinic.

Traditionally, the "hands on" approach to the study of law has been the Manitoba Faculty of Law's trademark. Recently however, Roland Penner, Dean of Manitoba's Faculty of Law, has taking a leadership role in the school's initiatives to improve access — particularly to Manitoba's aboriginal people. Aboriginal people represent approximately ten percent of Manitoba's population, and yet there are only a handful of lawyers to serve this large constituency.

Pro-active steps are being taken by the faculty to increase access to legal education. Efforts have been made to increase the effectiveness of outreach by increasing the amount of funding available for disadvantaged aboriginal students. More spaces are reserved for aboriginal, special, and half-time students. In fact, in 1992-93, the student body will consist of over twenty percent aboriginal, special, or half-time students. To support and assist in the transition to a more diversified student body, the position of Director of Academic Support Programs was established in 1990. Wendy Whitecloud, who has held the position since September of 1991, directs a hands-on tutorial program for aboriginal and special consideration students and provides counselling to all students in academic, social, and financial matters.

Manitoba's Faculty of Law was also one of the first law schools to offer a half-time program and it remains one of the most flexible. There are a total of sixteen half-time students currently in the program.

"For some years, we have been known as a good mid-range school with an emphasis on teaching but not on research and publications," comments Dean Penner. However, there has been a push in the last few years to increase publication and research through two projects. The first is the Legal Research Institute, housed at the Faculty of Law and funded mainly by the Manitoba Law Foundation. The Institute is involved with publishing monographs and organizing academic conferences on a variety of topics. Secondly, the Canadian Legal History Project brings in leading speakers on Canadian history.

WHERE THE PROGRAM COULD IMPROVE

Funding problems have become critical. Dean Penner stated that beginning in 1993-94, significant parts of the program might have to be cut or class sizes increased. The administration may not be able to continue to hire practitioners to supplement the courses offered by tenured faculty. This would mean a drastic reduction of third-year course offerings. Approximately one-third of the courses offered at the Faculty of Law are taught by practitioners hired as part-time or sessional lecturers. The Manitoba Law Foundation gave the Faculty of Law a one-time grant which covered the salary of part-time faculty last year. New sources of funding are being sought. "We are concerned about the future, but we are determined not to be overwhelmed," comments Dean Penner optimistically.

Manitoba's Faculty of Law has a stable body of experienced and respected faculty, but until recently there has been little opportunity for revitalization. The professors are very good at what they do, but there has been insufficient turnover allowing young faculty members to be hired, and to bring with them new ideas, teaching styles, and attitudes. Some significant hirings in the last four years have begun to turn this around.

The small size of the faculty and its practical nature lends itself to a highly structured curriculum that offers limited flexibility to take the few perspective courses offered. First year is completely compulsory as it is at all law schools in Canada, but in second year students only have one elective. In third year there is one compulsory course in the legal profession and professional responsibility, and the balance of the third year program is electives. As a result, there is a solid grounding in the traditional fields of the law, but in the students' opinion, there is not as much opportunity to get alternative viewpoints.

ON WINNIPEG

The University of Manitoba's campus is located on the outskirts of Winnipeg, about twenty-five minutes from downtown by bus, or fifteen minutes by car. If you own a car, it is advisable to apply for parking as soon as you are admitted. Parking space is very limited. Housing is available, and relative to Toronto and Vancouver prices, it is quite reasonable. A newer one-bedroom apartment might average around $450-$500/month whereas an older one-bedroom downtown might be around $400/month. Osborne Village is a popular area for students to find accommodation. It has the nickname "granola belt" because it is kind of a "hippyish" area, a remnant of the 60's with cafes and cheap rents. It is on a direct bus route which makes getting to campus easy and quick.

Extra-curricular activities are few and there really is not a very good social life connected to the Manitoba's Faculty of Law. It is a commuter school and not many students live in the residences.

The city of Winnipeg has a small-town atmosphere even though it is a city. Everyone seems to know everyone else. Winnipeg is known for its cold temperatures but take heart — the skies are mostly sunny, and spring is gorgeous starting about April when classes end.

WHAT THE STUDENTS SAY

(Pseudonyms have replaced the following students' names)

The Strengths of the Program

"The faculty and administration bend over backwards to help students who are having problems, or fall ill." Cameron LL.B. '92

"The faculty-student ratio is very high and for core courses you might have twenty-five students in the class. You feel the professor knows who you are." Lynn LL.B. '95

"The Dean and Associate Dean are very accessible and largely responsible for the relaxed atmosphere. The professors are equally accessible." Lynn LL.B. '95

"If you are going to practise in Manitoba you will meet the people you will practise with in the law school, since the legal community is quite small." Cameron LL.B. '92

"The practical aspects are excellent. We take legal methods where we learn how to do legal drafting and memo preparation, interviewing, counselling, negotiating, and advocacy. These courses put you into the situation of being a lawyer, for example, from drafting to moot courses. Some of these courses are conducted by practitioners too." Allison LL.B. '93

"University of Manitoba was the last place I applied to. I thought it was so impersonal and its brochure is the least impressive. They do themselves an injustice because, once you are admitted, they encourage a collegial atmosphere where study groups are formed and you work together like you will when you are a lawyer." Kurt LL.B. '93

"The new computerized lab opened up this year and there is good support from the library staff." Kurt LL.B. '93

"There is a strong feminist component and the University of Manitoba's first Gender in the Law course just started. This was quite a breakthrough." Cheryl LL.B. '93

"As a part-time student I can continue my education, and support myself.

Taking six years to complete the program would be too long, but one year part-time is great." Lynn LL.B. '95

"The standardized curriculum makes you well-rounded. There is a focus on corporate/commercial, more than anything else." Lara LL.B. '92

"We have a legal aid clinic. In second and third year you can volunteer. You deal with real people's problems ranging from landlord and tenant to some petty theft. It gives you an idea if you will like court or not, and when you are dealing with people you get a feel for the seriousness of the profession." Nicole LL.B. '93

Where the Program Could Improve

"The school could improve in offering more courses in current areas, such as environmental law and gender in the law. The core areas are covered well, but the topical subjects don't get the attention they deserve." Cameron LL.B. '92

"The size of the school limits diversity. It is a meat-and-potatoes curriculum and it specializes in practice." Kurt LL.B. '93

"There are very few visible minorities although they are trying to attract more native students. A native students' advisor was hired this year." Cameron LL.B. '92

"It's not a big school; therefore, there is not a variety of different ethnic groups." Lynn LL.B. '95

"The program is inflexible in terms of course choices. In first year there is no choice [this is true of all law schools], and in second year you only have one option. You have to take the required courses which I would rather not have taken." Cheryl LL.B. '93

"There is not much school spirit and politically it is quite apathetic." Cheryl LL.B. '93

"Students don't show up at law games and other events. There is not that much school spirit." Lara LL.B. '92

"You are very isolated from any other faculty." Allison LL.B. '93

"The faculty does not have that much money.... They are trying to get the legal profession to donate money to the law library." Nicole LL.B. '93

The Controversies

"There is some controversy over gender issues, and there is a perception that the faculty are old-fashioned and unwilling to change. There aren't many female professors and the ones that there are, are mostly at the junior level." Cameron LL.B. '92

"Feminism is kept quite quiet. There is no real controversy that stands out."
Cheryl LL.B. '93
"There is not a lot of heated debates. I guess we are kind of apathetic. The only thing people got really heated about was when the faculty asked for a contribution to an endowment fund. We are all pretty tolerant and that is what the province is like too. You always get people who are black or white on issues, but we disagree graciously." Nicole LL.B. '93

On Faculty

"Leigh Steusser teaches criminal law, advocacy, evidence, and coaches the Gale Cup. He was the best teacher I have ever had in my life. He knows how to teach and deal with people. Everybody from the timid first year to the cocky third year gets his message. [He wrote a textbook on advocacy]." Nicole LL.B. '93
"Phil Osborne teaches contracts and torts. He brings the cases to life. He likes the socratic method and encourages participation." Cheryl LL.B. '93
"John Irvine teaches property and torts. He has a very good grasp of the subject matter and has a very entertaining way of teaching." Cameron LL.B. '92
"Linda Vincent teaches contracts. She is very thorough with a wonderful sense of humour. She was able to get her point across with some give and take." Lynn LL.B. '95

Other Comments

"The University of Manitoba is a commuter school and approximately three quarters of the students are from Winnipeg; only a few live in residence." Cameron LL.B. '92
"Marks are not stressed. The professors are constantly telling us that C's are fine and that you shouldn't expect A's in first year. Marks are given to us in sealed envelopes, and it's your choice if you want to disclose them or not." Lynn LL.B. '95

McGill University

■ INQUIRIES

Admissions and Placement Officer
Faculty of Law
McGill University
3644 Peel Street
Montreal, Quebec
H3A 1W9
(514) 398-6602

*NOTE: There are three legal programs available at McGill's Faculty of Law: the three-year Civil Law (B.C.L.) program required to be admitted to the bar and practise in the province of Quebec, the three-year Common Law program (LL.B.) required to be admitted to the bar and practise outside of Quebec, and the National Program which students can enter at the end of their first year of either the Civil or Common Law program. The National Program is a four-year program which includes the first year of either the Civil or Common Law programs. The National Program allows students to graduate with both B.C.L. and LL.B. degrees at the end of four years. Approximately seventy-five percent of the students enroled at McGill's Faculty of Law choose the National Program, which gives them the choice to practise common or civil law anywhere in Canada.

ADMISSIONS INFORMATION

■ APPLICATION DEADLINE DATE FOR ADMISSIONS

1 February
1 March for CEGEP students currently completing their D.E.C. and applying to the Civil Law stream

■ REQUIRED TO SUBMIT

- Official copies of all university academic transcripts

- LSAT score report or Université de Montréal's test score for those applicants who prefer to write a test in French
- Personal statement
- Curriculum vitae
- Two letters of reference

■ **EDUCATION REQUIREMENTS**

LL.B. program requires two years of undergraduate study at a recognized university program.

B.C.L. program applicants can apply directly from a Quebec College of General and Vocational Education (CEGEP) although further studies at the undergraduate level may be required to be admitted to certain bars of the common law provinces.

Ability to read in both French and English is required, as materials in certain courses may be available in French only. In addition, occasionally an important course may only be offered in French in a given year. It is Faculty policy not to offer required courses in French only.

■ **AVERAGE GPA**

LL.B.: 80% or A- or 3.7
(range 69%-88%)

B.C.L.: CEGEP students	87%
University students	79%

range for both CEGEP and university students is 67% − 86%

■ **AVERAGE LSAT**

87th percentile

If the LSAT is written more than once, the scores are averaged. In some cases, applicants who prefer to write a test in French may write the test administered by the Université de Montréal.

■ **RATIO OF APPLICANTS TO REGISTRATIONS**

20.1 :1 LL.B.
6 :1 B.C.L.

■ **SIZE OF INCOMING CLASS**

LL.B.: 50
B.C.L.: 90-95

■ **CAN YOU DEFER ACCEPTANCE**

Only with the permission of the Associate Dean, Admissions. The maximum deferment is usually one year.

■ **APPLICATION FEE**

$40

■ **TUITION FEE**

The 1992-93 tuition fees are $1,916 for Canadian students and $7,464 for non-exempt foreign students

CLASS PROFILE

■ **AVERAGE AGE OF STUDENTS ENTERING THE PROGRAM**

LL.B. : 25
B.C.L.: 23

■ **PERCENTAGE OF THE CLASS WHO ARE WOMEN**

LL.B. : 49%
B.C.L.: 57%

■ **PERCENTAGE OF WOMEN WHO ARE TENURED FACULTY**

10%
Four out of forty professors are tenured and ten are tenure track.

■ **PERCENTAGE OF THE CLASS WITH**

two years or more of an undergraduate degree	LL.B. 6%
a three- or four-year degree	LL.B. 76%
a post-graduate degree	LL.B. 18%
two years or more of an undergraduate degree	B.C.L. 5%★
a three- or four-year degree	B.C.L. 53%
a post-graduate degree.	B.C.L. 14%

★*Note:* 28% of the B.C.L. class were CEGEP students

■ **PROFILE OF LL.B. POPULATIONS**

mature students★★	LL.B. 14%
native students	LL.B. 2%
mature students★★	B.C.L. 11%
native students	B.C.L. 2%

★★ A mature student is defined as someone who is over thirty years of age or who has been out of school for a minimum of five years.

OTHER RELATED PROGRAMS

Master of Law, M.B.A./LL.B., LL.B./M.S.W., Doctorate of Law
HALF-TIME PROGRAM: At the present time there is no half-time program at McGill's Faculty of Law.

ADMISSIONS REQUIREMENTS

Passive bilingualism is required for all programs. The option to express yourself in your mother tongue in class or during moots is always available, but the ability to read in both languages and an oral comprehension of the other language is required. While it is the policy of the Faculty of Law that obligatory courses not be offered in French only, in a given year, a non-obligatory but important course may be offered in French only. This situation took place in 1991–92.

No formula is used as part of the admission process. A holistic approach is taken considering the LSAT, GPA, personal statement, curriculum vitae, and references. The personal statement plays an especially important role in the committee's decision. "Students underestimate a well-written and well-thought-out statement. We are looking for flexibility of expression and clarity — what it shows us about you," comments Professor Jukier, Associate Dean. To calculate the GPA for admissions purposes, all years are used; however, Professor Jukier states, "If we see a bad first year but a good second year we will discount the bad year a bit. An upward trend is important. We give less weight to poor grades if an explanation is offered and supported with documentation." Some universities assign different values to their marking scheme; for example, a B at one university may have a range of 65-80% compared to a B from another school defining the range as 70-80%. To help equalize this, the admissions committee uses the marking system designated on the transcript. A master's degree can be an advantage and it will be looked at.

The study of law requires an analytical way of looking at things and good problem solving skills. These skills are tested by the LSAT and further evidence of these skills is looked for in the academic record. For students applying from fine arts programs, it is advisable to take electives in politics, philosophy, or logic courses in order that reasoning skills can be assessed.

There are no admissions categories for applicants, but the Admissions Committee does differentiate between regular applicants, mature applicants, and native peoples. With mature and native peoples, the admissions committee can show more discretion. Mature students need a minimum of a Diplôme d'études collègiales (D.E.C.), or two years of a university education. The mature student category at McGill's Faculty of Law can be defined as over thirty or out of school for a minimum of five years. Native applicants are encouraged to enroll in the Program of Legal Studies for Native People given at the College of Law of the University of Saskatchewan in the summer immediately prior to admission to the faculty, and acceptance may be conditional upon the successful completion of the course at Saskatchewan.

CHARACTER OF THE SCHOOL

McGill has integrated the study of civil and common law to such a degree within the National Program that the students seem to have a deeper understanding of the two systems and a tolerance of the differences. The relationship between Anglophone and Francophone students is friendly and respectful.

Both the University of Ottawa and McGill University offer the Civil Law and Common Law Programs, but the structure of the programs is distinctly different and this has affected the characters of the schools. McGill's Faculty of Law has chosen to integrate the two systems whereas the Faculty of Law at the University of Ottawa keeps the two systems separated. At the University of Ottawa the two programs are headed by different deans, administered by different admissions personnel, and there are two separate student law societies — the two solitudes. Yves-Marie Morissette, Dean of the Faculty of Law, describes the difference as follows: "At the University of Ottawa there are two realities present. We have one reality where there is a greater degree of integration. Over time our students realize that they have to know French and English and have at least a passive understanding of both official languages."

Tensions still exist between the two groups, co-existing in an Anglophone university in the largest Francophone city in Canada. The political tension of the national community however is set aside by the students. Political debates are avoided and the students are reluctant to confront constitutional issues, less they upset their "peaceful" co-existence.

"The most striking thing about our student body is how incredibly diverse it is. All parts of the country are represented and ten percent of the student body are foreign students. If there is an ethos, it is that it brings you into contact with people who are very different from you in a small school. There is tolerance developed at this institution. When you come out of here you don't despise the civil law or vice versa if you are in common law. You are not narrow-minded. They seem to get along because if anyone became intolerant they would all suffer," concludes Morissette.

STRENGTHS OF THE PROGRAM

The establishment of The Institute of Comparative Law and Legal Theory at McGill's Faculty of Law has had a strong influence on McGill's law program. The strength of the program comes from the comparison of the two systems of law that exist in Canada, and with that, a deeper understanding and appreciation of the two. "We have taken the direction of sophisticated comparative law. Unsophisticated comparative law is legal tourism, just the description of what happens. It has to have a theoretical perspective from law, and from that perspective you can look at different systems and go beyond to make comparisons," states Morissette.

The bisystemic and generally bilingual training gives the utmost mobility to graduates of the National Program. The B.C.L degree give you access to Quebec and the European countries of France and Belgium. The LL.B. allows graduates to practise law in every province except Quebec and some American States. The United States does not require an American law degree to practise law, only a law degree from a university program that has been accredited. The states of California, Massachusetts, New York, and Washington are readily accessible markets that can be accessed by writing an exam. This gives the program an international slant favouring the United States and Europe, compared to UBC's international interests with links to the Pacific Rim countries.

McGill's faculty also boast professors and students with backgrounds both national and international. Professors have obtained their initial legal training in five Canadian provinces: Quebec, Ontario, Manitoba, Saskatchewan, and Alberta. Others have been recruited from the United States, the United Kingdom, France, Belgium, the Netherlands, Yugoslavia, Australia, and New Zealand. Similarly, the five hundred undergraduate students are drawn from all ten Canadian provinces, several states in the United States, and a variety of European countries. In addition, McGill graduates have pursued their legal careers around the world. The varied geographic backgrounds of the students and faculty, the emphasis on comparative law, and bilingualism give McGill an international bent.

Students have the opportunity to become involved in the *McGill Law Journal*, which is student run. It is a bilingual professional journal that gives students experience in editing and writing. The McGill Legal Information Clinic is also student run. The service is limited to the McGill University Community; therefore, the diversity of problems may not be as great as if it served the city at large. However, it does provide the chance for upper-year law students to gain practical experience in providing legal counsel and information.

WHERE THE PROGRAM COULD IMPROVE

McGill University as a whole has a huge deficit of over seventy million dollars. The brunt of the budget restraints have hit the law library resulting in a collection of resources that is very strong in terms of Comparative Law and Air & Space Law, but it is not as diverse or comprehensive as it should be. As a result the law library will be given top priority during the next funding campaign. The law library at McGill University does not fall under the control of the Faculty of Law but rather the general library system. The Faculty of Law itself has not been limited by budget cutbacks in the last eight years. The number of faculty has stayed constant with a concerted effort to add marginally to the number of Francophone professors teaching in the civil law area.

The Faculty of Law at McGill has very expensive and focussed priorities. McGill's Faculty of Law aspires to an international slant in its curriculum and composition of its student body and faculty. This is supported by its commitment to the study of the two legal systems of common and civil law and the research conducted by the Institute of Comparative Law. As a result of these priorities a duplication of resources is necessary. Faculty who can teach both legal systems of law in both languages are needed as well as the research and library resources required to give adequate support. This may be causing McGill's limited financial resources to be distributed too thinly and narrowly.

ON MONTREAL

The Faculty of Law's campus at McGill is located in the heart of downtown Montreal. Living in Montreal's core gives students the opportunity to observe first hand the political tension surrounding our country's unity. However, the Faculty of Law itself tries to minimize the tension so as to be able to exist together peacefully. "Montreal is a terrific meeting place for French and English. Even though living in Montreal may be laced with tension, we can sit down and discuss the questions that we are facing less sensationally, since we are representative of every perspective in Canada," commented one student.

Montreal is a very reasonable place to live, both in terms of relatively low tuition fees relative to law schools outside of Quebec, and in cost of living. Rent is reasonable and the transit system is good allowing students to live farther out than the student ghetto surrounding the university where the rents are even more reasonable.

Language does become a problem which affects those who enjoy Montreal and would like to stay and practise law as a litigator. Only those who are completely bilingual would be able to succeed and even then it would help if you were also a Francophone.

WHAT THE STUDENTS SAY

The Strengths of the Program

"The National Program has served me well. I'm clerking in the Supreme Court of Canada and I wouldn't have gotten there if I wasn't bilingual and had a grounding in the two legal systems. Out of twenty-seven clerks from across Canada, five are from McGill. This is the highest number from any individual school." Nicole, articling student

"I think you learn more about the law and you are a better lawyer when you know about both legal systems. The experience humbles you and you don't think any one system is superior." Kabir LL.B. '93

"The atmosphere is very good. We have people from all walks of life, an equal representation of men and women, some, but not enough aboriginal students, and some students from Europe on exchanges. There is a lot going on such as weekly coffee houses, law games which take place every year, and a skit night that is held annually. All this develops camaraderie." Morton, articling student

"Bilingualism is a strength of the program. It is a pleasure to be sitting in class and hearing students answering and asking questions in both languages, switching back and forth, and no one minds." Lise B.C.L. '93

"If someone had said I would be working and studying in French I wouldn't have believed it two years ago. I worked in French last summer and took my first course in French this year. French isn't shoved down your throat, but there are so many opportunities to become bilingual if you try." Kabir LL.B. '93

"Professors get to know you by your first name. They often come to the Thursday afternoon cafés and chat. They make an effort to participate in student life beyond academics, and they are extremely knowledgeable in their fields." Lise B.C.L. '93

"There is a focus on business law courses, but the civil law program has the strongest focus because we are in a civil law province. . . . Most of our big name professors are in civil law but in general you get a good education in both legal systems." Erin B.C.L. '92

"McGill is known more as a theoretical institution, and I think this is good. They don't focus on the rules because they will change. They teach you how the rules were developed and how they have changed and then they go on from there. It is more important to know how to think." Erin B.C.L. '92

Where the Program Could Improve

"McGill is an old and conservative school and it is not the first to jump on the bandwagon to offer courses in native law, environmental law, or gender issues. There is only one course taught in Native law, and it is offered only every second year. Environmental law is better now that we have a professor who has this as an area of specialty. There is only one course in gender issues, but some of the younger professors use feminist legal issues in their courses." Nicole, articling student

"The two languages of instruction make it necessary to duplicate courses. As well, they have to keep up the Comparative and Air & Space areas because of the Institutes. This affects the type of holdings the library has. McGill's library has few American journals, and serious research often requires consulting American journals, so you might need to use inter-library loans or get a friend at a Toronto school to complete your research." Stephen, articling student

"The library has suffered due to lack of financing. I wrote a paper last term and I found it hard to find some journals. This is a real hindrance and faculty find it hard to keep up to date." Isabelle B.C.L. '92

"There is not enough emphasis on the practical procedural aspects of being a lawyer. They teach you how to argue, and point out strengths and weaknesses of old judgements. That is the biggest strength of the faculty. But they have given up the basic practical procedural training which becomes very important once you step out of the university." Morton, articling student

"A few big names have left the faculty since I have been here, and this might have been because of the political climate." Isabelle B.C.L. '92

"I could not take language courses as part of my degree. I think this is stone age thinking. If I want to practise in Montreal I have been told that I have to improve my French, but I can't do that by taking courses." Kabir LL.B. '93

Controversy

In 1991-92 a semi-obligatory, but important course was offered in French only and this caused a flare-up of emotional tension between the Anglophone and Francophone students attending McGill's Faculty of Law. The outcome of this was a clearly defined policy on the language requirement arrived at with the consultation of the Law Student Society.

"The central controversy is contingent upon being located in Montreal. McGill is supposed to be a bilingual faculty of Law when only twenty-five percent of the student body are Francophones. They are trying to increase the courses offered in French. This has not worked because the French course they added was a core course which Anglophones had to take. Some students didn't realize they would have to take courses in French. The law school is a jack of all trades and master of none. McGill has to decide whether it is an English or a French institution." Isabelle B.C.L. '92

"Language was definitely an issue this year [because of the semi-obligatory course taught in French]. At the outset it caused a little bit of tension, but it has dissipated and not divided us. The constitution is also an issue, but we try to discuss it in an objective way as possible to avoid political division." Lise B.C.L. '93

"I don't want to confront issues where we are going to disagree. The underlying tensions only resulted after the French course issue. That has died down but there is still some underlying tension. I try to disregard it. We are so aware of the situation in Quebec and law is practised so much in French in Quebec, and your texts are in French. You can't get away from it but we do get along." Erin B.C.L. '92

On Faculty

"The professors are superb as a rule. They are very accommodating and open on a personal level to help you choose any career in law that you want." Kabir LL.B. '93

"The faculty are sensitive to sexism and racism without hitting us over the head with it." Isabelle B.C.L. '92

"Blain Baker teaches administrative law. He treats students with respect and on an equal footing. He is very approachable about his course and other matters." Morton, articling student

"Professor Jukier and Professor Toope both challenge you. They teach you the rules but they go beyond that and they are very approachable." Erin B.C.L. '92

"Colleen Shepherd teaches Feminist legal theory and Family Law. She is very helpful and takes a lot of interest in the students. Professor Shepherd is also the advisor to the Women's Caucus." Nicole, articling student

Other Comments

"Some students leave after the third year with a Common Law or Civil Law degree, but other things being equal, the program is really geared to four years. I think you lose out on electives and other things you can get out of the law faculty if you leave after three years." Kabir LL.B. '93

Université de Moncton

■ **INQUIRIES**
École de droit
Université de Moncton
Moncton, N.B.
EIA 3E9
(506) 858-4564

ADMISSIONS INFORMATION

■ **APPLICATION DEADLINE DATE FOR ADMISSIONS**
30 March

■ **REQUIRED TO SUBMIT**
- Two official copies of all university academic transcripts
- Questionnaire enabling the respondent to elaborate on why they want to study law
- Two references letters from persons who can assess the applicant's intellectual capabilities
- French proficiency test for those who do not comply with the school's language requirements, as competency in both official languages is required.

■ **EDUCATION REQUIREMENT**
Normally a full undergraduate degree is required. For a three-year undergraduate degree program, the minimum number of years completed is two. For a four-year undergraduate degree program, the minimum number of years completed is three. For persons who have not completed their undergraduate degree program, the minimum cumulative GPA required for consideration by the Admissions Committee is at least 3.5 on a scale of 4.

- **AVERAGE GPA**

  3.2 based on a four point scale or B or 74% (range is not available)

- **AVERAGE LSAT**

  As in all other French Law Faculties in Canada, the LSAT is not a requirement for admissions. Good results on this test may positively influence the admissions committee, but a candidate will not be disadvantaged if he/she has not received a good result or chooses not to write the LSAT.

- **RATIO OF APPLICANTS TO REGISTRATIONS**

  5.0 : 1

- **SIZE OF INCOMING CLASS**

  49 (74 offers made)

- **CAN YOU DEFER ACCEPTANCE**

  No

- **APPLICATION FEE**

  $50

- **TUITION FEE**

  The tuition fee for 1992-93 is $2,050 plus student activity fees.

CLASS PROFILE

- **AVERAGE AGE OF STUDENTS ENTERING THE PROGRAM**

  26

- **PERCENTAGE OF THE CLASS WHO ARE WOMEN**

  51%

- **PERCENTAGE OF WOMEN WHO ARE TENURED FACULTY**

  25% (of a total of 12 full-time professors, 3 are women)

- **PERCENTAGE OF THE CLASS WITH**

two years or more of an undergraduate degree	11%
a three- or four-year degree	75%
a post-graduate degree	14%

■ **PROFILE OF LL.B. POPULATIONS**
mature students	11% (5)
aboriginal students	0%
visible minorities	n/a

OTHER RELATED PROGRAMS

LL.B./Master of Public Administration, LL.B./Master of Business Administration, a one-year Diploma in Common Law Studies (DipECL) for students from those countries who are members of the international "Francophonie" who have obtained a Licence in Law, and a conversion program is offered for students who have a diploma in civil law from the province of Quebec. This program extends over three semesters. There is no half-time law program at Université de Moncton.

ADMISSIONS REQUIREMENTS

Moncton's École de droit is a French program only and not bilingual. All courses are taught in French, exams and papers are written in French, and presentations are given in French. All students are required to be proficient in both official languages. Students graduating from the Université de Moncton's undergraduate programs are required to have a French course as part of their graduate requirements. Therefore, if applicants to Moncton's École de droit have been educated at another university and have not taken any courses in French, they will be required to take the French Proficiency test. The test is three hours long and applicants will be required to write a four hundred word essay in French. The minimum grade allowed is a C+. Applicants with a C average will be admitted conditionally and will be required to take a French course along with their law degree until they can pass the proficiency test with a C+.

A Law School Admissions Test (LSAT) score is not required. The LSAT is an American-based test and is written in English and this would disadvantage Canadian Francophones. The test d'admission en droit developed by the Université de Montréal's Faculty of Law is not used either because the administration felt it would prejudice students who were from outside Québec.

The majority of applicants to Moncton's Faculty of Law apply under the **Regular Category** of admission. The decision to admit in this category is based primarily on academic performance. No adjustment is made to the grade point average (GPA) before it is reviewed. All years of grades are taken into consideration and an upward progression of grades is looked for. If an applicant has a master's degree it is an advantage. The degree of difficulty of the undergraduate courses or a comparison of programs or institutions is not a factor. Regular applicants fill out a special questionnaire which gives them the opportunity to explain their grades and give additional relevant information. This is given some weight when deciding difficult cases.

Each year approximately one or two students are admitted under the **Mature Student Category** but there is no fixed quota. A mature student is defined as someone who is twenty-six years old and has been in the workforce for five years in an area related to law — for example, government, administration, or negotiating — with some degree of excellence. An applicant applying under the Mature Student Category will have more emphasis placed on their work experience than on their academic performance.

Aboriginal students are encouraged to apply under the **Native Student Category**. Aboriginal applicants who do not meet the general admissions requirements are encouraged to register for the eight-week preparatory course offered by the Native Law Centre at the University of Saskatchewan or the parallel course in French offered at the Université d'Ottawa/University of Ottawa's Faculty of Law. Successful completion of this course may result in admission to Moncton's École de droit.

CHARACTER OF THE SCHOOL

Moncton's École de droit has the smallest student body of any law faculty in Canada, with approximately 120 students in total. As a result the school spirit is high and the students get to know their classmates well. Moncton's École de droit is also the youngest law faculty in Canada. The young professors have more of a co-operative relationship between teacher and student rather than a hierarchical one. The professors interact with the students and often participate in the extra-curricular activities.

The composition of the class is made up of fifty to sixty-five percent of students from New Brunswick and the other fifty to thirty-five percent of students are from across Canada. These students bring with them many different points of view, but they have one thing in common — their desire to learn common law in French.

The location of the school, in the heart of Acadia, is responsible for a significant number of speakers and conferences on issues concerning Acadian rights. The program is very structured with few electives in second and third year, but students can chose their electives in the area of language rights if they wish. The Acadian focus is strongest in the extra-curricular and social life of the student body.

STRENGTHS OF THE PROGRAM

Founded in 1978, Moncton's École de droit was the first law school to offer students the opportunity to study common law in French and it remains the only French university in Canada to offer the joint Common Law and Master in Business Administration program in French. The Université d'Ottawa is the only other university in Canada to offer a French common law degree. The Centre International de la Common Law en Français, founded at Moncton's École de droit, has added an international dimension to the work of the school, which is now renowned in the international French world.

The Translation and Legal Terminology Centre is established at Moncton's École de droit, and for the first few years the faculty was immersed in the translation of the law and legal terminology into French. Now that the translation is complete, the faculty is analyzing how the study of law in another language transforms the common law. Moncton's École de Droit is focusing on the law school's minority context.

Before the study of common law in French was available, the admissions criteria for Francophone law schools put Francophones outside of Québec at a disadvantage. This led to an underrepresentation of Francophone lawyers outside of Québec. Moncton's École de droit seeks to offer Francophones outside of Québec good legal services and, if possible, to make professionals aware of the necessity of transforming both the social system and the judicial apparatus.

"We try to institute in our students a feeling that the law is an agent of change. We try to encourage a sensitivity to Acadian culture and to the French community outside of Quebec. This is evident in the way professors organize their courses, the publications and activities outside of the faculty . . . The professors are very involved in social and political issues regarding the double minority of French common law and Acadian heritage. This permeates everything we do," comments Pierre Foucher, Chair of the Admissions Committee and Law Professor.

WHERE THE PROGRAM COULD IMPROVE

As the youngest faculty of law in Canada, Moncton's École droit has not had as much of an opportunity to build its research and publication base as have more established law schools. Also, the number of graduating students has not reached a critical mass in the work force yet, so Moncton's École de droit is still relatively unknown to law firms outside of New Brunswick.

Moncton's École de droit stresses the fundamental areas of law, but its small faculty limits the faculty's ability to offer specialized courses and a variety of teaching styles. Also, there is no law review to give student legal editing and research experience.

The law building was at one time a residence for clergy and is not well-suited for the purposes of a law school. The library is housed in the musty basement, and overall the ventilation is poor. However, the one redeeming feature of the building is the chapel which also happens to be the largest classroom. One entire wall of the chapel is a stained glass window with an eastern exposure. When the sun streams in the atmosphere is very inspiring. A new building is on the fundraising priority list.

At present, there are no aboriginal students registered. This may be because most of the aboriginal community in New Brunswick are Anglophones, and aboriginal students in Québec more often attend civil law programs. There are few visible minority students registered at Moncton's École de droit. Francophones outside of Québec are in themselves a minority group which the school is dedicated to.

ON MONCTON

The greater Moncton area has a population of approximately 80,000 with a sixty/forty split between English and French respectively. The Université de Moncton's campus is a twenty-minute walk downtown, or if you want to take the bus, the transit system is good.

Accommodation is easy to find and a typical one-bedroom apartment is around $350 per month; two-bedroom apartments with all conveniences are around $440 per month. There are few apartment buildings, and most apartments are on the top floors of houses. General residence accommodation is available and if you are a law student you get first priority for a single room. University furnished apartments are also available and can be leased for eight months.

Living expenses in Moncton are increased by the province's high taxation. New Brunswick has an eleven percent provincial sales tax combined with the GST resulting in an additional twenty percent every time you go to the cash register.

Moncton is located two and a half hours from Halifax, which is the closest major centre, and only minutes from incredible beaches and lobster fishing.

WHAT THE STUDENTS SAY

(Pseudonyms have replaced the following students' names)

The Strengths of the Program

"The professor-student ratio is very small. Some of my second- and third-year classes had only six students in them. When I arrived they knew my name before classes even started and I felt like they knew me before I even arrived. It is like a family." Monette, articling student

"A strength is the relationship that the students have with the professors. The program is so new that the professors are young and you get a lot of contact with them. They come to the parties and this makes it easier to ask questions in class." Andre LL.B. '90

"The common law program is in French, but the textbooks are in English and so are most of your readings and therefore you are trained to be a bilingual lawyer. You learn the legal terms in French and English." Julie LL.B. '94

"Since you are studying Common Law in French it is helpful to have the Translation Centre on the third floor available to ask questions." Antoine LL.B. '92

"The atmosphere is the best thing. After six months, everyone knows everyone else which is good most of the time. There is a real team spirit and it is not competitive. Everyone helps everyone else just get through it." Rebecca LL.B. '93

"There is a very friendly atmosphere. The whole school and the faculty come out to the lobster party at the beginning of the year. One Friday a month there is a happy hour in the student lounge, and at the end of the year there is a graduation banquet." Jennifer LL.B. '92

"Contracts, constitutional law, and fundamental rights are two focusses of the law school. They have now graduated over one hundred students who are practising in French and for Acadians this is a big strength. Now Acadians can get justice and make sure the judge understands what they have to say in their own language. The law school is a key factor that has helped the Acadian community establish itself." André LL.B. '90

"Speakers have an Acadian slant and a lot of our professors are invited as jurists on national TV, but if you are not interested in minority language rights you will have the same education as in any other law school. The Acadian slant of the conferences and speakers is a plus." Julie LL.B. '94

"The moot court competitions are great and since there is a small student body you have a good chance of getting on the team. Moncton sends students to all the competitions." Monette, articling student

"There is a full-year class in advocacy which shows you all the practical aspects of litigation, motions, discoveries, trial interrogation, and moot appeal in front of real judges." Rebecca LL.B. '93

"We have people from almost everywhere in Canada. In my class we had people from all provinces except Prince Edward Island and British Columbia." Antoine LL.B. '92

"The library staff are great and very accommodating. They remember what you are working on and let you know if they find something that might help you." Monette, articling student

"There are lots of computers in the law school and you have access to Quick Law." Monette, articling student

"There are a large number of mandatory courses and law firms like this." Julie LL.B. '94

Where the Program Could Improve

"Since it is a small school they don't specialize and they are limited in faculty and courses.... You have to take two courses out of four different block areas. Some people like this, but others feel it limits their choices." Antoine LL.B. '92

"When students went back to their home province some law firms didn't know about the school. However, the more students we graduate the more we will get known." Julie LL.B. '94

"Eight people quit before Christmas and five or six can't come back. There will probably be about thirty-five students next year." [Forty-nine started the program.] Philippe LL.B. '94

"The building used to be a monastery and it is not very well suited to a law school. The library is in the basement and this is not good for the books. The ventilation is poor and it is not a good facility for lockers." Philippe LL.B. '94

"The courses were not overly practical, even the courses like criminal procedure and civil procedure were not practical. I never drafted a document and I did not know how it fit in the big scheme of things. The professors don't ever help you out in terms of what to expect when you are articling. . . . Not enough professors have practised law. One criminal professor had never gone to trial." Monette, articling student

Controversies

"There are not that many controversies at Moncton. We are working to improve things at the school and the administration is very open to suggestions. Two students sit on the school council out of approximately twelve positions." Rebecca LL.B. '93

"The gender issue was a controversy. Certain employers were not asking the same questions for men and women when they were hiring and this was a hot topic. The dean has brought this to the bar association." Antoine LL.B. '92

"The school is founded on linguistic issues and you get Acadian perspectives from the staff and faculty. Therefore, you get debates and different opinions since we have students from all over Canada." Antoine LL.B. '92

On Faculty

"Pierre Foucher is dynamic and motivates everyone. He is very knowledgeable in his area of constitutional law." Antoine LL.B. '92

"Fernand Landry is a good teacher. He teaches contracts and torts and is a practitioner who is very involved with the liberal government of the province." Phillipe LL.B. '94

"Andrea Boudreau-Ouellet is very well organized and available whenever you need her. She is involved in a lot of provincial and national committees and teaches property, wills, and real estate." Jennifer LL.B. '92

"Jacques Vanderlinden teaches history of law. He is a part-time professor from Belgium who is renowned in international comparative law and is very knowledgeable." Julie LL.B. '94

Other Comments

"Most of the students have to borrow money to study and student loans do not cover articling because it is not classed as study. Therefore, you can come out up to thirty to forty thousand dollars in debt and law firms expect you to have a car and dress well. You are still borrowing for the next five years." Andre LL.B. '90

"The job prospects are few. Think about it before you go. Some people who went directly from undergraduate didn't realize just how much work it was. They came because they couldn't find a job, not because they really wanted to be a lawyer. You should talk to students and lawyers to see what kind of a challenge you will have to meet." Julie LL.B. '94

"Getting an articling job isn't the problem. It is getting hired back that is hard. Don't wait too long to get legal work experience with a law firm." Jennifer LL.B. '92

"Get ready for three gruelling years. It is very intense and a heavy workload." Antoine LL.B. '92

"First year is the hardest. If you survive it you will be OK. Being organized is the key and coffee — lots of coffee." Jennifer LL.B. '92

"I really wanted to do my common law degree in French and to see something outside of Québec. For economic reasons I thought it was better to get a common law degree since the law schools in Québec are graduating a thousand students each year for a population of six million. Friends of mine graduating with civil law degrees were not getting articling positions." Rebecca LL.B. '93

"Realize that you cannot read everything and be open minded. It is a lot of work, but you have to be able to organize yourself the way you understand it. Don't be afraid to ask questions and this is easy to do since the professors are very accessible." Chloe LL.B. '93

University of New Brunswick

■ **INQUIRIES**

Admissions Office
Faculty of Law
University of New Brunswick
P.O. Box 4400
Fredericton, N.B.
E3B 5A3
(506) 453-4693

ADMISSIONS INFORMATION

■ **APPLICATION DEADLINE DATE FOR ADMISSIONS**

31 March
(All documentation should also be submitted by this date.)

■ **REQUIRED TO SUBMIT**

Regular Category

- Official copies of all university academic transcripts
- LSAT score report

Mature Students (in addition to the above)

- At least two letters of reference
- Personal statement of no more than 500 words

Aboriginal Students

- Official copies of all university academic transcripts
- LSAT score report
- Letters of reference are optional
- Personal statement is recommended

- **EDUCATION REQUIREMENT**

  Completed at least three years or equivalent of full-time academic study at a recognized university. (Ontario Grade 13 or Quebec CEGEP will be considered equivalent to one year of academic study at a recognized university.)

- **AVERAGE GPA**

  3.59 based on a 4.3 point grading system or B+ or 78%
  Range 2.84 — 4.19

- **AVERAGE LSAT**

  36 based on the old scoring system out of 48
  Range 25 — 44 (percentile score not available but a score of 38 is thought to be the equivalent of an 80th percentile)

- **RATIO OF APPLICANTS TO REGISTRATIONS**

  15.8 : 1 (the ratio for the class of 1992 is 17.5 : 1)

- **SIZE OF INCOMING CLASS**

  80 (158 offers were sent out)

- **CAN YOU DEFER ACCEPTANCE**

  No

- **APPLICATION FEE**

  $20 (The application fee will be increased to $25 as of 1993)

- **TUITION FEE**

  The 1992-93 tuition fee for Canadian residents is $2,350.
  The 1992-93 tuition fee for non-exempt foreign residents is $4,050.

CLASS PROFILE

- **AVERAGE AGE OF STUDENTS ENTERING THE PROGRAM**

  24

- **PERCENTAGE OF THE CLASS WHO ARE WOMEN**

  51% (in 1990-91 the percentage of women was 40%)

- **PERCENTAGE OF WOMEN WHO ARE TENURED FACULTY**

  6% (1 woman out of 16 tenured faculty members. Two women are in tenure track positions)

■ **PERCENTAGE OF THE CLASS WITH**

two years or more of an undergraduate degree	2%
a three-year degree	19%
a four-year degree	77%
a post-graduate degree	1%

■ **PROFILE OF LL.B. POPULATIONS**

(for the 1991–92 class only)

Native Students	1%
Minorities	n/a
Mature Students	5% (4)

A mature student is defined as an applicant whose experience, maturity, and outstanding qualities indicate an ability to successfully undertake the study of law. Post-secondary education is not required for admission as a mature student.

OTHER RELATED PROGRAMS

Students in either the B.A. or B.B.A. programs at the University of New Brunswick or the B.A. program at St. Thomas University may be admitted after three years of study toward their degree. Upon successful completion of first-year law, the B.A. or B.B.A. is awarded.

There is no formal half-time program at New Brunswick's Faculty of Law, although requests can be made to the Dean's Office to vary course loads. The degree must be completed within six years.

ADMISSIONS REQUIREMENTS

Basically, there are three categories for admission to the first year of the LL.B. program: Regular applicant, Mature applicant, or Aboriginal applicant. There are no quotas in place for the number of students admitted under these categories, but based on recent experience, two or three Mature students and one or two Aboriginal students are admitted each year on average.

Regular applicants make up the majority of the students admitted, and it is a clear-cut process based primarily on the index score generated by the admissions formula. The formula is comprised of the candidate's grade point average (GPA) and Law School Admissions Test (LSAT) score. The GPA is designated a weight of sixty percent and the LSAT is given a weight of forty percent. Before the figures are put into the formula however, some adjustments are made to the calculation of the GPA. Twenty-five percent of the candidate's lowest grades in their undergraduate degree are eliminated regardless of the year in which they were obtained. The admissions index score is then calculated and the scores are rank ordered from the top down. Sixty of the regular spots are filled in this manner. Candidates' files are reviewed to decide on the remaining twenty spots. Extra-curricular activities, employment experience, and a bilingual capacity are factors that are favourably regarded.

Mature applicants and **Aboriginal applicants** are not evaluated by means of a formula. A candidate's GPA, if any, and LSAT score are only two criteria considered along with significant achievements in their work history, examples of maturity, or other outstanding qualities that might persuade the committee that they can successfully undertake the study of law and justify special consideration in the admissions process. Reference letters, personal statements, and in the case of Aboriginal applicants, the successful completion of Saskatchewan's program of Legal Studies for Native People, will be taken into consideration.

New Brunswick's Faculty of Law does give regional preference in their admissions process. Approximately forty of the eighty spots are allotted to residents of New Brunswick or those who have undertaken their pre-law studies at a New Brunswick college or university. An additional thirty spots are reserved for applicants from Atlantic Provinces or those who have attended a university in the other Atlantic Provinces.

CHARACTER OF THE SCHOOL

UNB's Faculty of Law celebrates its one hundredth anniversary in 1992, giving it the distinction of being the second oldest university-based common law faculty in the Commonwealth. UNB's Faculty of Law is proud of its heritage, and this is reflected in its traditional character and highly structured program.

The program was developed to give students a solid, well-rounded legal education with more of a practical slant. The more traditional black letter approach to the study of law is often used, emphasizing the process and rules of the law.

To ensure that the basics are covered, there are many required courses. The first year of the program is compulsory, as it is in all law schools in Canada. However, five of the upper year courses are also compulsory and, in addition, students must take at least one course from each of the five compulsory areas of study — Business Organizations, Commercial Law, Property Law, Estates, and Perspective on the Law.

In September of 1992, UNB's Faculty of Law started its second century of legal education under the direction of a new Dean — Wade MacLauchlan. MacLauchlan himself is a graduate of New Brunswick's Faculty of Law and was previously a faculty member for eight years at Dalhousie's Faculty of Law. At Dalhousie, he was part of the transition from a traditional approach to legal education, to a study of law in a historical, social, and comparative perspective. MacLauchlan believes UNB should play to its strength, which he identifies as the effective formation of legal professionals. He says that the Faculty will continue to offer a strong core curriculum, and will diversify through further optional offerings.

The students and faculty at UNB's Faculty of Law are going through a period of adjustment, coping with issues such as women and the law that the new integrative approach encourages. However, the atmosphere is close-knit and friendly on the whole.

STRENGTHS OF THE PROGRAM

A good, well-rounded legal education with a historic commitment to teaching is the mandate of UNB's Faculty of Law. Current areas of development are environment and equity issues, as well as an increasing emphasis on professionalism.

A well-managed budget, and the support of the Beaverbrook Canadian Foundation have made it possible for New Brunswick's Faculty of Law to appoint the Mary Louise Lynch Chair in Women and Law, and to expand the faculty from eighteen to twenty within the last three years. The two new faculty positions were filled by women. This is consistent with the Faculty's affirmative action hiring policy that prefers women candidates.

New Brunswick is a bilingual province; therefore, there is a need for practitioners who are bilingual. Students have the opportunity to take two courses offered in French at UNB's Faculty of Law, and an exchange program to increase the opportunities students have to take courses in French towards their common law degree with Moncton's Faculty of Law is being investigated.

Interested students can develop their skills in legal editing by becoming involved with the *Law Journal*. The *Law Journal* is owned and published by the students themselves, with a degree of faculty support. The Faculty recognizes the value of the *Law Journal* by giving academic credit to the Editor-in-Chief and up to four Associate Editors.

Students interested in developing their oratory skills required for litigation roles will be interested in the faculty support and encouragement to take part

in mooting competitions. Academic credit is given to students who participate in the competitive moots. New Brunswick's law students have regularly
participated in the Jessup International Moot, The Laskin Memorial Moot,
the Tri-Lateral Moot, The Gale Cup Moot, and The Harrison Memorial
Shield Moot. Please see the chapter on *Unique Characteristics* for information
on school standings in mooting competitions.

The strong sense of cohesion among the students is perhaps the faculty's
biggest strength. Starting with a small class size of eighty first-year students,
the size is further reduced by sectioning the class into two groups of about
forty students each. Enrollment in upper-year courses ranges mostly between
fifteen and thirty-five. These small classes provide students with a less
intimidating atmosphere to ask questions and to get to know their classmates
and professors well.

At most law schools in Canada, final exams in first- and upper-year courses
count for one hundred percent of the final grade. A co-operative atmosphere
is re-enforced at New Brunswick's Faculty of Law by giving first-year students
the opportunity to write mid-term exams at Christmas, which count for
either forty percent, or twenty percent if they do better in their final exam.
A substantial number of upper-year courses have one hundred percent finals;
however, students have the option of writing papers or doing mid-term
exercises in many upper-year courses.

WHERE THE PROGRAM COULD IMPROVE

The strengths of UNB's Faculty of Law are also its weaknesses. The small size
of the faculty provides fewer resources and limits the diversity of courses
available. Developing an area of specialization is not possible, and a relatively
small selection of theory-based courses are offered, compared to those offered
at larger schools such as University of British Columbia, and Osgoode Hall
Faculty of Law. UNB's Faculty of Law is the most highly structured law school
in Canada.

In terms of faculty, the law school has the lowest number of women faculty
members of any law school in Canada. Steps are being taken to rectify this,
but for the near future, this is the situation. The faculty are seasoned with an
average of fourteen years of experience each. Certainly they are well respected
and knowledgeable, but a rejuvenation with younger professors bringing in
new ideas and teaching styles has not taken place.

Students attending UNB's Faculty of Law do not have the opportunity to
participate in a legal aid clinic.

ON FREDERICTON

New Brunswick's red brick campus is situated half way up the hill overlooking the St. John River. Housing is relatively expensive because Fredericton is a capital city, and there is a shortage of rental accommodation. If you choose to come in September to look for accommodation, you will still find something if you are not too selective, but if you want something close to campus and affordable, you should come early. An average rent for a one-bedroom apartment close to campus might be around $475/month or $200/month shared accommodation. Downtown Fredericton is only a fifteen minute walk away. The bus system in the city is poor, but taxis are very reasonable. A car is not necessary to get around Fredericton, but if you want to go to Halifax, the closest large centre, a car is more convenient than public transit.

The city of Fredericton is a quiet, attractive town with an economic base supported primarily by the university and government offices. The Saturday morning market on the waterfront downtown is an institution which dates back to the 1800s adds to the city's charm.

WHAT THE STUDENTS SAY

(Pseudonyms have replaced the following students' names)

The Strengths of the Program

"The size of the law school is a strength in that it is a small school with eighty students in first year. You get to know everyone and it is not intimidating. It is very self-contained, in one building, and the professors are very accessible. There is a low student-professor ratio and lots of opportunity to get involved in clubs and organizations." Nancy, articling student

"When we got here during orientation, the Dean asked us all to introduce ourselves to each other. It is a very friendly atmosphere and a celebration of how our backgrounds are different. It is so competitive to get in that once you get in they want to keep you." Leah LL.B. '94

"The number of compulsory courses such as Evidence, Business, Contracts, Torts and Constitutional Law, among others forces you to get a broad exposure and the basics before you move on to other things." Dan LL.B. '93

"UNB Law School is best able to prepare people for the traditional small town practice." Colleen LL.B. '93

"The library staff and the support staff are very helpful, and there is a good relationship between students and staff." Benjamin LL.B. '93

"It is taboo to be ultra competitive. At UNB, there is pressure to share knowledge and this may be partly because the Maritimes are community based. We feel like we are all in it together, except perhaps around the time we are looking for articling placements." Dan LL.B. '93

"There is a great sense of loyalty to the school. Everyone is involved with the Law Student Society or various groups and clubs. It is the one hundredth anniversary of the law school and there is a lot of pride in this." Benjamin LL.B. '93

"I participated in the Laskin National bilingual moot. It counts as a course and it builds your confidence. Standing up in front of judges and having things challenged is the nature of the competition, and it is good to compare your team with the other schools. I found that they were pretty much the same as ours, and that makes you feel good since we don't have access to the Supreme Court libraries or as many judges like the University of Ottawa does." Colleen LL.B. '93

Where the Program Could Improve

"The curriculum is geared towards black letter law [the rules and the process] and the practical aspects of law. This is necessary in first year, but this slant continues in upper years too. The curriculum seems to be lacking in theory content — especially in feminist theory and reality. Women only got the vote a while ago, let alone the right to sit on juries. We get a very one-sided view as opposed to what the law could be and where it is going. It is important in first year to get an idea of what the law is, who created it, as well as a historical and a women's perspective." Shala LL.B. '94

"UNB should have more academic courses, such as a course on Feminism. They do fly up some women professors from Harvard to teach one course in feminism and they do have a Perspectives in Law course, but it is weak. There should be more women on staff." Dan LL.B. '93

"I would like to have a curriculum where I could choose a good theory-based education and others could choose a more applied perspective if they wanted. We don't have this because we don't have the course selection, but also we have a lot of tenured professors who believe black letter law is what is necessary to get a job. It is important to have the curriculum opened up to legal theory because in practice you need to consider different aspects." Shala LL.B. '94

"There are only three required courses in second year, but you have to choose from different areas. This is fine for me but others aren't interested in one of these classes. The categories can be restrictive but the structure can be an advantage to have a well-rounded view of the law." Benjamin LL.B. '93

"The idea is that the people in law school tend to be a cut above everyone else. This isn't necessary." Benjamin LL.B. '93

"The research component needs improvement. We need more training in computer legal research and library research in general. Participating in the moots is a good way to learn how to use the library." Colleen LL.B. '93

"Currently, there is only one writing requirement and it is possible to get through your entire degree with only doing one major paper." Cameron LL.B. '92

"There is limited access to practical courses. The enrollment for civil trials, practice advocacy, and collective bargaining is limited to fifteen students, since a small class size is important." Nancy, articling student

"There isn't any support here for aboriginal students. Aboriginal students who come to UNB would have to be very prepared to look at life in a different way. The first thing you learn in property class is that the crown owns all the land and this is against everything I believe. You have to take it all in without giving in to the system." Karen LL.B. '93

"It is a more conservative school and corporate commercial is the strongest area, whereas I am more interested in aboriginal law. There aren't any courses in this area now, but there might be a land claims course next year. The faculty and students are becoming more receptive towards aboriginal issues, for example, in discussions in constitutional classes." Karen LL.B. '93

"There is no public legal aid. The Law Student Society is trying to change this by networking with the community to provide research support. They need to make better use of the school. The faculty are active in the community, but the students aren't used as the resource we could be." Colleen LL.B. '93

The Controversies

"The biggest issue is how women and the law have to be respected and treated as equal. It has to change through the curriculum and by the number of women on faculty. Hopefully, a women's chair will help this and educate both men and women in the law school who don't necessarily see a problem." Shala LL.B. '94

"There isn't one controversy that stands out but there is a touch of gender issues. The school is taking steps to correct this by introducing a Chair in Feminist Studies, a course in perspectives which includes a section on women and the law and they are flying up professors from Harvard to teach Feminist courses." Benjamin LL.B. '93

"There is a lack of understanding within the student body as to what it means to be a feminist, and the school is just getting into courses in this area." Nancy, articling student

"Women's issues are in the forefront and it is a reflection of what is going on on-campus in general. There are a number of discussions on woman's role in the law. I've never seen a group that were so consistently aware of the issue. This year our class has forty-one women and thirty-nine men." Leah LL.B. '94

"There is an emphasis on practical versus theoretical and the faculty are still struggling with how to incorporate the theoretical into the practical courses. Some are worried that the UNB's traditional strength in the practical side will be watered down by this movement." Colleen LL.B. '93

On Faculty

"Richard Bird teaches Corporation Law, Tax, and Corporate Finance. He is the type of person who could get the class laughing and get his point across. He makes the socratic method acceptable." Cameron LL.B. '92

"Beverley Smith is exceptional in his approach to law. He is a very credible and honest man who values integrity above all else and practises what he believes in. Just recently, he has written a text on professional conduct. He teaches Professional Conduct, Wills, and Trusts." Nancy, articling student

"Geoffrey Bladon teaches very practical courses such as Civil Trial and is the organizer of the competitive moots. He was a practitioner in Ontario and the Chief Justice of the Yukon, so he brought with him the realities of the real world and a perspective from the bench so that he could judge advocacy skills." Nancy, articling student

"Don Fleming teaches Torts and International Law. He is tough, but as a result, I really know my stuff." Karen LL.B. '93

Other Comments

"I didn't expect students to be so apathetic. They are not apathetic in terms of school but towards society in general. The students are wrapped up in their own careers and not caught up with the issues around them." Benjamin LL.B. '93

"There are three other aboriginal students, two chinese students, and no black people. I take part in class but I am not involved in the social activities. The way I look at society and law is very different from them and we don't share the same philosophy." Karen LL.B. '93

"Try and determine if you are committed to being a lawyer, because law school is just the tip of the iceberg. The real world is harder and the hours are longer." Nancy, articling student

"Remember to have confidence in yourself and trust in yourself. The skills that you have developed got you in and you can do it. It is easy though to get caught up in a panic." Leah LL.B. '94

Osgoode Hall Law School

■ **INQUIRIES**

The Admissions Officer
Osgoode Hall Law School
York University
4700 Keele Street
North York, Ontario
M3J 1P3
(416) 736-5040

ADMISSIONS INFORMATION

■ **APPLICATION DEADLINE DATE FOR ADMISSIONS**

1 February (for regular applicants)
1 May (for Native applicants)
The LSAT must be written no later than the December test date in the case of Mature applicants, and the February test date in all other cases.

■ **REQUIRED TO SUBMIT**

Regular Category

- Official copies of all university academic transcripts
- LSAT score report

In addition to the above, applicants in the Mature Category need

- Résumé
- Personal statement including "why law"
- Reference letters, at least two, from persons with a precise knowledge of the applicant's ability and potential

In addition to the requirements of the Regular Category, applicants in the Special Circumstances or Access Categories need

- Personal statement

■ **EDUCATION REQUIREMENTS**

Two full years of academic work beyond the Ontario senior matriculation level at a recognized degree granting institution.

■ **AVERAGE GPA**

3.64 or A- or 80% (range 3.24 — 4.20)

■ **AVERAGE LSAT**

83rd percentile (range of 44-99 percentile)
If the LSAT is written more than once, only the best test score is considered.

■ **RATIO OF APPLICANTS TO REGISTRATIONS**

10.5 : 1

■ **SIZE OF INCOMING CLASS**

330 (673 offers sent out)

■ **CAN YOU DEFER ACCEPTANCE**

No.
Osgoode retains all applications for one year. If reapplying the subsequent year, all you need to submit is a current application form and fee, and any new documentation to update your application.

■ **APPLICATION FEE**

$40

■ **TUITION FEE**

The 1992-93 tuition fee is $2,457 for Canadian students.

CLASS PROFILE

■ **AVERAGE AGE OF STUDENTS ENTERING THE PROGRAM**

23

■ **PERCENTAGE OF THE CLASS WHO ARE WOMEN**

47%

- **PERCENTAGE OF WOMEN WHO ARE TENURED FACULTY**
  23%

- **PERCENTAGE OF THE CLASS WITH**

two years or more of an undergraduate degree	20%-25%
a three-year degree	50%
a four-year degree	20%-25%
a post-graduate degree	4%

- **PROFILE OF LL.B. POPULATIONS**

Native Students	0% (2 students)
Visible Minorities	19% (63)
Mature Students	10% (33)

OTHER RELATED PROGRAMS

LL.M., M.B.A./LL.B., Master of Environmental Science/LL.B., J.S.D.
There is no half-time program at Osgoode Hall's Faculty of Law

ADMISSIONS REQUIREMENTS

Osgoode is the largest (common law) law school in Canada, normally admitting 330 students per year. To assist in the administration of such a formidable task, a formula has been devised for use in the admissions process for applicants in the **Regular category** only. The applicant's Law School Admission Test (LSAT) score and Grade Point Average (GPA) are the main criteria upon which admission is based. The LSAT score is weighted as the equivalent to one year of university work. It is converted into grade-point language and averaged in with *all* years of an applicant's academic record. All applicants' LSAT scores and GPAs are translated into a new standardized score using this formula. These standardized scores are rank ordered and applicants are given offers from the top down until the 240 Regular category places are eventually filled.

The Regular category admission scheme at Osgoode is, therefore, a "cut and dried" process. Extra-curricular contributions, work experience, ongoing social, physical, or economic disabilities, are *not* taken into account in making decisions with respect to this category of applicant. The only significant exception within this category occurs when students have had false starts or have, occasionally, faced exceptional circumstances adversely affecting their academic performance in a given examination, course, semester, or academic year. The Admissions Committee is authorized to delete the false start grades or the grades adversely affected by exceptional circumstances from the calculation of the applicant's cumulative GPA. The application material invites applicants who feel that they are entitled to such consideration to submit a statement requesting such consideration and explaining the circumstances with documentation where possible.

As a result of the formula approach for Regular category applicants, the length of a candidate's academic studies is neither an advantage nor a disadvantage. However, the structure of the formula can be an advantage for an applicant with only two years of undergraduate studies if their LSAT score is high. The reverse is also true in that a low LSAT score can be a disadvantage for an applicant with only two years compared to one with more years of university work.

A comparatively high percentage (20%-25%) of Osgoode students are admitted without a degree. This is reflected in the low average age of twenty-three years. (Please refer to the Comparative Statistics chapter.) According to Professor R.J. Gray, Assistant Dean, and a member of the Admissions Committee, "we have never had any reason to discriminate against the non-degree applicants. Academically, perhaps due to motivation, they perform slightly better than any other grouping in terms of the number of years of university work. In any event, we do not see any advantage to artificially and unnecessarily increasing the number of persons graduating from law school at age twenty-eight who have never experienced life in the permanent work force. Moreover, while not minimizing the value of under-graduate education, Osgoode has an abiding concern with access to the legal profession which, obviously, is directly affected by how long it takes to qualify for it."

It is for comparable reasons that Osgoode has no bias or weighting in its formula that favours applicants with graduate degrees. Again, according to Professor Gray, "In grade terms, while we accept them at face value, we frankly are somewhat sceptical of grades obtained in master's programs since we know that in such programs nobody ever gets below B." As a result, the Osgoode statistics show only four percent of students admitted in 1991-92 had graduate degrees.

Besides the Regular applicant group there are four other categories for entrance to Osgoode: Native Canadian, Mature Student, Access Program, and Special Circumstances. The admissions formula described above is not applied in these cases. The 1991-92 calendar states: "Osgoode Hall Law School is concerned that Indians, Inuit and Metis do not have substantial representation in the legal profession, and accordingly encourages applications from Native people." Usually, five or six offers are given to Natives. Two Native students were admitted in the class of 1991-92.

The Admissions Committee anticipates that eighty percent of the remaining places will be divided equally between the Mature and Access category applicants and twenty percent will go to the Special Circumstances category applicants. Within these categories, the mechanical process applied to Regular applicants is replaced by a more holistic approach. Here, work experience, past achievements, social and economic problems, disadvantages engendered by disability, extra-curricular contributions, and other unique factors are taken into account.

The definition of a **mature student** is one that turns twenty-six before 1 September of the year for which they seek admission, and has a minimum of five years of non-academic experience. No university education is required. The LSAT score and academic performance is given less importance; however, applicants must score in the 24th or higher percentile on the LSAT to be eligible for an interview.

Osgoode's calendar describes three basic types of mature students in order of priority given in the admissions process: those without a university background, or who have less than two years at university; those from groups under- or unrepresented in the legal profession; and those with two or more years of university. Mature students must have all documentation submitted by 1 February and write the LSAT no later than the December sitting. According to Professor Gray, Osgoode has more mature students than any other school.

The Admissions Committee has been given authority to relax the conventional admissions criteria in the case of two further categories of applicants. The **Access category** is for persons with good academic potential who have had to confront general social, educational, and/or economic barriers in the course of their education. The **Special Circumstances category** is for persons who have had their pre-law academic performances seriously affected by ongoing factors beyond their control such as illness, physical handicap, or problems of a compassionate nature, or by extraordinary involvement in worthwhile activities. Applicants must have a minimum of two years postsecondary education. Osgoode annually admits thirty-five applicants under the Access category and fifteen on a Special Circumstances basis.

CHARACTER OF THE SCHOOL

The size and diversity of Osgoode's students make it difficult to assign a character to the school, but adjectives such as hard working, aware, and competitive seem to describe common characteristics of Osgoode students.

Competitiveness and hard work are traits of all law students, since most of the students admitted are high achievers by the nature of the academic requirements. However, the competitiveness seems to be more apparent at Osgoode because there are twice as many students as in a middle-sized school. Steps have been taken by the administration to minimize the sometimes isolating affects of a large school. The incoming class of 330 students is divided into five sections of sixty to sixty-five students. Each section has all their classes together and this fosters close friendships and study groups. However, outside of this group, it is impossible to know most of the people in your year. One student commented, "I would be sitting in the lobby, waiting for an articling interview, and I would ask the other students waiting what school they went to. They said Osgoode and I didn't know them and they didn't know me either." Close friendships are made within small insular groups, but an overall feeling of cohesiveness among the students is missing. This lack of unity can make competition more intense. Being located only forty minutes from Bay Street might have an affect as well.

The student body at Osgoode is very diverse in terms of race, culture, age, and geographic representation. The curriculum is just starting to reflect this by offering such courses as First Nations and the Law and Rights of Indigenous People. Students have formed their own support groups and are actively involved. There is a Native Law Students Association, The Nelson Mandela Law Society, The Osgoode Hall Italian Cultural Society, The Osgoode Hall Jewish Students Association, The Women's Caucus, and Osgoode was one of the first Law Schools to have a Lesbian/Gay Caucus.

Osgoode has one of the more diverse student bodies at faculties of law across Canada. A tension and political backlash has often accompanied diversification at other law schools. This also exists at Osgoode but it is not as divisive. The student body seems to be more tolerant of the differences that diversity brings. This may be because of the anonymity that a large student poulation brings. If you do not choose to become involved in the political aspects of the school, you do not have to.

STRENGTHS OF THE PROGRAM

Osgoode's curriculum covers all areas of the law but, according to the Dean of the Faculty, James C. MacPherson, its strength lies in Public Law. The York University Centre for Public Law and Public Policy was established at Osgoode in 1986 and its focus on research enriches Osgoode's curriculum in this area. In addition, the outstanding faculty in Public Law gives students the opportunity to be taught by leaders in their fields. Peter Hogg is thought by many to be Canada's best constitutional lawyer and his writings have been cited often in the Supreme Court of Canada. John Evans is also pre-eminent in Administrative Law. Specialty courses in Environmental Law, Labour Law, Municipal Law, and Occupational Health and Safety Law are also offered. Osgoode has also created a major interdisciplinary research institute — the Centre for Public Law and Policy — which brings together faculty, students, and external experts to engage in public law research, conferences, and special lectures. International Law, especially in the areas of criminal and human rights, is also strong.

There are fifty full-time faculty and approximately fifty part-time faculty (mostly judges and lawyers) teaching at Osgoode. The curriculum at Osgoode is one of the largest and most diverse in Canada. No compulsory courses are required after first year, giving students the utmost flexibility to study whatever might interest them from the wide array of courses offered. University budget constraints have not adversely affected Osgoode.

To complement academic legal education, Osgoode has put into place four intensive clinical programs in Advanced Business Law, Criminal Law, Immigration and Refugee Law, and Poverty Law at Parkdale Community Legal Services. Approximately one hundred second- and third-year students have the opportunity to engage in hands-on or simulated experiences of being a lawyer through these programs. Each intensive lasts a full semester. Students are chosen by lottery except in the case of the Poverty Law intensive where an interview is used as the selection criterion.

Students are involved in the full spectrum of a poverty lawyer's work in the Poverty Law intensive at Parkdale Community Legal Services. A rigorous week of training in clinical skills is required prior to this intensive. Students meet and interview clients, develop strategies and tactics, counsel, negotiate, and appear before courts and tribunals. As well, students become involved in community education and development.

The Intensive Program in Criminal law places students with a judge, Crown attorney, or criminal defense lawyer for a ten-week period. In their placements, students engage in legal research, writing, and are involved in the interviewing, negotiation, trial, and sentencing processes. The program also includes simulation exercises conducting prosecutions, defending at least three criminal cases, and interviewing and negotiating. In addition, two major papers are required.

The objective of the Intensive Program in Immigration and Refugee Law is to expose students to a challenging series of seminars, clinical placements, and supervised research work. The program consists of three modules focusing on the Law of Admission to Canada, the Law of Exclusion from Canada, and the Law of Refugee Protection. Within each module, students have a two-week placement abroad at an embassy, an international organization, or at a Canadian location.

The Advanced Business Law Intensive builds on the knowledge gained in previous business courses with advanced discussions in corporate and tax law. It is also intended that students develop some insight into the broader theoretical and ethical considerations that confront a business lawyer throughout his/her career.

There is also another type of clinical program at Osgoode, namely The Community and Legal Aid Services Program (CLASP). CLASP is a student-run legal service organization with clinics at Osgoode and in the nearby Jane-Finch area. It provides legal education and assistance to people of low-income, and engages in legal research and law reform initiatives. Prerequisite extra-curricular volunteer work with the program is necessary prior to applying to the academic program. Students will engage in advocacy training, perform casework, supervise junior students, present a law reform or community development seminar, and receive a program of individualized counselling supervision emphasizing personal reflection and awareness.

"Osgoode is a national law school, not just an Ontario school," states MacPherson. Faculty come from all over Canada, including Professors Pierre Marc Johnson, former Premier of Quebec; Allan Blakeney, former Premier of Saskatchewan; and Ian Scott, former Attorney General of Ontario. These professors, who taught at the law school for periods of one to two years, contribute to the national flavour of the school. Also, approximately eighty students per year are admitted from provinces other than Ontario. This national representation of faculty and students invites their perspectives to be part of class discussions.

On the international scale, Osgoode students can apply for exchanges with the Faculty of Law, University of Kobe, Japan, or the Southwest Institute of Political Science and Law, Chongqing, China. In 1991-92 visiting professors from the United States, France, Confederation of Independent States (formerly the Soviet Union), and Japan will also add to the international atmosphere.

Students also have the opportunity to become involved on a voluntary basis with the *Osgoode Hall Law Journal*. The law review is staffed and edited by upper-year students in collaboration with members of the faculty.

WHERE THE PROGRAM COULD IMPROVE

There is a concern among the students interviewed that the balance between the practice aspects of the law versus the interpretation and the "why" of the law is not being maintained, and that the time spent on the interpretation of the law is at the expense of the required skills to practise law. The diversity of the student body brings to the fore many political viewpoints. However, these are not as divisive as they could be because of the anonymity afforded by the size of the school.

The size of the program is another concern. Although much has been done to foster school spirit, compared to other law faculties, Osgoode's sense of community is not as great. With an incoming class of 330 students each year, the experience can be overwhelming. Outside of a close group of friends, nurtured by the small sections in first year, it is harder to get to know people. After first year, students can choose their courses from a good number of courses and the core groups established in first year tend to disperse. This is compounded by the fact that a significant number of students come from the Toronto area and commute.

The physical location of York University's campus was a major source of dissatisfaction, as were the windowless classrooms in the Law building itself. These areas are dealt with more fully under the sections "What the Students Say," and "On North York."

ON NORTH YORK

North York is part of Metropolitan Toronto, although to get downtown by public transit requires a bus and subway trip of approximately one hour. By car it is a half hour drive, depending on the traffic. Most students have a car and say they would feel isolated without one.

York University's campus is large and sprawling and is located in the middle of a very busy traffic area near Jane and Finch, one of the highest crime districts in Toronto. Safety was a concern of the women interviewed but less of a concern for the men. An escort service has been put in place by the university.

Overall, the campus is very windy and barren of trees. The law building itself, however, does have a stand of trees nearby. A recent twenty-two million dollar building campaign was responsible for the addition of York Lanes commercial centre which houses doctor's offices, grocery stores, retail outlets, and a dance club. York Lanes has almost everything you need and this helps minimize the out-of-the-way location of the campus.

It used to be difficult to get residence accommodation, but the building campaign was also responsible for constructing new residences and renovating existing ones. Six hundred housing units, less than one hundred metres from the law school, are now available. Some rooms in residence are reserved for out of province law students and last year every Osgoode student who wanted a room in residence obtained one. Osgoode now has probably the best student housing situation of any metropolitan law school. Osgoode's student body also has a significant number of commuters.

Socially, there are many resources. There is a very active intramural sports program at Osgoode. The highlight is perhaps the Osgoode Touch Football League which has about fifty co-educational teams playing all autumn. The Metropolitan Track and Field Centre is on-campus and is available to students. There are also lunch-time concerts, a bird sanctuary, and York's own art gallery.

WHAT THE STUDENTS SAY

(Pseudonyms have replaced the following students' names)

The Strengths of the Program

"Osgoode's curriculum covers all areas, but it is very strong in constitutional law. It has a very strong academic orientation towards the law and I think the study of law is moving in that direction. Law is becoming more and more a multidisciplinary field." John LL.B. '92

"There is a good variety of courses offered and you can specialize. I am interested in tax law and there are still courses left that I haven't taken." Arlene LL.B. '92

"The students have a heightened awareness of social problems. You come out of the school with a more sympathetic viewpoint. Osgoode is more left and socially aware than some law schools." Jo-anne LL.B. '92

"The people make the place. The name Osgoode Hall is synonymous with great professors. They [the faculty] are great legal minds and this scares you off sometimes and intimidates you, but for the most part they are very approachable." Desmond LL.B. '92

"The library is the largest in the country and the Commonwealth." Clifton, articling student

"There are numerous clubs, committees and sports. You can be part of the high school project, legal aid clinic, equality committee, admissions committee, woman's caucus, or the musical society, etc." Jo-anne LL.B. '92

"Osgoode is a progressive law school and it is big on fairness [referring to the Clinical Intensives selecting their students by lottery]. There is no going through the transcripts and saying the cream will get the edge." Clifton, articling student

"The John White Society and other groups bring in very good speakers who expand on what is going on in the classroom." Jo-anne LL.B. '92

"Groups of law students go out and have sessions with high school students.

They explain to them about legal fields and their options. They encourage black students to apply as well as other students." Desmond LL.B. '92

Where the Program Could Improve

"It is common for students to get substantially lower grades in law school than they expected. It is hard to deal with and it spurs you on to do better and work harder. In first and second year you are thinking of getting a job, and if you are in corporate law it is even more competitive since the Bay Street firms weed you out according to grades. This causes more competition." Arlene LL.B. '92

"When I was in first year, I felt that Osgoode was extremely competitive what with students not wanting to share their summaries, etc. We independently formed our own study groups and shared summaries amongst ourselves, but not with those who were not in our group. Now that we have our articling jobs it isn't as competitive. There is some perception out there that Bay Street is where you should be and large firms select by virtue of marks for their first cut." Jo-anne LL.B. '92

"Perhaps there are too many students. In first year there are sixty students per section. It is very important in first year to be able to communicate with others to talk through ideas and this is difficult." John LL.B. '92

"Osgoode has a huge population. You would assume that you would know the people in your year, but you don't really get to meet them. At Osgoode a lot of people have completely different experiences and this is positive since not everyone can be the same, but it might take away from the closeness." Luping, articling student

"Corporate law or strict business is perceived by students and even some faculty to be an area of weakness." John LL.B. '92

"A lot of the corporate commercial courses are not taught by full-time professors but rather by practitioners. They were good, but it was hard to get to see them and there wasn't the same type of continuity. You didn't know what to expect from year to year. Professors devote themselves to their courses and their students whereas practitioners have their own careers and teaching is on the side. Osgoode has to get more full-time staff in terms of corporate commercial law." Luping, articling student

"The diversity reflects the student population, but the courses reflect the status quo. That is why natives and black students want courses that reflect the student body and not the mainstream view. It's difficult to change things, but the law school is where you start because it is a reflection of who we are as Canadians." Desmond LL.B. '92

"Every year you have to rank your courses. I have never had any problem, but many students can't get the course or professors they want. For example, it is very difficult to get into Professor Hogg's or Professor Young's courses or small seminars." John LL.B. '92

Controversies

"There are three dominant controversies at Osgoode: controversy involving feminist issues, issues of race and colour, and the strong policy bent some of the professors have in their teachings. There is a lot of concern among Osgoode students that they are not getting the requisite skills required to practise. I have learned so much from the controversy that I don't regret it taking place. However, the problem is that some of the more radical and extreme members of Osgoode's feminist movement tend to alienate people like myself that really want to learn about the issues." John LL.B. '92

"There are factions within the different groups because of the diversity, but it lends itself to the strength of the school. There are times when they are vociferous, but there are many forums either through the school newspaper or elsewhere where you can express yourself without restraint. You can't have everyone conforming. Not everyone thinks the same. We come from different backgrounds and ethnic groups." Desmond LL.B. '92

"The objectionists would write an article with their viewpoint and they would get a response. Then the objectionist would respond even stronger. As a student, you know the issues exist, but the writing makes them more controversial than they really are. There are a few active people, but there are a greater number who are passive and have viewpoints but don't want to get involved." Arlene LL.B. '92

"Osgoode encompasses all political issues. The students bring issues into the mainstream courses as I did on regional issues. There is a very active woman's caucus and native group, and as a result of their presence it has had an effect on developing the curriculum, ensuring certain perspectives are offered. Some would say that the political goings on were too much and a down side, but I don't think there is ever too much political debate. Law school is more than a legal education. It is an experience to learn an awareness of country, people, regional issues, political viewpoints, race, and feminist issues." Clifton, articling student

"There is definitely some tension. This is inevitable because the type of people you have in law school have strong opinions. Some are doing poverty law and are working in a clinic, and there are those that want to make a lot of money. You are going to have conflicts. . . . A lot of people from privileged backgrounds still want the law to be the old boys school. I see it changing but I also see resistance. It's not particularly worse at Osgoode than at other schools. The controversy has opened my eyes to a lot of things. Coming from a middle class white background, I was shocked by the reactions of some of the students in class to feminist professors and this experience has made me more of a feminist." Angela LL.B. '93

"In some of my first-year core courses they were heavily policy driven (eg. I didn't even open the rules). This is an ongoing debate. Is it [law school] a training ground, or training the mind in critical analysis. In my view, some balance is required between skills and a way of thinking. It is dangerous in core courses in first year if you don't touch the black letter law. Some balance is required as well as giving students an opportunity to choose." Clifton, articling student

"It is important to have a proper balance and sometimes the weight is shifted far more to the policy side. Students leaving some courses taught by certain professors often feel that they leave the course without the requisite knowledge to practise." John LL.B. '92

"There are some professors and some courses which are very much policy oriented, but at the same time there are other professors, especially practitioners, that are very applied. The professors have a spectrum of political views and you can pick and chose. Out of the thirty courses I have taken, I would say only four or five have been too policy-oriented. In first year you don't get to choose your professors so you could end up with more of a policy focus, but after first year you can choose. You are able to avoid the policy orientation if you really want to." Arlene LL.B. '92

"Policy versus black letter law [the practical side] is not really a controversy since that is why Osgoode and Toronto were started to begin with." Luping, articling student

On Faculty

"Peter Hogg is recognized as the foremost authority in the country in constitutional law. He is also a very good teacher and presenter." Desmond LL.B. '92

"Peter Hogg (constitutional law), John McCamus (contracts), and Mary Jane Mossman (family and gender and equality law) are fantastic and very approachable." Jo-anne LL.B. '92

"Alan Young, who teaches criminal law, is regarded as the most popular and best professor at Osgoode." John LL.B. '92

"Mary Jane Mossman teaches family law. She teaches without intimidating." Arlene LL.B. '92

Other Comments

"Price of education [at all law schools] is a problem. Not a lot of people can afford to access the education that we are preaching as being so important." Desmond LL.B. '92

"My opinion of Osgoode has changed since first year. Now I am very pleased but in first year I commuted. I found York as a whole was a commuter school and I found it hard to get to know people. I am living in residence now and I am able to get more involved with committees and get to know the professors better." Jo-anne LL.B. '92

Université D'Ottawa/
University Of Ottawa*

■ **INQUIRIES**

Chair of the Admissions Committee
Faculty of Law
Common Law Section
University of Ottawa
57 Louis Pasteur
Ottawa, Ontario
KIN 6N5
(613) 564-4060

***NOTE:** At the Université d'Ottawa/University of Ottawa it is possible to obtain a degree in civil law, which is required for practice in Quebec, or the common law, which is required for all provinces in Canada except Quebec. For information on the civil law degree please see the Université d'Ottawa under the civil law section. The common law section described below is divided into the English common law section and the French common law section.

ADMISSIONS INFORMATION

■ **APPLICATION DEADLINE DATE FOR ADMISSIONS**

1 February

■ **REQUIRED TO SUBMIT**

English Common Law Section

- Official copies of all university academic transcripts
- LSAT score report (if an applicant's native tongue is not English, the LSAT score may not be as heavily weighted)
- supplementary application form

French Common Law Section

- Official copies of all university academic transcripts and/or CEGEP transcripts
- An LSAT score is not required
- Supplementary application form

■ **EDUCATION REQUIREMENTS**
the equivalent of two full years of undergraduate studies

■ **AVERAGE GPA**
79.5% or A- or 3.7

■ **AVERAGE LSAT**
80th percentile

■ **RATIO OF APPLICANTS TO REGISTRATIONS**
22.1 : 1 English
3.4 : 1 French

■ **SIZE OF INCOMING CLASS**
120 English
60 French

■ **CAN YOU DEFER ACCEPTANCE**
No

■ **APPLICATION FEE**
$15 application fee plus a $30 evaluation fee. Both are non-refundable.

■ **TUITION FEE**
The 1992-93 tuition fees are $2124 for Canadian citizens (this includes general fees) and $7,181 for non-exempt foreign students.

CLASS PROFILE

■ **AVERAGE AGE OF STUDENTS ENTERING THE PROGRAM**
26 English
24 French

■ **PERCENTAGE OF THE CLASS WHO ARE WOMEN**
53% English
57% French

- **PERCENTAGE OF WOMEN WHO ARE TENURED FACULTY**

    35% (6 of 17 tenured faculty but out of 32 full-time faculty [i.e. tenured and tenure track] there are 16 women or 50%)

- **PERCENTAGE OF THE CLASS WITH**

two years or more of an undergraduate degree	n/a
a three-year degree	n/a
a four-year degree	n/a
a post-graduate degree	n/a

- **PROFILE OF LL.B. POPULATIONS**

    10% (12) Native Students — English
    2% (1) Native Student — French
    16% (25) Visible Minorities — English
    15% (9) Visible Minorities — French
    13% (15) Mature Students — English
    7% (4) Mature Students — French

OTHER RELATED PROGRAMS

M.B.A./LL.B., Diploma in legislative drafting
Master of Law degree with four areas of specialization: International Law, Constitutional and Administrative Law, Human Rights, and Comparative Law. An LL.D. Doctoral program in research is open to those who have already demonstrated a capacity for scholarly research and writing.
HALF-TIME PROGRAM: There is a limited half-time program available in the Common Law Section. These places are available to students who have been admitted to the full-time program, but who, due to pressing personal needs, prefer to study half-time.

ADMISSIONS REQUIREMENTS

The application form used to apply to University of Ottawa's Faculty of Law, Common Law Section, is structured to allow opportunities for disclosure in the areas of social, economic, racial, and cultural perspectives. Applicants can apply under the following categories: general student, mature student, native student, or special circumstances categories. The mature student is described as someone who may or may not have the minimum two years of university but does have five or more years of non-academic experience. There is no age requirement for a mature student.

The admissions process requires that each candidate's file be reviewed completely. The file is made up of a student's grade point average, their LSAT score, and additional information. A formula is not used in the admissions process at Ottawa's Faculty of Law; rather, a holistic approach is used. However, in the general category, academic standing and the LSAT score are the primary factors determining admission. There is room on the supplementary application form to explain false starts or other factors affecting the applicant's LSAT score or academic record. Two-thirds of the 180 students admitted are placed in the general category.

For applicants whose LSAT and academic record do not fall easily into the accept or reject pile, the personal statement and additional information becomes very important. Significant achievements in extra-curricular activities or community involvement are factors that are looked for. A neat and well-written statement that is expressed logically will be regarded favourably. The law school is looking for well-rounded candidates who will make a contribution both to the student body and the profession.

In an attempt to have a student body of prospective lawyers be representative of the people they will one day serve, the University of Ottawa's Faculty of Law, Common Law Section, has broadened its admission categories over the last three years. A pro-active recruitment of racial and cultural minorities, persons with disabilities, and persons who are economically disadvantaged has become a priority. Three years ago less than five percent of the entering class represented racial minorities. In contrast, the 1991-92 class was comprised of fifteen to twenty percent racial minorities, including persons from the Aboriginal Communities. Thirteen aboriginal students and approximately thirty racial minority students were part of the entering class. The administration at the University of Ottawa is in the forefront of having a student body which is coming closer to representing society. In the Common Law Section as a whole, there are approximately twenty-five Aboriginal students and the number of racial minority students is over sixty.

Many law faculties are changing, or at least reviewing their admissions criteria to focus on diversifying their student body. However, the University of Ottawa is one of the few faculties of law to support their policy by hiring a staff member to aid the transition. Three years ago Joanne St. Lewis, Director of the Education Equity Program, was appointed to implement and support the new policy.

"Once we have admitted these students, you have to conceptualize the program. Are you assimilating them or trying to have the environment reflect their contribution?" asks St. Lewis. "The number of minorities has increased to the point now where they have reached a critical mass and they feel safer in voicing their opinions." St. Lewis comments, "People are not willing to live with discomfort . . . and they are scared of change." Therefore, St. Lewis spends time trying to empower people and encourage mutual respect. St. Lewis is directly responsible to Donald McRae, Dean of the Faculty of Law, Common Law section. If St. Louis has difficulties with either staff or students, regarding issues of equity, she deals with them directly with the full support of the Dean.

THE CHARACTER OF THE SCHOOL

The University of Ottawa's Faculty of Law is unique in Canada and maybe the world. The two main legal traditions of Civil and Common law are taught in the same faculty and the same building. Within the Common Law Section, applicants can choose to study both in English and French, but they do not have to be bilingual. The combination of Common Law in English and French, and the presence of Civil Law in French, makes the University of Ottawa's Faculty of Law distinct. Add to this a pro-active admissions policy, and you have a very complex community that does not always cohabit peacefully.

National unity issues have perhaps heightened the existing tensions between the French Civil Law and English Common Law students. Friend-ships between the groups are neither natural nor forthcoming. Both groups are housed in the same building to encourage integration but, for most students, interaction is negligible. The development of camaraderie and understanding is time consuming and must be purposefully sought out. Most students have neither the time nor the inclination.

The University of Ottawa has taken steps towards making the Faculty of Law reflect the contribution of their diverse student body and is willing to live with the necessary discomfort in order to grow. Certainly controversy exists, but it does not seem as volatile or bitter as some other law schools. Perhaps this is due to a supportive administration that has already experienced one transition — when the profile of their faculty changed to fifty percent women.

"The University of Ottawa is a school that is going forward at quite a pace. New ideas are being tried. Some are troubled by the change and others welcome it," observes Dean McRae.

STRENGTHS OF THE PROGRAM

The strength of the University of Ottawa's Faculty of Law lies in the area of public law. "Ottawa is not a corporate commercial centre and this tends to flavour our approach. Other areas of strength depend on individual faculty member's expertise. We have a number of courses on feminist analyses, criminal law, and taxation, but they are all related back to a public law orientation," comments Dean McRae.

Located in the nation's capital the Law School has a sense of being part of the political scene. Students are given the opportunity to watch the proceedings of the Supreme Court of Canada, and prominent people such as Madam Justice Bertha Wilson are Scholars-In-Residence. In addition to the University of Ottawa's Faculty of Law library, students have access to the libraries of the Supreme Court of Canada (the richest and most important of law libraries in Canada), the Department of Justice, other libraries of departments and institutions of the Federal Government, and the National Library of Canada.

The University of Ottawa's Faculty of Law library itself serves the needs of both the common and civil law sections. It also contains an important collection in Comparative Law, Constitutional Law, Administrative Law, International Law, and Human Rights which are the fields of concentration for Graduate Studies in the Faculty of Law.

The Human Rights Research and Education Centre, established in the Faculty of Law in 1981, has developed the largest public collection in Canada of human rights documents. *The Canadian Human Rights Yearbook* is an annual refereed journal of scholarly articles. Law students in second and third year can participate as student editors.

The *Ottawa Law Review*, established in 1966, is recognized as one of Canada's leading scholarly legal periodicals. Approximately fifteen senior students have the opportunity to act as editors on the board of the *Review*. Previously, the selection criteria for these prized editorial positions was based on a narrow definition of academic excellence. To remove systemic barriers and increase the diversity of perspectives represented on the editorial board, the criteria have been changed to place more weight on the editing skills and specific background required to fill the positions. Experience as an editor on the *Review* is highly regarded by firms recruiting for articling positions. Student's experiences are enriched by training in legal research, accurate written expression, and an in-depth investigation of a variety of problems.

In terms of hiring, the University of Ottawa's Faculty of Law has not suffered as much as other schools in terms of budget cutbacks. Hiring in the French Common Law Section is expanding. Currently there are nine faculty members and plans are in place to build this to fifteen, with three positions added in 1990. In the English Common Law section, eight faculty members have been hired in the last five years.

In the words of McRae, "hiring ought to track the equity program. Our faculty should reflect the aboriginal, ethnic, and physically challenged as does the student body through our educational equity program." In keeping with this vision, two aboriginal faculty have been hired. This represents the highest number of aboriginal faculty at any Faculty of Law in Canada.

WHERE THE PROGRAM COULD IMPROVE

Although the concept of having French and English, Common and Civil Law together to encourage interaction seems rational, in reality it does not achieve its goal to the extent one might think. The Common Law and Civil Law Sections are quite isolated physically — in that they are on different floors — and administratively, in that there are two Deans, two admissions processes and administrations, and two separate student societies. There is, however, significant integration, co-operation, and understanding among the two language groups studying common law (English Language Program and Programme Français). A definite and concerted effort on the part of the student will be required to take advantage of the opportunity that exists.

The number of courses taught in French available to French Common Law students is significantly smaller than the English Common Law curriculum. This is due to the difficulty of getting faculty whose native language is French, but who have been trained in the common law system. Also the number of French books in the library is comparatively few compared to those in English.

ON OTTAWA

The campus of the University of Ottawa is situated in the heart of downtown, a ten-minute walk from the Rideau Centre, the Market, and the Rideau Canal. The Faculty of Law is completely self-contained in Fauteux Hall. Student lockers are in the basement, classes are all held in Fauteux Hall, and the library is on the top two floors of the five-storied building. Overground tunnels give accessibility to cafeterias, some residences, and social science buildings.

One student described the winters in Ottawa as "real winters," cold but fun with events such as Winterlude and skating on the canal. In February, the faculty and students get together and organize a Law Show with skits and satire. In the summers, the bike paths are great.

Ottawa has the atmosphere of a small town. "It's a quiet bureaucratic town that goes to sleep after 5 pm — a very relaxed atmosphere to study in," commented one student. If excitement is what you are looking for, the bars in Hull stay open until 3 am. It is a moderately priced city to live in, with a one-bedroom apartment within walking distance priced around $400. The vacancy rate in Ottawa is about one percent. There is no problem finding accommodation but it is not a tenant's market. In Hull the vacancy rate is 4.5 percent and it is cheaper, but fewer people choose Hull. Residence accommodation is also available.

WHAT THE STUDENTS SAY

(Pseudonyms have replaced the following students' names)

The Strengths of the Program

"You feel like you are close to the action being in Ottawa. Courses and moots in particular are dovetailed with the Supreme Court and you can watch the proceedings and find out what happened. You can call up the lawyers that have been on the case or get the "factums" [documents] on the case from the court." Edward LL.B. '92, English Common Law Section

"The University of Ottawa gives you a very practical legal education. There are a lot of practitioners teaching non-core courses and they bring a different point of view — real world rather than academic." Claude LL.B. '91, articling student, French Common Law Section

"The French Common Law program has small classes of 60 students as opposed to 120 in the English Common Law. In first year all your classes are together. It's kind of like being in high school again because you are seeing the same people all the time. You get closer to the people and get to know them, but on the other side, you become isolated. You are different because you are a Francophone." Danielle LL.B. '92, French Common Law Section

"The program is in French and there is value in that in itself. There is also job-related value. The job market for the French program is still open whereas the English majors are afraid the job market is drying up. I would encourage people to take the program in French if at all possible since you can practise in French and English." Luc LL.B. '92, French Common Law Section

"Doing my law degree gave me an opportunity to do a tremendous variety of things, for example, student legal aid in the AIDS community in Ottawa, tutor to first-year law students, and I worked on the *Canadian Journal on Women and the Law* and the *Human Rights Journal*." Anne LL.B. '91, articling student, English Common Law Section

Controversies

On Diversity

"There is a beginning of a commitment to affirmative action in the admission process, hiring of faculty, and the role students are playing in setting the agenda of the school, but we are not there yet. There is more work to be done in support for changes in the school. . . . This is a school where things are really changing and that's not always an easy process; that is why the University of Ottawa is either looked at very positively or very negatively." Suzanne LL.B. '92, English Common Law Section

"When we [black caucus] presented a budget to the caucus they didn't want to give us the money. We united with the women's group and the aboriginal group who were also having problems getting money for their projects. This almost caused a schism. I had to discuss this even with good white friends, and it created discomfort with others." Diane LL.B. '92, English Common Law Section

"The middle ground is becoming smaller. They are either part of the change or they are resisting it. The present administration has made a concerted effort to be more representative of the real world and the backlash against it is becoming more noticeable. But because of the change, people with an interest in these areas are coming here for that reason." Suzanne LL.B. '92, English Common Law Section

"The Equity Education Director, Joanne St. Louis, is an incredible resource. When I first came here I didn't think one person and a program could do very much, but I have turned my view on this 180 degrees." Edward LL.B. '92, English Common Law Section

"On the surface it's harmonious. It goes through some upheavals and then it levels off. I see the good side too. People are making the effort. I get tired of sensitizing people to different perspectives and different groups, but I hope it's working." Diane LL.B. '92, English Common Law Section

French/English Issue

"There is a very hot political and divisive atmosphere between the English and French. The clique of French Civil and Common Law students stick together and you have to make the effort to get to know each other. I happen to like the political conflict. I liked that the English side kept us on our toes. When you go out into the workplace you are going to have conflicts. People are not speaking the same language nor do they have the same beliefs. I went to law school knowing that it wasn't going to be all roses. I went there to gain something. There is conflict but it is beneficial." Claude LL.B. '92, French Common Law Section

"I expected to improve my French but I see a great obstacle between the two groups. The French Civil Law section is very different. They are younger, coming out of CEGEP mostly from Quebec, and fairly separatist. This carries over to their attitude toward the English students. They are a different culture and they are set apart. . . . There really isn't time and you have to make so much of an effort that it isn't really worth it." Allan LL.B. '92, English Common Law Section

"I think that some of the English people come because of the bilingualism and when they get here they see that the French have their own radio station and other institutions but they are expecting it to be the same. Bilingual to them means that there is a compromise and they'll get along. All bilingual means is that there are courses in each language." Luc LL.B. '92, French Common Law Section

"One of the things that attracted me to the University of Ottawa was the English and French mix. Was I ever surprised by the lack of harmony and the politics. It was really hostile. As a result it turned me off. I don't even talk French any more. The French are on the first floor and the English on the third and never the two shall meet." Diane LL.B. '92, English Common Law Section

"A lot of English resent the fact that you have to be fluently bilingual in Ottawa to get a government job. Even if you are bilingual it's not good enough. You have to have French as your first language." Diane LL.B. '92, English Common Law Section

Where the Program Could Improve

"The professors are younger on the French Common Law faculty than on the English side and they are more challenging, but the school can go further." Claude LL.B. '91, articling student, French Common Law Section

"There is a problem with law school evaluation. Final exams or essays are one hundred percent and the amount of work you put into a course is not necessarily reflected in your mark." Allan LL.B. '92, English Common Law Section

"The traditional legal methodology of teaching is the Socratic method. The new professors that are hired are younger and don't teach this way. The Socratic method is a very humiliating experience where you are called upon by your last name at a time when you might not want to be. The biggest part of law is not teaching you law, but developing an attitudinal shift. They do this on purpose and it is an assaultive experience." Anne LL.B. '91, articling student, English Common Law Section

"The school could improve by having more teachers who are more fluent in French. There was a course I was going to take in International Private Law. I dropped it because the professor's French was so bad. There are very few French-speaking professors available." Danielle LL.B. '92, French Common Law Section

On Faculty

"Administrative law is a real strength with leading names like Edward Ratushny. The faculty of law also has a very strong family law and feminist legal studies with Elizabeth Sheehy." Edward LL.B. '92, English Common Law Section

"The University of Ottawa's Faculty of Law offers courses in every area and is strong overall, but it doesn't have very highly specialized business courses like construction business law or advanced security law courses." Edward LL.B. '92, English Common Law Section

"Great dean and professors. They are very approachable and willing to discuss things." Diane LL.B. '92, English Common Law Section

"The difference from first year and now is like night and day. Dean McRae hired from alternate communities every opening he got. He openly stated that he was interested in all aspects of the law and he said it in print in the student paper. Affirmative action and drawing out minorities is working — there are problems but its working." Anne LL.B. '91, articling student, English Common Law Section

"Strong in traditional areas, especially in tenant and landlord act with Professor Joseph Roach." Danielle LL.B. '92, French Common Law Section

Other Comments

"Coming to law school was a radicalizing process for me. It forced me to confront the reality behind some of the abstract things I'd been thinking and made me work more actively towards these things." Suzanne LL.B. '92, English Common Law Section

"It is disconcerting how absolutely powerful the law can be and how absolutely wrong it can be. Law school has made me far more aware of privilege. When you leave law school you have a tool that others don't and lawyers haven't done enough to confront what they are doing with that privilege." Suzanne LL.B. '92, English Common Law Section

"I got a really good education. I learned to read, research, and argue and through legal aid I got an excellent practical education. But I wouldn't encourage anyone to go to law school." Anne LL.B. '91, articling student, English Common Law Section

"You can tell there are still a lot of rich people in law school and it is perpetuated. In the French Common Law program it is not so much that way." Danielle LL.B. '92, French Common Law Section

Queen's University

■ **INQUIRIES**

Registrar
Faculty of Law
Macdonald Hall
Queen's University
Kingston, Ontario
K7L 3N6
(613) 545-2220

ADMISSIONS INFORMATION

■ **APPLICATION DEADLINE DATE FOR ADMISSIONS**
1 February

■ **REQUIRED TO SUBMIT**

Regular Category

- Official copies of all university academic transcripts
- LSAT score report
- TOEFL score may be requested where English is a second language

In addition, Special Applicants will provide

- Two letters of academic or personal references
- Personal statement

■ **EDUCATION REQUIREMENT**
Two full years of academic work at a recognized university

■ **AVERAGE GPA**
80 or A- or 3.7 (range: 72%–92%)

- ■ **AVERAGE LSAT**
  81st percentile (range 44 – 99)
  If the LSAT is written more than once, the scores are averaged but trends are noted and individual extra-ordinary scores are also noted.

- ■ **RATIO OF APPLICANTS TO REGISTRATIONS**
  20.2 : 1

- ■ **SIZE OF INCOMING CLASS**
  160

- ■ **CAN YOU DEFER ACCEPTANCE**
  No

- ■ **APPLICATION FEE**
  $30 non-refundable

- ■ **TUITION FEE**
  The 1992-93 tuition fee is $2,324 — Canadian or Landed Immigrant. This includes student interest fees. The 1992-93 tuition fee for International Students is $6,692 plus student and faculty fees of $431.

CLASS PROFILE

- ■ **AVERAGE AGE OF STUDENTS ENTERING THE PROGRAM**
  26

- ■ **PERCENTAGE OF THE CLASS WHO ARE WOMEN**
  46%

- ■ **PERCENTAGE OF WOMEN WHO ARE TENURED FACULTY**
  10% (3 out of 32) Three other women are on staff but not tenured.

- ■ **PERCENTAGE OF THE CLASS WITH**

two years or more of an undergraduate degree	5%
a three-year degree	30%
a four-year degree	50%
a post-graduate degree	15%

- ■ **PROFILE OF LL.B. POPULATIONS**

Native Students	2%
Visible Minorities	15%
Mature Students	20%

OTHER RELATED PROGRAMS

LL.M., and Master in Philosophy/LL.B.

HALF-TIME PROGRAM: Six half-time students were admitted in 1991-92. The requirements for admission and application deadline date are the same as those for the full-time program. Part-time students are not restricted in terms of the courses they can take except by the ballot process. All courses are given during the day.

The part-time program at Queen's Faculty of Law is in the third year of a three-year pilot program. Both Virginia Bartley, Registrar, and John Whyte, Dean, agree it is almost certain that the program will continue. The number of students is small and probably will not grow significantly. Full-time students can apply to transfer into the part-time program for compassionate, financial, or career-related reasons. It is also possible for part-time students to apply to transfer into the full-time program. Students have a maximum of six years to complete the program, and students are required to take at least three courses per term (half the full-time load).

ADMISSIONS REQUIREMENTS

The major criterion determining admission for most students is the academic average and LSAT score although no formula is used. The admissions committee is looking for an upward trend in grades and a consistently strong record. Virginia Bartley, Associate Dean and Registrar of the Faculty, comments that "applicants can't rely on just doing a qualifying year with a previously average academic background. The qualifying year is quickly disappearing as an entry guarantee."

The length of a consistently strong record is important. Three years of solid academic achievement is preferred. It is possible to be admitted after only two years of undergraduate work; however, higher academic standards are required to be competitive with applicants with longer records. Most students find that their grades in first- and sometimes second-year university drop significantly from what they obtained in high school. Thus, obtaining good grades in the first three years can be difficult. The majority of students complete their degree prior to being admitted.

The admissions committee at Queen's Faculty of Law does not work on a quota system under an affirmative action policy. However, they hope to have twenty percent of the incoming class made up of special applicants and fifty percent women students, comments Virginia Bartley. Gaps in an academic or work history are noticed and should be accounted for in applications.

An applicant whose academic record and LSAT score are not strong enough for admission as a regular applicant may presently apply for consideration as a special applicant under the following categories. The admissions process will undergo substantial change over the next year. An applicant may be admitted if he/she

- has demonstrated sustained or distinctive achievment; or
- is a Canadian Indian, Inuit, or Métis; or
- has suffered from a seriously disadvantaged social or economic background; or
- has a substantial record of activity on behalf of persons in disadvantaged circumstances and intends to continue such activity after obtaining a legal education; or
- is physically handicapped; or
- is a mature student.

The mature student category can be misleading, in that age alone will not make an applicant competitive. "An applicant can't simply be getting older or go out and work for a lawyer for a couple of years and rely on a great reference. Ten years ago you might have been able to gain admission with a couple of years work experience and a mediocre average. Mature students now have upwards of ten years of quality experience," states Virginia Bartley. Most applicants in the mature student category have completed one year of an undergraduate program, but some have only a few university courses or no university courses at all.

At some universities, native students applying to law school are required to take a "pre-law" summer program at the University of Saskatchewan as part of the requirements for admission. This is not required in all cases by Queen's Faculty of Law.

THE CHARACTER OF THE SCHOOL

The Faculty of Law at Queen's University is committed to improving inequalities between women and men, and among minorities in our society. There is a long-standing tradition at Queen's Faculty of Law of stressing the interaction of law with the social and human context. There is only one compulsory course in second year, allowing students the flexibility to take comparative and critical theory courses if they choose.

A strong theme of justice issues and legal theory underlies all courses at Queen's Faculty of Law and this has attracted a group of students that hold very strong views on social issues. On the other hand, Queen's overall reputation of tradition and conservativism attracts another group of students who have money, power, and status as their ambition. The integration of social values into all courses has resulted in a student body with various groups holding very strong views on feminism, black letter law, and equity issues.

John Whyte, Dean of Queen's Faculty of Law, comments, "In the classroom you will be confronted by questions of law and social value all the time." The integration of social values into all courses has caused a split between students who feel this prevents them from learning the basics and those who feel that a more holistic approach to the study of the law is vital. The faculty are also divided on this issue. To this, Whyte's rebuttal is, "Professional education is for one's life work — practical but aggressively critical." He does not apologize for the stand the Faculty of Law has taken. Instead, he sees it as a strength. Whyte describes Queen's Faculty of Law as having a "reputation for openness and change, progressive and reformist." John Whyte will be stepping down as Dean of Queen's Faculty of Law in June of 1992. However, in his opinion, "social evaluation is not about to go away."

THE STRENGTHS OF THE PROGRAM

Queen's aspires to do well in a significant number of areas of the law, but in John Whyte's opinion it is number one in Canada in Criminal Law, Critical Legal Studies, Evidence and Procedure, Family Law, Feminist Legal Studies, and Public Law. Queen's is also strong in Taxation, Health and Legal Theory (perhaps second to the University of Toronto), International Law, Constitutional, and Administrative Law. Business Law has not been a traditional area of strength but, nevertheless, there are a number of advanced courses in this area. Queen's Faculty of Law does not have courses in Admiralty Law or Oil and Gas Law.

Three unique opportunities for students attending Queen's Faculty of Law are Legal Aid, the Correctional Law Project, and the Chinese Law Programs. In 1991, Queen's Legal Aid celebrated its twentieth birthday. The mandate of the program is to give law students an opportunity to participate in the life of the community and to provide improved legal education and greater amounts of quality legal research, states the spring 1991 issue of the *Queen's Law Reports*. Today, upper-year students appear as agents in proceedings before administrative tribunals. First-year students assist upper-year students on court and tribunal files and participate in researching and writing opinion letters. After mandatory training sessions, approximately 150 law students participated in Queen's Legal Aid during the 1990-91 academic year — nearly one-third of the student body. Queen's Legal Aid has grown and developed to the point that currently students are supervised by two full-time lawyers and managed by a Student Executive, elected annually by the organization's membership. Its educational value was clearly recognized in 1991 when Faculty Board of the Faculty of Law approved an academic credit for legal aid work done by third-year students.

Upper-year students enrolled in Clinical Correctional Law are eligible to participate in the Correctional Law Project. Kingston has ten federal penitentiaries located within a twenty-mile radius of the city. This proximity allows students to provide legal advice, assistance, and representation in the area of correctional law to inmates. Student members of the Project appear before the National Parole Board, institutional disciplinary courts, and assist in other matters under the supervision of the two Project lawyers.

The Chinese Law Programs offer selected Queen's faculty and students the opportunity to exchange with Chinese legal scholars and students. Queen's was the first Canadian law school, and among the first in North America, to offer courses in Chinese Law. Lectures and seminars by visiting Chinese scholars contribute to the program.

WHERE THE PROGRAM COULD IMPROVE

The atmosphere at Queen's Faculty of Law could be described as turbulent. Each student interviewed commented that if you were not willing to have your beliefs challenged, Queen's was not the place to be. As a result of this there is a lack of camaraderie amongst the students. A significant number of students describe themselves as the "silent majority." They feel strongly that the critical theory emphasis is taking away from their legal education and would prefer a more these-are-the-rules-and-this-how-to-apply-them approach, often referred to as black letter law. This group of students is especially opposed to the study of Business Law from a critical theory approach. Business Law is not a traditional area of strength at Queen's, but they do have all the basic courses as well a limited number of advanced courses. However, dissatisfaction with this area stems more from the critical theory emphasis.

Budget restraints have seriously impaired Queen's Faculty of Law in its ability to hire new faculty and to maintain and improve its physical facilities. John Whyte states, "we are not participating in new generations of hiring. You cannot stay out of the hiring game without suffering." The last significant period of hiring occurred five years ago.

The physical facility of Macdonald Hall, which houses Queen's Faculty of Law, has been outgrown. All of the lecture halls and seminar rooms are located in the windowless basement level, creating a dungeon-like atmosphere. Classrooms are not accessible by wheelchair. The law library is unable to expand due to physical limitations. It is putting up a valiant attempt to maintain its position as a top facility, but it is only a matter of time before space problems severely limit one of the more important cornerstones of the faculty. The Law Faculty is currently engaged in capital fundraising but improvements will not be seen for several years.

ON KINGSTON

The campus of Queen's University is compact. A person could walk from one end of the campus to the other in less than ten minutes. It is situated in the centre of town fifteen minutes from downtown by foot. The architecture consists of ivy-covered limestone buildings which adds to the tradition-rich history of the university.

The city of Kingston has a small-town atmosphere with a population of 69,000. One student commented, "It is comforting to go into a nightclub and run into people you know." Kingston is a university town, home to Queen's University, Royal Military College, and St. Lawrence College. Its economic base is predominantly made up of institutions (post-secondary schools, ten penitentiaries, and several government offices), tourism, and some industry.

A common form of transportation is the bicycle. Most students live within five minutes of the university in the "ghetto" immediately surrounding the university. Housing prices have been described as moderate.

WHAT THE STUDENTS SAY
(Pseudonyms have replaced the following students' names)

The Strengths of the Program

"I think Queen's has a strong program because it offers a wide range of courses. If you are interested in alternate perspectives and legal theory, which I tend towards, you can do that, or you can also do corporate law." Elizabeth LL.B. '92

"You have the freedom to design your own program and there is a good selection. I didn't have a problem with the balloting system, but you have to be careful in balloting to maximize your chances since seminars are small." Yolanda, articling student

"There is no ranking done on transcripts or on bulletin boards." Chris, articling student

"I had a picture of the *Paper Chase* in my head when I came but it's not that way. It's very user friendly. I feel that there are a lot of resources and I'm not stuck out there. Everyone is very helpful from the professors to the secretaries." Ellen LL.B. '94

"They divided us up into small sections [in first year], and the professor invited us over to his house. There is a singular sense of purpose where we are all doing the same thing at the same time." Vincent LL.B. '94

Opinions of the "Silent Majority"

"Queen's is a school that really cares, except that some people think it should embrace their particular point of view. I might not agree with what they are saying, but if you want to learn about them you can. The choice is out there for us to take. I have no criticisms of the school. Be prepared for an enlightening experience and to be forced to confront fears and realities." Joseph LL.B. '92

"Queen's has become known as an alternative program. There are more critical courses than strictly core courses compared to other schools. This is healthy in the long run, but the administration and the professors are focused on the politically aware people. You have to be prepared for the pitfalls. In first year you are fighting each other tooth and nail. In second year you ignore each other or there is talking behind your back. In third year you can tolerate each other." Robert LL.B. '92

"Queen's is attracting students with a variety of points of view, all of which are strongly held. The students are set in their ways and are not swayed that much. Queen's is still a conservative school. The faculty are split as are students. Silence passes as tolerance . . . in fact, the tolerance isn't there in terms of the silent majority. Minds or opinions won't be changed. It is a scary thing that I've probably become more conservative over the last three years." Dave LL.B. '92

Where the Program Could Improve

"The faculty is lacking in visible minorities, especially native people. Native students do not have to take the law school preparation course offered in Saskatchewan any more, but they still aren't coming due to lack of support. This is partly because of the size of the community." Elizabeth LL.B. '92

"You have to ballot for courses. I couldn't get into Land Transaction even though I tried every year." Chris, articling student

"Last year we lost three teachers and maybe only one was picked up by contract. They get teachers on special consignments but that does not give the development and growth needed to become part of the community." Chris, articling student

"The physical plant could be described as 'the dungeon.' The classes are in the basement and there are no windows. The library is quite crowded and is at the point of bursting at the seams. Also, the computer facilities are not restricted to just law students and this can be a problem." Robert LL.B. '92

Controversies

"Law schools attract two diametrically opposed groups. One group is attracted to a helping profession and the other wants to make a lot of money. Being volatile is not an unhealthy thing. It is a good representation of what is going on in society. Law school is not exempt from homophobia, sexism, etc." Elizabeth LL.B. '92

"Social issues are addressed in all courses. For example, in a taxation course, a feminist approach was brought in and unequal tax breaks for men and women were discussed. Some students said, cut the social commentary and just teach me taxation. This controversy is a strength." Chris, articling student

On Faculty

"Labour law is very good but you may not have as good a selection in business law. . . . The faculty are personable and the staff are very helpful." Yolanda, articling student

"Queen's is strong in the criminal field. It is also progressive in labour law taught by B. Adell. Two strong professors in criminal law are D.R. Stuart and R.J. Delisle who are published authors in the field. Martha Baily and Tony Pickard are good in their respective fields of family and criminal law." Joseph LL.B. '92

"The basic security courses are good. The teachers come from Toronto or Ottawa. Thirty students in my year went to major law firms on Bay Street." Chris, articling student

"Librarian Denis Marshall is by far the most knowledgeable legal researcher. He gives a credit course on how to research which will improve client service." Joseph LL.B. '92

Other Comments

"I didn't realize that there was so much sexism before I got to law school. I couldn't believe the comments in criminal classes about rape etc." Elizabeth LL.B. '94

"The students that were admitted as regular applicants are cut from the same cloth in terms of ambition, outlook, and social backgrounds despite the admission policies." Dave LL.B. '92

"It's hard to come up against people who will go out into the world and have the power that a law degree gives you. But you don't give up the fight." Elizabeth LL.B. '92

"I found law was more than I thought it would be. I possessed the skills but thought that I wouldn't fit, but I can. There is enough of a diversity that, given time, I think I can find a place. The law can fit the student instead of having to change to fit the law." Elizabeth LL.B. '94

"Don't doubt yourself, just do it and it all comes together." Elizabeth LL.B. '92

University of Saskatchewan

■ **INQUIRIES**

Admissions Committee
College of Law
University of Saskatchewan
Saskatoon, Saskatchewan
S7N OW0
(306) 966-5874

ADMISSIONS INFORMATION

■ **APPLICATION DEADLINE DATE FOR ADMISSIONS**

15 January Early Admission
15 March Regular Admission

■ **REQUIRED TO SUBMIT**

Regular Applicants

- Official copies of all university academic transcripts and official certificates equivalent to senior matriculation of the Province of Saskatchewan, indicating the subjects completed and the standing obtained in each subject. (Current students who have a student number attending University of Saskatchewan are exempted from providing transcripts or certificates.)
- LSAT score report

Special Applicants (in addition to the above)

- A personal statement identifying and explaining all special circumstances
- Relevant supporting documentation such as medical reports
- Details of any relevant occupational experience or community involvement
- Letters of reference

Native Applicants (in addition to the
Regular Applicants requirements)

- Successful completion of the Program of Legal Studies for Native People, held in the summer months at the College of Law

■ **EDUCATION REQUIREMENT**

Two full years of academic work beyond the senior matriculation level, including at least 12 credit units in the humanities or social sciences, at a recognized university or the equivalent of such work.

■ **AVERAGE GPA**

3.41 based on 4.3 point scale (range 2.83 – 4.17)
This is roughly equivalent to a B+ or an 80% average.

■ **AVERAGE LSAT**

74th percentile (range 47th – 99th percentile)
The February sitting of the LSAT is the last available date for admission in September.

■ **RATIO OF APPLICANTS TO REGISTRATIONS**

10:1

■ **SIZE OF INCOMING CLASS**

110 (210 offers sent)

■ **CAN YOU DEFER ACCEPTANCE**

No

■ **APPLICATION FEE**

$35   The application fee is waived for those with a University of Saskatchewan student number.

■ **TUITION FEE**

The 1992-93 tuition fee is approximately $2,500.

CLASS PROFILE

■ **AVERAGE AGE OF STUDENTS ENTERING THE PROGRAM**

25

■ **PERCENTAGE OF THE CLASS WHO ARE WOMEN**

50%

- **PERCENTAGE OF WOMEN WHO ARE TENURED FACULTY**
  24% (6 women out of a faculty of 25 are tenured)

- **PERCENTAGE OF THE CLASS WITH:**

two years or more of an undergraduate degree	6%
a three-year degree	59%
a four-year degree	9%
a post-graduate degree	3%

- **PROFILE OF LL.B. POPULATIONS**

Native Students	10% (11)
Visible Minorities	5% (5)
Mature Students	n/a

OTHER RELATED PROGRAMS

Second degree programs in a Bachelor of Arts and Science and an LL.B., and a Bachelor of Commerce and LL.B. can be completed in five or six years respectively. A Master of Law in the areas of Public and Private Law is also offered.

A part-time program is available to accommodate applicants whose family commitments, financial necessity, or occupational involvement prevent full-time study, and a written statement outlining the reasons why full-time enrollment is not an option is required. The same application deadline date and academic requirements apply for both part-time and full-time applicants. Part-time students must take at least a half course-load and be able to take the majority of their classes during the day.

ADMISSIONS REQUIREMENTS

There are two categories of admission at the Saskatchewan's College of Law — Regular and Special. The majority of the 110 students are admitted from the **Regular Admissions Category** where the primary criteria is the applicant's grade point average (GPA) and the Law School Admissions Test (LSAT) score. Both the GPA and LSAT score are put into an admissions formula where they are both designated an equal weight of 50 percent. The resulting index score is a major part of the admissions decision. The GPA used is based on the best two years. This allows students who do not get off to a very good start in their post-secondary education to still be competitive.

Applicants whose index scores fall into the "grey zone," meaning they are not a clear admit or reject, will have other factors taken into consideration, such as whether they did their degree on a part-time or full-time basis, the level of courses taken in upper years, and an upward progression of their grades.

In an effort to have the student body reflect a variety of backgrounds and experiences, Saskatchewan's College of Law also admits candidates from the **Special Admissions Category**. Academic criteria may not reflect an applicant's true potential due to reasons beyond their control. Therefore, applicants who have experienced cultural or economic disadvantages, physical impairment, a learning disability, or a significant interruption of the pursuit of post-secondary education are judged on the evidence they provide the Admissions Committee showing they have the ability to successfully complete the LL.B. requirements. The LSAT score will usually be given significant weight, but it is not required that a candidate have the required two years of university education. Other achievements through work or community involvement and an explanation of the nature of the educational disadvantage or interruption of studies should be outlined in the personal statement. Supporting letters of reference are also factors considered in the decision-making process.

For Native applicants applying under the Special Admissions Category, the successful completion of the Program of Legal Studies for Native People, held in the summer months at the College of Law, will be considered by the Admissions Committee as a special supplementary predictor of success in law school. For more information, please refer to the chapter on *Native People and Access to Legal Education.*

Candidates with particularly strong academic backgrounds who have completed at least two years of university, or are seeking admission as a special applicant, are encouraged to apply by 15 January. Decisions will be made in February, and those who are not accepted at this time will be reconsidered later with the regular applications.

Saskatchewan's College of Law is a regional school that gives preference to applicants who are Saskatchewan residents, or residents of the Yukon Territory, Northwest Territory, Prince Edward Island, and Newfoundland, since they do not have a College of Law. In 1991-92, eighty-seven of the 110 places were filled by candidates from these provinces or Territories.

CHARACTER OF THE SCHOOL

Saskatchewan's College of Law is a program that emphasizes what is behind the law, and how it affects people. In addition to the study of law as rules and process, there is a strong legal theory component in the curriculum. What is known as the legal theory cluster includes courses in liberalism, feminist analysis of law, critical legal studies, general jurisprudence, and legal theory in the subject areas of torts and contracts. A flexible curriculum provides students with the opportunity to explore these areas. Only one course and a writing assignment is required in the upper years of the program.

Saskatchewan's College of Law is a school of the new regime. The College of Law is going through a transition period. Studying law in the context of social issues, including feminist analysis, has caused some friction among the students. A small group of female students have a "Women and the Law" organization and a small group of the men have a "Men and the Law" counterpart, with intolerance on both parts. The faculty are clear in their mandate to move towards equity and maintain their theoretical emphasis, and are guiding the students through the transition. However, for the most part, the atmosphere is friendly.

The College of Law is committed to initiatives that enhance education equity. It is particularly renowned for its encouragement and support of Aboriginal students. The Program of Legal Studies for Native People was established at the College in 1973 and has been widely supported as a national program since that time.

Of the other three law faculties in the prairie provinces, Saskatchewan's is probably less applied than the other programs, although outside the classroom students have the opportunity to get involved with the publication of a refereed journal, the *Saskatchewan Law Review*, or the campus legal services clinic, and mooting competitions.

STRENGTHS OF THE PROGRAM

Aboriginal Law and human rights are areas of strength at Saskatchewan's College of Law. The Native Law Centre is part of the College of Law and its mandate is to promote the development of the law and legal system in ways which would better accommodate the advancement of native communities in Canadian society. At present, the Centre is involved with a pre-law orientation and screening program, a research and publication program, library services, seminar series, and it acts as a community resource centre. In the next couple of years the College of Law hopes to appoint a Research Director who will increase this strength further.

Two courses are offered in the area of Aboriginal Law — "Indian and Aboriginal Law," and "Advanced Studies in Aboriginal Law," but it is more that just the courses and the Centre that makes this area strong. For the aboriginal students themselves, there is a sense of community and genuine commitment. Approximately two-thirds of aboriginal students take the Program of Legal Studies for Native People offered through the University of Saskatchewan either as a pre-requisite to law school or as an opportunity to meet other aboriginal students who are applying to law schools. Therefore, there is already a familiarity to the university and a connection that has been established.

In the area of human rights the College of Law has an endowed chair — the Ariel F. Sallows Chair of Human Rights. This attracts people of international stature on a rotational basis. The incumbent of the position teaches a course on human rights specific to their area of expertise as well as continuing their research.

The College of Law works in co-operation with the department of Political Studies in the Faculty of Arts and Science to jointly participate in interdisciplinary study. A conference was held on "Post-Meech Lake" where they looked at the legal constitutional aspects and took an interdisciplinary approach in the analysis of problems. Students were encouraged to register for the conference. The College of Law hopes to form a similar relationship with environmentally related departments, having just applied for an Environmental Legal Chair.

The Legal Assistance Clinic offers students a chance to start working with real people and their legal problems and to put into context what they have been learning. The Clinic offers free legal assistance to people who cannot afford the services of a lawyer. Student participation in the work of the clinic was institutionalized by the College of Law to the extent that a clinical law course was created as a third-year elective.

Students can also become involved as editorial staff or contributors to the *Saskatchewan Law Review*, which is published semi-annually. Research articles and comments of practising lawyers, academics, and law students are printed. Second- and third-year students are given credit for their participation, and in addition, they receive training in careful and thorough research and in concise and accurate writing.

In all years, students gain experience in preparing cases for argument and in presenting these arguments in a court room setting. The College of Law is actively represented in many of the mooting competition and gives participating students three credits towards their LL.B. program when they compete in the Jessup Moot Court Competition in International Law, the Gale Moot Court Competition, and the Laskin Memorial Moot Court Competition. The College of Law has had a strong presence in these competitions. Please see the chapter on *Unique Characteristics* for information on standings.

WHERE THE PROGRAM COULD IMPROVE

The small size of the faculty does not allow for the richness or range of curriculum of the larger schools, such as University of British Columbia, Osgoode, or Université de Montréal. For their size the curriculum is quite good, but it does not have the benefit of having courses offered in multiple sections to allow students to pick convenient times or professors with different teaching styles and viewpoints. One area where they are short of faculty is in corporate commercial law.

The school does actively support mooting competitions and provides students with the opportunity to become involved with Clinical Legal Aid, but the number of students who can take advantage of them are small. Continued budget constraints could force the College of Law to discontinue the Clinical Legal Aid service.

Saskatoon is physically remote from the country's major urban centres. The faculty tries to compensate for this by frequently bringing in guest lecturers and sponsoring conferences. There have been at least one, and sometimes two major conferences in recent years and some renowned speakers that they have had in the past are Elijah Harper, Preston Manning, Benoit Bouchard, and Chief Justice Dixon.

ON SASKATOON

The campus of the University of Saskatchewan is gothic in appearance, with old stonemason buildings interspersed with lots of trees and wide open spaces that give an impression of tradition. The law school itself is housed in an attractive, modern building. Downtown is a ten-minute walk from campus and there is plenty of housing near the university. If you wish to live farther away, the bus system is good. A typical two-bedroom apartment rents for around $425 per month and a one-bedroom averages around $300 per month.

The Saskatoon Field House is a recreation complex adjacent to the campus that houses nautilus equipment, tennis, and track and field. Students receive a number of free passes to the complex.

Saskatoon in often referred to as the "City of Bridges" situated on the Saskatchewan River. Students describe it as a friendly city with lots of parks and places to walk and bike. During the summer there are buskers on the sidewalks, and a Shakespearean Festival by the River. In the winter, its prairie location contributes to the cold, sometimes reaching forty-five below celsius and averaging between fifteen and twenty below celsius.

WHAT THE STUDENTS SAY

(Pseudonyms have replaced the following students' names)

The Strengths of the Program

"There is a strong Public Law, Administration, and Constitutional Law focus." Mark LL.B. '92

"The academic support program for part-time and first-year native students is a strength. They help you with study skills, and memo-writing. The College is hoping to broaden it to include other groups too." Lise-Anne LL.B. '92

"There are quite a few native students and I think it adds to the school because we draw on a wide variety of backgrounds." Mark LL.B. '92

"There are a lot of seminars and I find it easier to speak up in smaller groups. The seminars also gave you the opportunity to write papers rather than have your mark based on a final exam." Lise-Anne LL.B. '92

"The mooting program is very strong and well supported. Last year the Jessup moot team won the world title. This year I was on the Gale Cup and we won the nationals." Lise-Anne LL.B. '92

"The whole attitude in the College is very refreshing and open-minded, from the faculty to the students." Daniel LL.B. '93

"It is not a large college so you get to know your classmates well. When you are doing your undergraduate degree you just feel like you are one of the many, but at law school you feel like you know your classmates and you feel closer to them. People from all years attend the social functions and the faculty often participates too." Tom LL.B. '92

"The clinical law program takes about ten students per term and places them in legal aid, native alcohol centre, Saskatchewan Psychiatric Centre, the Youth Detention Facility, and solicitors' offices. It is great because it helps you deal with people as clients and ethical issues, and at the same time help people. The classroom component taught you how to communicate with clients and explain things. The Clinic is always in jeopardy due to funding constraints." Nelly, articling student

"The Legal Follies is a variety show which runs for two nights and is a real hoot. It is written by students and performed by students and faculty. It really pulls the college together and raises money for a charity. Approximately 210 students out of 300 get involved. I'll remember it the most about law school." Tom LL.B. '92

"There are lots of opportunities to participate. There are ten curling teams and different levels of football from the 'Professionals' to the 'Wobbly Ankles.' " Tom LL.B. '92

Where the Program Could Improve

"There is not enough selection in the corporate commercial area. The college is small and needs a few more professors to increase the selection in this area." Ted LL.B. '94

"The College cannot expand their faculty due to limited funding, so they have to depend on downtown lawyers. Since they have a practice, these courses have to be offered in the evening and this is difficult for single parents. In first year, however, if you have children they will put you in a section where classes start at 10 am instead of at 8 am so you can get your children off to school." Lise-Anne LL.B. '92

"The practical end of things could be improved. There are courses like Trial Advocacy where you do mock trials and the Clinical Law Program, but only ten students are allowed in first semester and eight in second semester in Trial Advocacy, and the Clinical Law Program is in danger of being discontinued due to funding cutbacks." Lise-Anne LL.B. '92

"If anyone is physically disabled, it would be very difficult for them to have access to the library." Lise-Anne LL.B. '92

"We have a system of balloting since almost all our upper-year classes are electives and you have to have a method of choosing. Classes are restricted in size and faculty, and there is a complicated process seen by some to be unfair. You choose your classes in the spring and hope that in September you get them. You don't know your class schedule or your exam schedule until September. Because of this, I ended up taking classes in second year that I didn't have the appropriate background for. For the most part though, people got what they needed and wanted." George, articling student

"There is a notable political colour to the faculty. At least three quarters of the faculty are staunchly left wing." Tom LL.B. '92

Controversies

"Gender problems have been ongoing. There is a small women and the law group that struggles to change things and then there is the men and the law group and we have had our problems. The faculty set up a program on equity in the law school and have worked hard identifying problems and barriers." Lise-Anne LL.B. '92

"It is necessary to take a legal theory class [which puts law in a social context and brings out issues of feminism, economics, race and culture etc.]. A lot of people don't like it and don't feel it is important and others feel that the understanding of theory is very important since it is out of theory that concepts are developed." George, articling student

"There is an ongoing creative tension on gender issues and societal justice. The poorest group in society tend to be women and there is a progressive women's rights group at the College, but they do not represent the majority of students. There is tension but there is also tolerance. It is a constructive process." Mark LL.B. '92

"Definitely, gender issues have been the focal point of Saskatchewan's College of Law controversies. Events that have taken place have people opening up and talking about the issue to understand and communicate with each other. There is more support from the faculty than your classmates. The faculty have implemented policies to prevent gender discrimination and have gender neutral language in class." Nelly, articling student

"There is a strong emphasis on feminist issues. There were more first-year women than men in my class and the trend has continued. There is such a strong emphasis on feminist issues that it has become uncomfortable for a lot of men to attend Saskatchewan's College of Law, since you have to measure every word that comes out of your mouth. You would think that a law school would have an exchange of ideas but you can't if it isn't what the feminists want to hear. There is a real growth of radical feminism." Tom LL.B. '92

On Faculty

"The faculty are very supportive and approachable about both classwork and personal problems." Lise-Anne LL.B. '92

"A definite strength is the faculty. I found them very open and helpful. As an aboriginal student just finished with the summer program, I found they went out of their way to make sure we were comfortable and that we would succeed." Daniel LL.B. '93

"Faculty involvement with students issues, such as gender equality, is a strength. The faculty try to find out what the student needs are and what is going on." Nelly, articling student

"Mary Anne Bowden teaches Property. She get students turned on to law in their first year." Mark LL.B. '92

"Ken Cooper-Stephenson uses a gentle socratic method. He doesn't challenge you to the point of intimidation, but he is very knowledgeable and is able to impart that knowledge without lecturing. He is able to pick up on differences on opinion and is conscious of different approaches and brings those out as well. He is able to incorporate a lot of legal theory into his class so you are not just learning concepts but the underpinning for everything." George, articling student

"Ron Cuming teaches Commercial Law and he is very well-informed on sales of goods law and debtor creditor and he is very concerned about students." Mark LL.B. '92

"Donna Greschner teaches Constitutional Law and is very good, and is also a strong feminist." Lise-Anne LL.B. '92

"As Dean, Peter MacKinnon tries to understand students' concerns and be empathetic. As a teacher, he inspires student discussion and makes everyone feel worthwhile." Nelly, articling student

"Jean Ann Smith teaches Contracts and Administrative Law. She knows her material and is fairly approachable. She is very much into the philosophical angle of the law." Victor LL.B. '92

Other Comments

"Think good and hard about going to law school. I took law because it offered other alternatives and I may be forced to explore them. Practising may not be an option due to the job market. If you want private practice, the opportunities are limited right now due the downturn of the economy. Firms are downsizing all over the place. Opportunities are not there that were there a few years ago in Alberta and Saskatchewan." George, articling student

"Law school is a great experience but it is tough. First year is a type of controlled insanity, but you come out of it stronger and it builds a camaraderie that lasts forever." Mark LL.B. '92

"Don't go into law school expecting to learn the law. You learn a way of thinking and analyzing. I think it is important to develop good friendships because it is a very stressful place." Nelly, articling student

"When you get into law school and you look back at what you did in undergraduate, you wonder how you got by. You have to condition yourself to the heavy workload in law school. You have to do your homework every day and if you miss you have to make it up." Tom LL.B. '92

University of Toronto

■ **INQUIRIES**

Admissions Office
Faculty of Law
78 Queen's Park
Toronto, Ontario
M5S 2C5
(416) 978-3716

ADMISSIONS INFORMATION

■ **APPLICATION DEADLINE DATE FOR ADMISSIONS**

1 February

■ **REQUIRED TO SUBMIT**

Regular Applicant

- A signed application form
- Official copies of all university academic transcripts
- LSAT score report
- A personal statement

Mature Student

- All of the above plus a curriculum vitae
- Up to two letters of reference to be received by February 15

Native Applicant

- Brief description of their aboriginal status and any connections they may have with their community plus the items listed above under regular applicant

■ **EDUCATION REQUIREMENTS**

Three full years of academic work at a recognized university

- **AVERAGE GPA**

   83.3 or A- or 3.7 (range 78.5 – 94.1)

- **AVERAGE LSAT**

   93rd percentile (range 79.6 – 99.5)
   If the LSAT is written twice, the Admissions Committee will consider both scores and any explanation the candidate wishes to offer. Normally, the higher score is accepted.

- **RATIO OF APPLICANTS TO REGISTRATIONS**

   13.3 : 1

- **SIZE OF INCOMING CLASS**

   179 (297 offers sent out)

- **CAN YOU DEFER ACCEPTANCE**

   No.
   The admissions office retains materials submitted by applicants for two years following the year of application.

- **APPLICATION FEE**

   $40 non-refundable

- **TUITION FEE**

   The 1992-93 tuition fee for Canadian citizens is $2,230.
   The 1992-93 tuition fee for Visa students is $7,474.
   Both fees includes student society fees.

CLASS PROFILE

- **AVERAGE AGE OF STUDENTS ENTERING THE PROGRAM**

   25

- **PERCENTAGE OF THE CLASS WHO ARE WOMEN**

   51.4%

- **PERCENTAGE OF WOMEN WHO ARE TENURED FACULTY**

   13.5%

- **PERCENTAGE OF THE CLASS WITH:**

   | two years or more of an undergraduate degree | 1.7% |
   | a three-year degree | 31.8% |

| a four-year degree | 53.6% |
| a graduate degree | 12.3% |

■ **PROFILE OF LL.B. POPULATIONS**

| Native Students | 8 |
| Visible Minorities | 28 |

Minority students % as of 91/92 first year class is 20.11%
(This figure was arrived at by name search only)

OTHER RELATED PROGRAMS

LL.B./M.B.A., M.B.A., LL.B./M.S.W., LL.B./Ph.D. (Philosophy), a Master's
of Law and a Doctorate.

HALF-TIME PROGRAM: The half-time program at the Toronto's Faculty of
Law is designed to accommodate students who are unable to attend on a
full-time basis because of financial difficulty, health or physical disability, or
family commitments. No half-time students were admitted in 1991-92 and
two students were admitted in 1990-91.

Admission requirements are the same for both half-time and full-time
programs. Financial assistance, including scholarships, bursaries, and loans is
available to half-time students. Half-time students must complete the program
in six years and be able to attend classes when normally scheduled, i.e. during
the day and early evening.

ADMISSIONS REQUIREMENTS

There are three categories under which students can apply for admission to
Toronto's Faculty of Law — the regular, mature, and native categories. Within
the **Regular Category** of admissions a number of factors are taken into
consideration. These include *academic factors* based on an applicant's grade
point average (GPA) and Law School Admissions Test (LSAT) score, and the
non-academic factors such as the response to disadvantage due to adverse
personal or socio-economic circumstances, barriers faced by cultural or
linguistic minorities, motivation and involvement in academic and non-academic activities, and the impact of temporary or permanent physical handi-
caps. Applicants are urged to bring this information forward in their personal
statement. Interviews are not granted due to the large number of applicants.
No formula is used in the admissions process and each file is reviewed in its
entirety.

In terms of the academic factors, the cumulative averages are used in the admission process but false starts are excluded. False starts occur when students find themselves in the wrong program and do not excel until they switch to the program that matches their interests. Another example of a false start could be that the students begin university without really knowing why. They lack motivation, lose interest, and quit. Sometime later they decide on what they want to pursue and return to school and are successful this time.

The cumulative average is only the starting point. Academic transcripts are closely looked at to see how the grades were achieved. For example, the types of courses, level, and what year they were taken in, and an applicant's grade in relation to the class average are taken into consideration. The admissions committee is looking for an increasing progression of difficulty in the courses taken. Taking a first-year course in fourth year and getting an A may carry less weight than taking a senior course in their final year and receiving a B.

The University of Toronto's Faculty of Law is among the most highly selective law schools in North America and has the highest standards in Canada, based on a combination of undergraduate academic record and LSAT score.

The academic factors do have the greatest weight in the decision making process, but when two candidates have identical competitive academic standings, the non-academic factors are given serious weight.

"Students should regard their undergraduate degree as an end in itself and they should take courses because they are interested in them and really do well. Then, if they decide to go to law school, they are prepared. Getting into law school should not be your exclusive goal because more applicants are rejected than accepted," comments Joan Lax, Assistant Dean and Director of Admissions. The competitive average to be admitted to Toronto's Faculty of Law has increased every year. However, Ms. Lax encourages serious candidates to re-apply if they are not successful the first time. Applying more than once does not prejudice a candidate's application. "Every year we do admit some that were rejected the year before. Not that standards are lower but because there is more information. One more year of good grades can make the difference."

In the **Mature Admissions Category**, mature is defined as those applicants who have five or more years of non-academic experience, and may or may not have at least two years of undergraduate study. The academic factors are not given as much weight as in the regular category of admission. Instead, the Admissions committee may give greater weight to other evidence of their ability to study law successfully, such as experience or success in other non-academic environments.

First Nations people including Indians, Métis, and those of Inuit heritage are under-represented in the legal profession and Toronto's Faculty of Law is attempting to encourage applications from First Nations people by giving them special recognition in their admissions policy under the **Native Category**. For native applicants who may not have had the opportunity to adequately prepare for law school the summer orientation course in legal studies is available through the Native Law Centre at the University of Saskatchewan.

An increased priority has been given by some law schools to admit groups that are underrepresented in faculties of law. The admissions committee at Toronto's Faculty of Law reviewed its admission policy in 1990 and currently does not have a preferential policy for groups other than Natives. (The Faculty has had a preferential policy for Native applicants since 1975.)

"It was premature to change to a preferential policy for groups other than natives until we had a better understanding. We are trying to find out who is applying and what happens to their application in our admissions process," states Joan Lax. A voluntary survey was conducted in 1990-91 of all applicants in terms of culture, race, socio-economic status, and linguistic ability. When the resulting data has been analyzed, recommendations may be forthcoming. In the meantime, the administration has an Outreach Program which is run by the Director of Student Affairs in co-operation with students and alumni from minority communities.

CHARACTER OF THE SCHOOL

Toronto's Faculty of Law has a long-standing reputation of having the strongest commercial law area in the country. The influence of Bay Street, located only blocks away, is felt in the areas of easy access to practitioners, fund raising, and recruiting. However, over the past three or four years the administration has made a concerted attempt to diversify this image. The significant increase in faculty with interdisciplinary backgrounds, the development of a Perspectives course in first year, and other more interdisciplinary courses contribute to a broad range of courses. It is a traditional law faculty that is making a strong commitment to making the transition to a faculty with a more diversified focus, but it is still in the early stages.

The high standards of admission and the corporate focus attract a group of very bright and competitive individuals. However, once they are admitted to the program these same individuals seem to band together. Competitiveness still exists, especially around exam time and articling interviews, but it is a healthy competitiveness and not one of ripping out pages in reference texts or hiding needed resources. On the whole, the atmosphere at Toronto's Law School seems to be a congenial one.

STRENGTHS OF THE PROGRAM

There is no doubt that the close proximity of Bay Street gives Toronto's corporate/commercial area of the law a strong advantage. Accessibility to top practitioners that can be drawn on to teach, be guest lecturers, or to preside over moot courts is readily available. Toronto's strategy to cope with budget constraints has been to integrate faculty from other sectors of the university. The administration has been able to add thirteen to fourteen faculty members in the last five years. Some of these appointments were cross-appointments with the Faculties of Social Work, Management, or Philosophy. In fact, over half of the members of the Law Faculty are cross-appointed to one or more of the fourteen faculties, departments, and centres at the University. "This integration and bringing in of new people has helped us to maintain our momentum and keeps us on the cutting edge," comments Robert Sharpe. Integration has enabled Toronto's Faculty of Law to begin to offer a varied range of courses, different teaching approaches, and legal theory.

The first year of study at Toronto's Faculty of Law covers Civil Procedure, Constitutional Law, Contracts, Criminal Law, Property, and Torts. A similar first-year program exists at all Common Law programs in Canada but it is enriched by the small-group program and an additional course in Perspectives on Law.

The small-group program ensures that students are taught one of their first-year courses with a class size of only sixteen. The first-year experience of law school can be quite stressful as students used to academic success learn what is expected of them in a school of law. The small group helps to minimize this as friendships are forged and a mentor-like relationship is encouraged with a faculty member. The small group also offers a friendly environment to begin to learn the techniques of legal research and writing.

Perspectives on Law, or Bridge program as it is sometimes called, is the seventh course in the first year curriculum. Toronto's Faculty of Law calendar states that it was introduced in 1986 to reflect the increasingly theoretical and interdisciplinary approach to law and to ensure that a perspective element would be introduced into the first year. During four one-week periods spread evenly throughout the year, students are exposed to the intensive examination of legal history, law and economics, legal philosophy, feminist analysis of the law added in 1988, and race and culture difference added in 1991. During each bridge week, instruction is suspended in four of the remaining six courses on a rotational basis and at the conclusion of each bridge the students are evaluated by a written assignment.

Upper-year students can take advantage of the short-term Distinguished Visiting Professors of Legal Theory initiated in 1986, and be involved in the

University of Toronto Faculty of Law Review journal as editors, as well as many other opportunities.

In 1991, the Law Library at Toronto's Faculty of Law moved into the new Bora Laskin Law Library. This spacious, carpeted, and air conditioned facility was made possible primarily from the strong support of alumni. Individual carrels and tables are powered for the use of personal computers and several study rooms are available for students to book.

The goal of the Faculty of Law is to be the pre-eminent centre for research and of teaching law in Canada, and to be one of the great law schools in the common law world. In support of Toronto's goal to be a national school, one-third of its student body comes from outside Ontario and from virtually every province and the Territories. The students have studied at most Canadian, numerous American, and some universities abroad.

WHERE THE PROGRAM COULD IMPROVE

The administration at Toronto's Faculty of Law are taking significant steps to change the school's image from that of a commercial law faculty. However, a significant number of students are still attracted to Toronto's Faculty of Law because they want to be in the heart of one of Canada's biggest commercial centres and at a school where corporate commercial law is very strong. As a result, there seems to be a pressure within the student body itself to work for a large, prestigious firm on Bay Street. It is hard to curtail the effect of this lingering perception when corporate commercial is still, and probably always will be, very strong.

Toronto's Faculty of Law prides itself on its high academic standing but such high standings are in themselves self-selecting of a predominantly white upper-class student body who have had access to a good academic foundation. As a result, it does not offer a very diverse student body, either in background or in ambition. Students from across Canada do make up the student body but there is a conservative homogeneousness that is a common denominator.

ON TORONTO

The Faculty of Law is self-contained in two historic buildings, Flavelle House and Falconer Hall on the downtown St. George campus of the University of Toronto. Both buildings were private residences at one time. The buildings are ivy covered and stately. The surroundings are park-like with mature trees partly blocking the busy metro scene. Immediately behind the law school is

Philosopher's Walk, to the north is the Royal Ontario Museum, Bloor Street, and the Yorkville area, to the south is Queen's Park where the provincial Parliament Buildings stand.

A car is not necessary due to the excellent subway system in Toronto. The subway provides quick access to all parts of Metropolitan Toronto and is steps away from the front door of Falconer Hall. Parking costs are very high and accommodation off-campus with parking is hard to come by.

Applicants from outside Ontario are given priority in securing accommodation in the four law residences which accommodate twenty-two first-year law students in single rooms. Applications are enclosed with the offer of admission and rooms are allocated by May 15. In 1990-91 residence rents were in the range of $340 to $550 per month compared to a private apartment off-campus at $550 to $700, or $750 to $900 per month for a one- or two-bedroom unit respectively. One student mentioned that to live modestly in Toronto off-campus cost approximately $10,500 per year.

WHAT THE STUDENTS SAY

(Pseudonyms have replaced the following students' names)

The Strengths of the Program

"There was a sense that you are on the cutting edge. There were a lot of good speakers coming in during the intensive courses offered in the first two weeks of term. You were very busy because of the extra hours but it was exciting. You felt you were part of the research and you were able to talk to people who were experts in their field." Deborah, articling student

"I am involved in the Work in Japan Program that was just initiated this year. Even though it takes up a lot of my time and it is a big commitment, it has been one of my best experiences. During the year [second year] I take six hours a week in Japanese language instruction. Actually, it's more like ten to fifteen hours if you count the work outside class and all of this is non-credit work. During the summer I will be doing thirty hours a week in Japanese instruction to prepare me for working for a year in Japan. I will take a leave from law school to do this. Hopefully I will be working with the Yamaha corporation in a smaller Japanese city which will force me to learn the language." Kevin LL.B. '93

"SLAM, Students in Law for the Advancement of Minorities, has evolved and there is a cordial working arrangement with the faculty. Faculty are now more sensitive to what minorities have to say. They have added a new course — Race, Culture and the Law — and a new bridge component on race and culture. These were things SLAM asked for. They could add cultural awareness to other courses as well as the separate program." Paul LL.B. '92

"The bridge weeks in first year are really useful. I am more interested in feminism so I would probably have taken those courses anyway, but you are getting this education as part of your curriculum. It is important to society that you be aware and it might even change your goals in life." Karyn LL.B. '92

"The law school is stately and there is a lot of pride there. It can be a bit intimidating and not what you may be used to, depending on your background. The faculty are friendly and the students will be your friends for life since you have been through so much together." Ian LL.B. '92

"There is competition. There is no doubt that the students are very bright but they compete within themselves and it is not cut-throat. I don't know of a single instance when somebody wouldn't have helped me and it's the same with the students in the law firm I am articling in. There was the attitude that we [the administration] picked you, you are the best. We believe in our selection process and we are here to help." Deborah, articling student

"The program is only competitive in a very healthy way. I was an undergraduate at U of T directly across the road from the Faculty of Law. I was expecting it to be a very cold, heartless place, but it isn't." Cecilia, articling student

"[Toronto's Faculty of Law] is stronger in the business areas than left-wing socialist type courses." Deborah, articling student

"If you are interested in working in Toronto, access is right there, but I wasn't headed for Bay Street. I picked Toronto because it was the best law school." Ian LL.B. '92

"I came with the thought that U of T had a corporate image but there are so many alternate ways of thinking about the law which are incorporated into the curriculum that I think this is changing. You are exposed to many different ideas and they are mandatory. You can't turn a blind eye to them. As a lawyer you have the power to make certain changes. There never used to be legal aid and now there is. So we should be aware of the issues." Karyn LL.B. '92

"My interest in academia is average and the school offers more than enough to stimulate my interests. For those who are highly interested in being a prof, or really like the academic side, it is ideal." Karyn LL.B. '92

Where the Program Could Improve

"Because the professors are the best in their field, they may not be the best teachers. If a professor is less than the best, he/she may be able to understand why the student doesn't understand." Ian LL.B. '92

"The handbook shows hundreds of courses offered but after you take out all the ones that were cancelled there weren't that many. I actually had to pick some just because they fit." Kevin LL.B. '93

"They could be more sensitive to people not wanting to work downtown on Bay Street." Ian LL.B. '92

"My father was a lawyer on Bay Street, and I had worked in his office during the summers. I had always assumed that this was what I wanted, but I started to feel trapped on Bay Street. This time around I've decided I don't want to go to Bay Street and I am not going to article in Toronto. The program was very Bay Street oriented, not so much in terms of courses or recruiting, but most of the practitioners are from Bay Street and they are major financial contributors to the program. They have a high profile on campus. Now, however, there are two positions on the alumni committee. One position has to be filled by someone who is not Bay Street bound, to ensure that other interests are represented, and that students are exposed to non-Bay Street lawyers as well." Jill LL.B. '92

"The student body is not diverse. It is skewed very heavily towards white but it is pretty equal in terms of male and female. I would have liked more contact with people with totally different backgrounds than mine. There is a lot of sameness in where they are coming from, why they came to law school, and where they are going. They may be falling in line with the conservative nature of U of T. They all seem to want corporate commercial, securities, or tax law and go downtown. I don't know if this is why they originally came to law school or because all the head faculty are from that area." Ross LL.B. '92

"The University of Toronto has no visible minority professors. We get a very one-sided view of life. It is a big problem with the faculty." Kevin LL.B. '93

"As a coloured male, I feel left out. There is a lack of sensitivity to other perspectives. A lot of the law is taught from a white perspective and some cases in criminal law show decisions that are culturally biased. You would think that the professors would comment on this, but they don't." Paul LL.B. '92

"The number of minority students is not an accurate reflection of the general population. For example, there are five or six oriental students, one black student, and one East Indian student in my class. You can count them. Most of the minorities are in the mature student group." Paul LL.B. '92

"The school shies away from black letter law. If you are interested in being a legal scholar, this is the place to be. This probably goes back to having the best profs since they are the most academic. If you intend to be a practising lawyer, perhaps the focus of the courses could be more towards black letter law in addition to critical studies." Ian LL.B. '92

"Just to be admitted you have to have a high LSAT score even if you have a high GPA, and this makes you wonder if the test should that heavily weighted. Your GPA is based on a your work over a period of time whereas the LSAT is only representative of your performance on the day of the test." Karyn LL.B. '92

"The university could offer more flexibility. The seminars dealing with racial and feminist issues are not given many credit hours, so you have to take tax or labour administration to fill out your program." Ross LL.B. '92

"There is no integration with the rest of campus. Having been at Queen's and Western as an undergraduate, you got to know the rest of campus. You used the recreational facilities. U of T is so big and the law faculty is kind of an entity to itself. You don't take advantage of the whole university community." Jill LL.B. '92

The Controversies

"Law school has been patriarchal white male and upper middle class. Now there are over 50 percent women and affirmative action, but you are still going to get minorities who are also the elite among their own culture. Something else has to be there besides just affirmative action. A diverse background of lawyers would better understand a diverse group of people. It is a strength that U of T is getting different cultures, but it is still in its infancy." Ian LL.B. '92

"Compared to three years ago, the experience I've had in the law school is richer. There are a number of students older than thirty and there are more minorities." Jill LL.B. '92

"The main controversy is between the economic and the feminist analysis schools. They don't understand each other. It is a schizo learning process. One perspective looks at a case from one side but never mentions the other and vice versa. It is almost like no one is admitting that there is another valid perspective." Ross LL.B. '92

"In the feminist bridge the issues were reproduction technology and abortion. We only heard from one side since only the feminist professors wanted to be involved. The organizers should have gone out of their way to find someone to represent the other side. Questions during the session that were not in alignment with the feminist view point were shot down. I felt cheated." Kevin LL.B. '93

On Faculty

"The professors are usually the people who wrote the book in their field and it is exciting to learn from them." Ian LL.B. '92

There was no consensus as to who the best professors were. Therefore the following were only mentioned by individual students.

"Dean Sharpe is very positive and he summarises case law very well in every class." Kevin LL.B. '93

"Michael Trebilcock taught me contracts. He organized his material in an entertaining way and taught it such that it was possible to study from my notes. Ideas and themes emerged and it all made sense at the end." Deborah, articling student

"Arnold Weinrib teaches tax and property and I like his clear approach." Paul LL.B. '92

"Martha Shaffer teaches family law. She is a young professor and is very good. She has a feminist perspective and is open to criticism of the feminist point of view in class." Jill LL.B. '92

Other Comments

"Everything is just getting better. Student groups are forming within the school, for example the native group and minorities. Dean Sharpe places importance on them because everyone is welcome to express their ideas." Karyn LL.B. '92

"I chose U of T because I had heard all these great things about it but I had never been to Toronto. Coming in on the 401 with six lanes of traffic was quite an experience. It was a shock to me. Compared to the University of British Columbia where I had done my undergraduate, it was incredibly expensive. The area around the university is a busy cosmopolitan area, whereas surrounding UBC there was a very nice residential area, golf course, woods and ocean." Cynthia LL.B. '90, practising lawyer

"Most people are happy to be here. We think of our school as being number one and we are expecting good job offers." Kevin LL.B. '93

University of Victoria

■ **INQUIRIES**

Admissions
Faculty of Law
University of Victoria
P.O. Box 2400
Victoria, British Columbia
v8w 3H7
(604) 721-8151

ADMISSIONS INFORMATION

■ **APPLICATION DEADLINE DATE FOR ADMISSIONS**

31 March (Applicants applying under the Regular Admissions Category described below are strongly encouraged to submit applications by 31 December of the preceding year as offers will begin to be made prior to Christmas.)

■ **REQUIRED TO SUBMIT**

Regular Category

- Official copies of all university academic transcripts
- LSAT score report
- Application form which requests information on academically related extra-curricular activities, community involvement, work experience, and personal characteristics

Special Access or Native Category

in addition to the above
- Two references

- **EDUCATION REQUIREMENT**

    Three full years of academic work at a recognized university towards a degree.

- **AVERAGE GPA**

    3.62 or B+ or 79 (range 3.19 − 4.22)

- **AVERAGE LSAT**

    88th percentile (range 63rd − 99th percentile)
    For candidates applying for entry in September 1992, LSAT scores will be accepted based on tests written since June 1982.
    For candidates applying for entry in September 1993 or later, only scores on LSAT tests written on or after 10 June 1991 will be accepted.

- **RATIO OF APPLICANTS TO REGISTRATIONS**

    18.5 : 1 (279 offers given)

- **SIZE OF INCOMING CLASS**

    100

- **CAN YOU DEFER ACCEPTANCE**

    No

- **APPLICATION FEE**

    $40

- **TUITION FEE**

    The 1992-93 tuition fee is $2,521 for Canadian students and $3,825 for non-exempt Foreign students.

CLASS PROFILE

- **AVERAGE AGE OF STUDENTS ENTERING THE PROGRAM**

    26

- **PERCENTAGE OF THE CLASS WHO ARE WOMEN**

    53%

- **PERCENTAGE OF WOMEN WHO ARE TENURED FACULTY**

    28% (7 women out of 25 tenured faculty)

- **PERCENTAGE OF THE CLASS WITH**

two years or more of an undergraduate degree	NO RECORD
a three-year degree	77%

| a four-year degree | NO RECORD |
| a post-graduate degree | 5% |

■ **PROFILE OF LL.B. POPULATIONS**

Native Students	5% (5)
Visible Minorities	n/a
Mature Students	4%

OTHER RELATED PROGRAMS

LL.B. Co-op Program, Master of Public Administration/LL.B.
HALF-TIME PROGRAM: No-one applied for half-time status in the fall of 1992. The requirements for admission and application deadline date are the same as those for the full-time program. All first-year courses are given during the day, but a number of regular courses in second and third years are offered in the evenings. Half-time students are required to take a half course-load and they have six and a half years to complete their degree.

ADMISSIONS REQUIREMENTS

Victoria's Faculty of Law is "attempting to get the best and the brightest," comments Lyman Robinson, Chair of the Admissions committee. The administration is aggressively trying to recruit excellent applicants, and one way of doing that is to make very early offers of admissions. Admission decisions are made before Christmas on files that are complete. Applicants from Ontario should especially take note of this since Ontario law schools will not give out offers of admission until after 31 March.

Within the **Regular Category** of admissions, a formula is used in the admission process which assigns a seventy percent weight to the candidate's grade point average (GPA) and thirty percent to their LSAT score. Grades in all undergraduate courses are used to determine the GPA for applicants with three years of university completed. However, applicants with a four-year degree can drop from three to five of their worst full course equivalents. This prevents students from being penalized for getting off on the wrong foot.

No effort is made to judge the degree of difficulty or level of courses making up a candidate's academic record. The courses do have to be academic in nature and therefore, performance courses in music or physical education programs are not used. When the value for the GPA is calculated, the emphasis is on the undergraduate degree. Master's degrees are considered, but it comes down to a subjective decision of the committee as to how much weight they are given. The rigour of the program is an important factor.

The two main criteria used in the decision-making process are the GPA and LSAT score, but four other factors are taken into consideration: extra-curricular activities, community involvement (for example, volunteering at a hospital, assisting the United Way, or political involvement), work experience including practicums and co-op experiences, and personal characteristics such as perseverance or tenacity, shown by paying your way through school or juggling extra-curricular commitments. Points are then awarded to each of these factors and they are then added to the formula. In 1992, eighty of the one hundred positions were filled by regular applicants. Additional points, allocated for factors other than GPA and LSAT, made a difference for fifteen of this group. No formal interviews are granted, but applicants are seen if it is requested.

In September of 1992, fifteen students were admitted under the **Special Access Category** of admission. This category provides applicants with the opportunity to obtain a legal education who may not have had a chance due to physical, cultural, or financial disadvantage, or family responsibilities. Students with or without completed university courses fall within this category. A more holistic approach is taken in the admissions process and the admissions formula is not applied. Evidence is looked for that will persuade the admissions committee that the candidate will succeed in law school. Achievements at work or through public or community activity would be one indicator, as well as academic performance in any educational or training program, and a demonstrated ability to write effectively at a law school level.

The **Native Category** is in response to the concern of Victoria's Faculty of Law that the number of people of Indian, Métis, and Inuit backgrounds are underrepresented in the legal profession. Applications from Canadian Native people will be considered on an individual basis. Factors such as academic performance, LSAT, employment history, personal interviews, and letters of reference are considered. Depending on a native applicant's background, an offer may be made conditional upon the successful completion of the Program of Legal Studies for Native People conducted by the Native Law Centre at the University of Saskatchewan. (Please see chapter on *Native People and a Legal Education*.)

CHARACTER OF THE SCHOOL

The students at UVic's Faculty of Law, housed in the Begbie Building, refer to their law school as "Begbie High." Like in a small high school, this group of one hundred first-year students gets to know each other intimately. The students are self-contained within the law building. They go to class, study in the library, talk to their professors, and have their lockers all within "Begbie High."

There is a tendency at all law schools in Canada to isolate themselves from the rest of the university environment, and life in general, and this effect is magnified at Victoria's Faculty of Law. As UVic is isolated from the mainland of British Columbia, Begbie Building is also isolated from the majority of the campus. The original university buildings form a natural grouping, with the law building on the periphery. The small student body, along with the isolation of the law school, promotes close friendships and a sense of camaraderie.

UVic has recently had a change of deans and focus. Maureen Maloney, Dean of UVic's Faculty of Law, has as her mandate making the study of law reactive to current issues in society. "Diverse social issues such as the Charter, attention to race and gender issues, global interest in the environment, and the complexity of maintaining diversity and unity in Canada all fall under the legal umbrella," states Ms. Maloney in her introductory message to students. This vision of law as both interdisciplinary and inclusive seems to run counter to UVic's "introspective atmosphere" where the previous emphasis was on the fundamental and traditional aspects of the law. As accompanies all change, there is some tension during transition; however, a very close camaraderie still exists among the student body.

STRENGTHS OF THE PROGRAM

A major emphasis of Victoria's Faculty of Law is on Public Law, since it is located in Victoria — a major centre of government. Interested students have the option of participating in a Public Law intensive term during their second or third year. The Public Law Term probes the nature of policy formulation and decision making in governmental departments and agencies, as well as the role of the lawyer in the context of the administrative and legislative processes. The evolution of public law is analyzed and discussed in terms of the historical and current societal values and issues. A clinical placement may be arranged for each student. Term-long programs are also offered in Business Law and Planning, and Criminal Law. These terms are offered once every two or three years and provide a balance between practice and theory. Practitioners and governmental officials are brought in and legal skills are taught. A Clinical Term where students are placed in a downtown law clinic under the direction of a Faculty Director is offered for a full term's credit in each of the Fall, Spring, and Summer terms. All of the term programs are intensive and integrative.

Victoria is located on the Pacific Rim and, in co-operation with other university departments, the Law Faculty is developing an expertise in legal issues which are becoming more important as contacts with the Asia-Pacific Initiatives increase. The Centre for Asia Pacific Initiatives is located in the Law building. An exchange program with Chulalongkorn University in Bangkok, Thailand, or other acceptable foreign institutions for one term in second or third year may be arranged. Courses such as International Business and Trade Law, Asia Pacific Law, and International Law are listed in Victoria's Faculty of Law calendar. Victoria's Faculty of Law and British Columbia's Faculty of Law both have Asian initiatives, but they do not compete. British Columbia concentrates more on Japan, China, Hong Kong, and Korea.

Another highlight of the curriculum is the Legal Process course which takes place in the first three weeks of first year. The Legal Process course offers students an overview of law, including an analysis from many perspectives and the institutional structure of the Canadian legal system. Consistent with Victoria's common theme of studying law as part of society, the values reflected in the Canadian legal system as well as issues of professional responsibility are explored. Basic legal skills, such as reading statutes and case law, are taught and a background is laid for upper-year courses. The students are divided into groups of twenty, and two faculty members are assigned to each group. Students quickly make lasting friendships and have a supportive non-threatening atmosphere in which to make their transition into law school.

Victoria's Faculty of Law is the only law faculty in Canada to offer a Co-operative Law Program. This innovative program was established in 1990 and gives students the opportunity to gain practical experience plus earn money during their legal education. The first year of the program is full-time and then it alternates four months of classes and four months of work placement. The placements increase the length of the regular law program by eight months. Students get experience in job search skills by applying for postings and going through the interview process to obtain their placements. Placements are not confined to British Columbia. A few students have been placed in London and Bangkok. Students applying to the Co-operative Law Program must meet the requirements for the regular program and indicate that they would like to be considered for the Co-operative Law Program. Thirty qualified students are then selected by lottery.

WHERE THE PROGRAM COULD IMPROVE

The small size and close-knit student body is a strength of Victoria's Faculty of Law. However, the high school atmosphere can also be a weakness depending on how comfortable you are in an environment where everyone knows so much about you. There is also little representation of the significant Chinese population native to British Columbia, although other racial or ethnic groups of British Columbia are represented. The population of the city of Victoria, for the most part, is not racially diverse. The majority of the students are of the traditional make-up of law schools — white, upper-middle class. If you are coming from a large cosmopolitan centre, there may be a significant adjustment period.

Course selection was a concern of the students interviewed. All law schools offer a more limited version of courses than is outlined in their calendar in accordance with the availability of faculty to teach them, scheduling, and the demand for the various courses. However, the special term programs in criminal and business law have not been offered in the last three years and the public law term is only offered once every two or three years. This makes it quite possible for students to miss this opportunity all together. The limited selection of courses is also a concern to students participating in the Co-operative Law Program. One academic session of the Co-operative Law Program is offered during the summer and the course selection is more limited than during the regular terms because there are so few students in the program.

ON VICTORIA

Victoria's Faculty of Law calendar is the only law faculty to have colour pictures in its calendar — and with good reason. One photograph shows the historic and picturesque shoreline of Victoria with a sailboat leisurely departing. Other pictures set the scene by showing students eating and studying outdoors on the patio attached to the law building, and the Dean flipping fresh fish and hamburgers on an outdoor barbecue. It is no wonder that Victoria has the highest number of lawyers per capita of any city in North America. It is a lovely place to live. Winters are short, with mild temperatures around nineteen degrees celsius returning by March, and Victoria has more sunshine than the mainland. The bicycle is the main mode of transportation around campus.

University of Victoria's campus is located northeast of the city of Victoria, about a half-hour bus ride from downtown and ten minutes from the beaches. The campus is situated in the middle of a very affluent residential area which creates a problem for students seeking accommodation. The rental market is tight, and finding accommodation close to the school can be difficult since few people living in the area rent out rooms. Shared accommodation can cost approximately $300-350 or a one-bedroom apartment might be around $500. It is advisable to come early to find a place to live. The law building itself, Begbie Building, is a new brick building named after British Columbia's first Justice of the Supreme Court and has excellent mooting facilities. The Diana M. Priestly Law Library is housed within Begbie Building and is an excellent resource.

The city of Victoria is a government town with a social life that is more family oriented, and has a high percentage of people who are retired. For a faster pace, Vancouver is about a half-hour drive to the ferry, an hour and a half on the ferry to the mainland, and twenty to thirty minutes to get downtown Vancouver. In 1992, the ferry cost $29 one way or $5.50 to walk on board.

WHAT THE STUDENTS SAY

(Pseudonyms have replaced the following students' names)

The Strengths of the Program

"The three-week legal process component at the beginning of first year was very helpful. No other courses took place during this time and it helped you to meet other students. It also gives you a good grounding in how to read a case and do a brief." Kurt LL.B. '93

"The smaller size attracted me because it allows for specialized attention and more direction on major research papers." Kurt LL.B. '93

"The classes are not that big. In first year they divide you into smaller groups of twenty-five to thirty and you have almost all your core courses together. The smaller groups makes it easier to ask questions." Tina LL.B. '93

"UVic's program is progressive. They are willing to tackle new ideas such as different teaching formats, integrating feminist legal theory, clinical terms, the co-op program, and exchanges with Asian Pacific countries." Kathryn LL.B. '92

"The atmosphere is co-operative and competitive only at times. The co-operation starts in first year with the buddy system [first-year students are paired up with second-year students]. Our policy within the library is very trusting. The faculty stresses co-operation. We know they aren't trying to fail us and they don't openly rank us." Kathryn LL.B. '92

"It is a really comfortable environment and a nice place to go to everyday. You know everyone and it is really relaxed and informal. There is a sense of community." Neal LL.B. '93

"It is very friendly. About half the students are from B.C. and the rest are from everywhere. Noone really knew anyone in the city when they arrived so you turn to each other. People are really co-operative." Kimberly LL.B. '94

Where the Program Could Improve

"UVic is a small school and therefore there is a lot of gossip. It is like a high school. We even call it 'Begbie High' [after the name of the law building Begbie Building], but you also get a lot of support from the other students." Kurt LL.B. '93

"It is definitely political and since it is a small school there is a lot of labelling going on, but the atmosphere is still pretty good. It is a small school so it is kind of high schoolish." Louise LL.B. '92

"You don't know in advance whether the courses in the calendar are going to be offered so you can't plan ahead." Louise LL.B. '92

"Upper-year classes are limited to twenty-five to fifty students, but because it is a small school a course is only offered in one term and you might not get the courses you want." Tina LL.B. '93

"In the co-op program we have one summer academic term where the selection is very limited and you may have to take courses you don't want. You are also kind of cut-off from the other students so there is less opportunity to socialize or get to know others." Kimberly LL.B. '94

"UVic is a good school for a well-rounded education but it is not a good school to specialize; for example, in the area of criminology, there are only three criminology courses offered and one is a mandatory course. This is due to the small size. The trade-off is worth it though. A more well-rounded education will help me if I decide to change my focus later on. A lot of students come in thinking they know what they want and they often change their mind." Kathryn LL.B. '92

Controversies

A couple of years ago, the administration, in co-operation with the students, developed guidelines for law firms interviewing students for articling positions as a result of inappropriate questions that female students were asked during the interview process. These guidelines were put into place to prevent discrimination of students who were married, had children, or were handicapped. This created some controversy as it was not received favourably by most law firms and some students felt it would affect their search for articling positions.

"The big controversy is gender. There has been a big push to increase awareness of this and it creates a feeling that it is being pushed on you — that you have to be politically correct. . . . Some students are very supportive of the changes being made. Others believe it in principle, but not in the way they are going about it and some feel bound and gagged." Tina LL.B. '93

On Faculty

"You get to know a lot of the professors on a first-name basis. They don't make you feel like you should be in awe of them. It is a very open and friendly atmosphere." Laurel, articling student

"Terry Weuster teaches Secured Transactions. He gave the lowest marks in school but he was very concerned that we learn and really challenged us. He brought in outside, real life examples and taught at a very practical level. In my last year, he won the teacher of the year award." Laurel, articling student

"Donovan Waters is a leading Canadian authority on trusts." Laurel, articling student

"Mary Anne Waldron teaches Real Property, Secured Transactions, and Contracts. She is very well prepared. As soon as you get the course material, you know what to expect and what to prepare for. She covers everything." Neal LL.B. '93

"Associate Dean Donald Casswell is very good. He teaches Evidence, which is a very convoluted subject matter, but he gave us a good framework of analysis that was easy to understand." Kurt LL.B. '93

"James Cassels teaches Contracts, Remedies, and Legal Theory. He is really approachable, knowledgeable, and has a clear style. He integrates policy and does it in a way that doesn't create a backlash. He puts it together in a way that isn't shoved at you." Kathryn LL.B. '92

Other Comments

"When you are in first year it is stressful, but remember you are not going to fail out. It is important to keep things in proper perspective. Everyone else is feeling the same way you are." Kimberly LL.B. '94

University of Western Ontario

■ **INQUIRIES**

Student Affairs Officer
Faculty of Law
The University of Western Ontario
London, Ontario
N6A 3K7
(519) 679-2111 ext. 8425

ADMISSIONS INFORMATION

■ **APPLICATION DEADLINE DATE FOR ADMISSIONS**

1 February

■ **REQUIRED TO SUBMIT**

- Official copies of all university academic transcripts
- LSAT score report
- Completed questionnaire requesting information on scholarships, extra-curricular activities, work experience, and adverse circumstances
- TOEFL score may be requested where English is a second language

Mature students and native people must submit:

- Two letters of reference
- Personal statement explaining why they do not qualify as a regular applicant

■ **EDUCATION REQUIREMENTS**

Two full years of academic work at a recognized university

■ **AVERAGE GPA**

80% or A- or 3.7 (range 75% – 91%)

- **AVERAGE LSAT**

    89th percentile (range 43rd – 99th)
    If the LSAT is written more than once, the scores are averaged.

- **RATIO OF APPLICANTS TO REGISTRATIONS**

    17.8 : 1

- **SIZE OF INCOMING CLASS**

    155

- **CAN YOU DEFER ACCEPTANCE:**

    No

- **APPLICATION FEE**

    $30

- **TUITION FEE**

    The 1992-93 tuition fee for Canadian citizens is $2,272 which includes
    the student activity fees.
    The 1992-93 tuition fee for visa students is $7,517 which includes the
    student activity fees.

CLASS PROFILE

- **AVERAGE AGE OF STUDENTS ENTERING THE PROGRAM**
    25

- **PERCENTAGE OF THE CLASS WHO ARE WOMEN**
    46%

- **PERCENTAGE OF WOMEN WHO ARE TENURED FACULTY**
    17%

- **PERCENTAGE OF THE CLASS WITH**

two years or more of an undergraduate degree	12%
a three-year degree	33%
a four-year degree	48%
a post-graduate degree	7%

- **PROFILE OF LL.B. POPULATIONS**

Native students	3
Visible Minorities	n/a
Mature Students	19

OTHER RELATED PROGRAMS

LL.B./M.A. Program in Law and Philosophy, M.B.A./LL.B., Exchange programs with the Université Laval at Québec City (Diplôme de Français Juridique) and Case Western Reserve University in Cleveland, Ohio, Joint Program with Université Laval at Québec City (where students may obtain a degree in the other legal system), and a Ph.D. in Philosophy with a specialization in legal philosophy.

HALF-TIME PROGRAM: There is no half-time program at the University of Western Ontario

ADMISSIONS REQUIREMENTS

According to P.G. Barton, Associate Dean (Students Affairs), "We are looking for someone who has chosen a discrete area of knowledge and focussed in on it. A four-year degree with a major is given more weight but this is only in marginal cases. If you have a three-year degree with an eighty-five percent average you would probably get in." The University of Western Ontario's calendar states, "the Admissions Committee places special emphasis on undergraduate programs that have been challenging and concentrated in a particular area of study, programs in which applicants have taken a number of honours or equivalent courses in that area, as well as courses tending to develop reading and writing skills." A master's degree is not an advantage when applying for admission to Western's Faculty of Law.

A formula is used to aid in the admission process at Western's Faculty of Law. The formula is based on a combination of the candidate's Grade Point Average (GPA) and Law School Admission Test (LSAT) scores. Recently, the weighting of the LSAT score has been reviewed. Admissions personnel at the University of Western Ontario believe that the LSAT can separate people out at the lower and upper ends of the scale, but it is not as effective for most of the applicants who fall somewhere in between. As a result, the admissions committee has lowered the weight given to the LSAT from approximately twenty-five percent to approximately twenty percent in the admissions formula.

The admissions committee at Western's Faculty of Law sets aside twenty of the 155 first year places for outstanding students with only two years of university education. The committee makes a concerted effort to try and get the brightest of students in this category to come to Western's Faculty of Law by sending out offers of admission early in the spring. Therefore, it is advisable to submit the Law School Application Form and supporting documentation as early as possible. Typically, students with only two years completed of their university program tend to have averages around eighty-four or eighty-five percent.

Another ten of the 155 spaces are reserved for mature students. The term "mature student" at the University of Western Ontario is defined as a person who is at least twenty-eight years of age but does not have the required ten or more university credits to qualify for admission in the regular category. Mature student applicants are reviewed based on their experience, maturity, and outstanding achievements. All mature students are interviewed and the LSAT score is used only as a base line. A score in the fiftieth percentile is considered a good indicator of whether an applicant can handle the rigour of law school. The applicant's achievements are weighted more heavily in the decision making process than the LSAT score and the academic average.

The remaining 115 to 120 spots are filled with candidates in the regular admissions category. For students in this category, academic performance and the LSAT score are the primary criteria on which the decision of admission is based. A minimum of a 150 LSAT score and a seventy-five percent GPA is used. The average is calculated using the best three years of post-secondary education. Therefore, it is possible to eliminate the effects of a poor first year by completing more than three years of post-secondary education.

CHARACTER OF THE SCHOOL

What stands out most about the character of Western's Faculty of Law is the strong sense of camaraderie amongst the student body. This feeling of being part of the institution begins in first year. The incoming class of 155 students is put into small groups of sixteen. As a group, they take one of their six courses together and learn the skills of legal research, writing, and oral advocacy. They band together as they start the sometimes frightening process of trying to figure out what is expected of them.

The compulsory nature of the curriculum reinforces their bond. First year is completely compulsory, as it is at all law schools. However, a core of four courses in second year, two in third year, and two compulsory electives in Law in the International Setting and Philosophy of Law must be taken in second or third year. All students graduating from Western's Faculty of Law have these courses in common. The curriculum at Western's Law School maintains the highest number of compulsory courses of any university in Ontario.

Admission of diverse groups in terms of race, culture, and economic background is at its infancy at Western's Faculty of Law, resulting in a relatively homogeneous student body that is white, and middle to upper class. This will undoubtedly change as efforts by the Law Foundation of Ontario continue to advocate the diversification of student bodies at all faculties of law.

Despite the friendly atmosphere, there is still controversy and at Western's Faculty of Law the faculty are at the heart of it. Gender issues are the source of an ongoing debate among faculty who either feel it takes away from the fundamentals, or those who feel it is an integral part of the law. Students are also caught up in the debate, but it is fuelled by the faculty.

STRENGTHS OF THE PROGRAM

The strength of Western's Faculty of Law lies in the area of taxation, labour law, family law, and the applied side of constitutional law according to P. Mercer, Dean of the Faculty of Law.

The National Tax Centre, directed by Professor Brian J. Arnold, was established by the Faculty of Law in 1981. It is dedicated to pursuing independent research on all aspects of Canadian income taxation and to providing quality continuing education programs in taxation for lawyers and others interested in the Canadian tax system. There are four full-time faculty members in taxation at Western. As a result, students interested in income tax law and policy can elect to take a concentration in Taxation. A decision to register in the taxation concentration is made at the end of the first term in second year.

Students who wish to achieve a high level of fluency in written and spoken French for professional reasons, but have an insufficient background in French, can take advantage of the Diplôme de Français Juridique. It is a three-year program offered in conjunction with the LL.B. program and with the co-operation of the Department of French.

Exchange opportunities exist with Case Western Reserve University in Cleveland, Ohio and Université Laval. Under the auspices of the Canada — U.S. Law Institute, a number of students in third year are permitted to spend one term at the School of Law at Case Western Reserve University. The program exposes students to legal problems in the American legal system. For third-year students who want to study the Civil Law in French, one term can be spent at Université Laval. Financial support is available for both of these exchanges.

Students can experience the practicalities of the legal profession by participating in Community Legal Services. For over twenty years students have been helping people in the community deal with landlord tenant disputes, summary convictions, criminal, and quasi-criminal problems. Participation in this program is voluntary.

WHERE THE PROGRAM COULD IMPROVE

Over time, the number of faculty at Western's Faculty of Law has decreased due to budget constraints. In the last five years, only six full-time faculty have been appointed. This reduction in faculty has limited the ability of Western's Faculty of Law to offer a wide range of courses in specialty areas such as Environmental Law, Native Law, and Immigration and Refugee Law. The student body is seriously lacking in diversity of race, culture, and economic backgrounds. The administration is attempting to change this by devoting more attention to access issues.

At other schools the Law Journal, which publishes articles and notes relating to the law, is completely student run. The *Canadian Journal of Law and Jurisprudence* at Western's Faculty of Law is run by the Faculty of Law and the Department of Philosophy. Only students of proven ability are given the opportunity to assist as student editors.

ON LONDON

London's nickname, "The Forest City," hints at the quiet tree-lined streets that are home to the university. Western's rolling green campus is a ten-minute drive from downtown London. The city itself was described by students as "slow moving and stalwart," "a small town that thinks it is a big town." The economy is geared to students with a good selection of bars and pubs.

On the surface it seems like an affluent town, but the east side of London is not. Student housing is not concentrated immediately around the university, so public transit is relied on. The bus system is adequate but frequent transfers are necessary to get from point A to point B. Downtown is only a twenty-five minute walk from campus. Most students, however, do have cars. Parking costs have increased drastically in the past few years to $150/year. The vacancy rate for apartments is fair and apartments are moderately priced.

London has a good symphony orchestra and theatre and Toronto is only a two-hour drive away.

WHAT THE STUDENTS SAY

(Pseudonyms have replaced the following students' names)

The Strengths of the Program

"Before I entered law school, I had no idea of what law school was about. Two years of volunteering with the Community Legal Services clinic helped me to decide what I wanted." Roger LL.B. '92

"There are a lot of social activities. Life is really centered around the law school and you have the opportunity to meet people and to get a good legal education at the same time." Matthew LL.B. '92

"The student body is the strongest point. Although there is competition, the students get along with each other. There is very little snobbishness between years. It is close knit, fun and it made my experience there worthwhile." Lin LL.B. '91

"The size of the classes is a strength. In first year there is the small group context. The incoming class of 155 students are put into groups of sixteen. We were given the opportunity to meet others and learn from them. I met my best friend in my group." Matthew LL.B. '92

"The librarians like Pat McVeigh are fantastic. They get to know your names quickly and they are very supportive in general. They ask you what you are working on and keep it in mind, and if they find anything they'll help you. If you need a book they'll even find the person who has the book you need and ask them to share." Susan, articling student

"No one has ever had to leave the library to find sources. The library staff is even better — George Robinson, Pat McVeigh, and Marianne Welch. Mr. Robinson, the head librarian, even comes in on late shifts." Matthew LL.B. '92

"It is a more personal and warm atmosphere. Books aren't hidden on one another. You are supportive of one another and help each other, which is odd because the marking scheme is not conducive to this. It works on the bell curve so you are competing with each other." Susan, articling student

"There is a great range and diversity of the student body in terms of age and experience. Some worked for ten years without a degree before coming to law school. There is no range in terms of ethnic groups like there is at the University of Toronto in downtown Toronto.... The description of Western as a WASP country club is partly true. I had expected that from the stories I had heard about Western, in that it was attended by well-to-do people who had not wanted for much. I prepared myself for that. Being a Chinese woman, I expected to stay on the fringes but I was very surprised. A lot of the students are well-to-do, but I didn't find them aloof. There is a range of people who haven't been advantaged for their entire life." Lin LL.B. '92

"There are a high number of mature students. I just turned twenty-two in my first year and in my small group of sixteen there were four people that were over thirty. It is good to meet people who have different experiences." Matthew LL.B. '92

Where the Program Could Improve

"There ought to be more of the clinical aspects of teaching law like they have in medical programs. There is only the legal clinic, which is completely voluntary. Clinical is sort of overlooked. There is more emphasis on the theory than on the practical side." Roger LL.B. '92

"Legal research and advocacy is not emphasized here. Law schools teach you theory. Practising lawyers tell us that what we are learning in law school won't help us. Why aren't they teaching us things we will need ten years from now? We are not prepared for the world of work, but at the same time there is the opportunity to get the skills in clinical legal education, trial process and external moot program, but you have to pursue it." Matthew LL.B. '92

"The admissions policy is bringing in a homogeneous student body coming from the same backgrounds (upper middle class). It should be more varied in terms of economic background. If you are going to work in the public sector you should understand your clients, who tend not to come from the upper middle class. The admission review is in its infancy. The pressure is coming from traditional means of affirmative action with an emphasis more on race and gender than economics." Roger LL.B. '92

"I think tenure should be abolished. Universities are carrying individuals who have no business teaching. We have had to let people go who are committed and bright. The funding squeeze is killing them. We don't need as many law schools. Universality is a crock. Close a few down and distribute the money and concentrate on producing good lawyers or charge higher tuition at all of them." Gordon, articling student

"Commercial law is offered and it is an important course, but it is taught by a practitioner who volunteers his time. If he decides not to teach, that course simply would not be offered. They [Western] claim to be a big business school but they don't even pay this professor. All the money is being channelled into the library and not the faculty." Eleanor LL.B. '92

"From my limited perception, Western is seriously falling behind the other law schools in respect to upcoming issues in the law such as environmental law, native law, and immigration. There is only one course offered in environmental law and there is not much material in the library — you could put it all in one briefcase. It is treated like a boutique course when in reality it is a really relevant area. They have an environmental law course because everyone else does and it is taught by a practitioner rather than by someone who studies and does research in that area full-time. Native law does not exist and immigration and refugee law is only taught once every other year." Roger LL.B. '92

"The grading system rewards exam writing skills and not analytical abilities. I learned how to play the game, figuring out what the instructors want and the extent of what I needed to know. I focussed on the right thing to perform and do well but I don't have the same insight of the law as some who were getting C's." Gordon, articling student

"Do something to dispel the perception that Western's Law School is a WASP country club and promote more applications from diverse groups. There are no black students in a student body of 450. I am Chinese and the number of Chinese students is less than ten." Lin LL.B. '92

Controversies

"The school is very sensitive to sexism, possibly over-sensitive. There are a lot of very strong feminists. There has been a division between faculty. It didn't affect my education though. It was sometimes like living in a house where parents were fighting and you're not a little kid so you kind of look at them and say 'come on.' It made me angry because I wanted them to settle their differences.... Two women professors were let go at the end of their three-year contract because there wasn't enough money and it was felt that efforts were not strong enough to keep them on. The feminist faction, both men and women, also wanted more courses in women and the law and other feminist courses. The older professors felt this wasn't where their focus is. There is fighting over limited resources. Some people think it should be spent on fundamental courses and others think it should be spent on more human rights, women and the law, and sexual harassment courses." Susan, articling student

"There is a big debate and faculty infighting, but it doesn't affect the quality of education unless you are politically active and want to align yourself. The professors are human and people have differences. It will be the same when we are working in law firms. If you don't have a socialist, right-wing feminist viewpoint, then you don't have to take those courses. There was more of a debate in first year than now. There were some great discussions of feminism, but these divisions are not evident now to the average student." Matthew LL.B. '92

"There are a lot of talented faculty, but lately there has been a lot of debate on issues such as sexual harassment, feminism as opposed to more traditional views, and this has had an impact. It has led to a little less tolerance which was at its height a couple of years ago, but it is getting better now. In the past, the professors were spending time on philosophical debates among themselves and some students felt that this was to the detriment of their educational experience. Recently the professors have been refocusing their attention on teaching." Lin LL.B. '91

"The faculty is not all that responsive to students. The faculty divisiveness over gender issues, the building fund, and the letting go of two women professors who were on contract is destructive to their relationships with the students. I don't have that much trust in faculty members. They don't have that much time for you and that is annoying when you are paying tuition. Some professors will give you hours of their time, such as one of the women professors they let go." Eleanor LL.B. '92

On Faculty

"The tax option is the best in Canada, taught by five or six professors with sterling credentials. Professor Arnold appreciates the fact that it is a dry course and proceeds very slowly and hammers in the basic concepts." Roger LL.B. '92

"Dean Mercer is great. He has a lot of integrity, a great sense of humour, and is young and smart." Susan, articling student

"I think there are excellent professors in trusts and wills and family law. Many of them have written the texts that we are using in class." Matthew LL.B. '92

"Despite the faculty being troubled in the last few years, they have been very supportive — far better than my undergraduate experience. I have never been just a number. They care and take an interest in their students." Lin LL.B. '92

Other Comments

"It's [Western's Faculty of Law] is a great place to go to law school. It might not be the best, but it's a great place to be. There is more to a good legal education than academics. You have to know how to deal with each other." Matthew LL.B. '92

University of Windsor

- **INQUIRIES**
    Admissions Office
    Faculty of Law
    University of Windsor
    Windsor, Ontario
    N9B 3P4
    (519) 253-4232 extension 2925

ADMISSIONS INFORMATION

- **APPLICATION DEADLINE DATE FOR ADMISSIONS**
    1 February

- **REQUIRED TO SUBMIT**
    - Official copies of all university academic transcripts
    - LSAT score report
    - Reference letters
    - A personal profile

- **AVERAGE GPA**
    Information on GPA averages and ranges was not made available. The admissions policy at the University of Windsor does not use GPA as a determinative criteria. The GPA is only one of the seven criteria considered to determine admission.

- **AVERAGE LSAT**
    Information on LSAT averages and ranges was not made available. The admissions policy at the University of Windsor does not use the LSAT as a determinative criteria. The LSAT is only one of the seven criteria considered to determine admission.

■ **EDUCATION REQUIREMENT**

Two full years of academic work at a recognized university after senior matriculation

■ **RATIO OF APPLICANTS TO REGISTRATIONS**

16.5 : 1

■ **SIZE OF INCOMING CLASS**

145 (325 offers were sent out)

■ **CAN YOU DEFER ACCEPTANCE**

No

■ **APPLICATION FEE**

$25

■ **TUITION FEE**

The 1992-93 tuition fee is $2,277 for Canadian students and $7,510 for non-exempt foreign students.

CLASS PROFILE

■ **AVERAGE AGE OF STUDENTS ENTERING THE PROGRAM**

27

■ **PERCENTAGE OF THE CLASS WHO ARE WOMEN**

52%

■ **PERCENTAGE OF WOMEN WHO ARE TENURED FACULTY**

28%

■ **PERCENTAGE OF THE CLASS WITH**

two years or more of an undergraduate degree	17%
a three-year degree	34%
a four-year degree	30%
a post-graduate degree	17%

■ **PROFILE OF LL.B. POPULATIONS**

MATURE STUDENTS: this is not a separate category at Windsor's Law School and therefore no accurate statistics were available

NATIVE STUDENTS: five native students are attending the program

OTHER RELATED PROGRAMS

M.B.A./LL.B., and joint J.D./LL.B. program in conjunction with the University of Detroit Mercy Law School.

HALF-TIME PROGRAM: Three half-time students were admitted in 1991-92. The requirements for admission and application deadline date are the same as those for the full-time program. Part-time students have a maximum of six years to complete their degree and they must prove to the committee that they are disadvantaged, or have exceptional family circumstances which make them unable to attend full-time. Most courses are given during the day.

ADMISSIONS REQUIREMENTS

Fifteen years ago Windsor's Faculty of Law instituted an admissions policy which personifies their theme — Access to Justice. They cast aside the concept that good prospective lawyers could be identified by excellent grade point averages (GPA) and Law School Admission Test (LSAT) scores only. Instead, "we assess each candidate as human beings rather than as solely an academic being," comments Donna Eansor, Associate Dean. Academic and LSAT performance are only two of the seven criteria considered and, of the seven, the LSAT score is probably the least significant.

The seven criteria used in the admissions process are: career objectives, community involvement, LSAT scores, personal accomplishments, personal consideration, university program, and work experience.

All years of the university program are considered, but individual circumstances are taken into consideration. For example, if a student did poorly in Commerce but improved significantly when they found their niche in Arts, their first year would be eliminated and considered as a false start. Positive trends are looked for, as well as whether a full-time or part-time course load was carried, and the degree of difficulty of the courses. Master's degrees are considered along with other academic achievements.

Work experience, including part-time, summer and/or full-time, will be analyzed for its indication of organizational and administrative skills and initiative. Certification or training programs will also be considered.

Evidence of an ability to meet the intellectual rigours of a law program are looked for, but next in importance is the candidate's potential to contribute creatively and meaningfully to the law school and the community. Thus, community involvement is carefully looked at. A high level of commitment and the nature of the contribution will be assessed.

Personal accomplishments in the areas of extracurricular activities, hobbies and special accomplishments whether in high school or university, artistic or athletic achievements, communication skills, and languages spoken are just a few areas which might be highlighted — whatever might add value to the mix of the student body.

The admissions committee will be looking for candidates who have direction and are able to express it in a well thought-out career objective. For example, what area of the law is of most interest to you and why. What will you do with it once you have your law degree?

Personal considerations such as illness, bereavement, unusual family responsibilities, or other such circumstances which may affect an applicant's qualifications will be noted.

An LSAT score valid within six years is required but is not weighted heavily. All of this information is asked for in detail on Windsor's Faculty of Law application form. Filling out this extensive and probing application form is the first test of a candidate's commitment. Interviews are not granted so the application form is the method of presenting your best self. Fill it out carefully. If you think it is onerous to complete, think how time consuming it is to read when it is one of two thousand applications.

Windsor's Faculty of Law uses no other categories of admission as it is believed by the administration that the existing policy already covers them. However, there is a special admissions policy to encourage Native Canadians to pursue a legal education. Again, this is consistent to the Access to Justice theme as Native Canadians are underrepresented in the legal profession. If a Native Canadian applies under this policy they may be required to take and successfully complete the eight-week Program of Legal Studies for Native People offered each summer by the Native Law Centre at the University of Saskatchewan. Automatic admission is given when these conditions are met. The LSAT is waived as can other criteria.

CHARACTER OF THE SCHOOL

Established in 1968, Windsor is the youngest faculty of law in Ontario. Perhaps because of this Windsor has decided to make innovation its trademark. Its theme was Access to Justice before access was popular. For this faculty, access to justice begins with access to a legal education. Windsor is reaching out to people who have confronted and overcome adversity. The admissions policy emphasises why the candidate wants to become a lawyer and how they see themselves helping their community once they have obtained their law degree. To have such direction, and the experience to give credibility to such goals, the process tends to favour older applicants, people who have come to the realization that they want to pursue law a little later. For many it is a second career. Windsor's average age of twenty-seven is one of the oldest of all the law schools.

The atmosphere among the students is more laid back and co-operative, with the majority of the students interested in the practical aspects of their studies and intent on getting on with the practice of law.

Students have the freedom to choose their courses in second and third year with only two mandatory half-course requirements after first year.

STRENGTHS OF THE PROGRAM

The access to justice theme is the backbone of the research focus at Windsor's Faculty of Law. Windsor pioneered the research in the area of pre-paid legal services in Canada. Seven professors out of a faculty of twenty-five are involved in researching access to justice issues. Several other faculty members have a special interest in Law and Development in relation to Third World development. Courses such as "Access to Justice: Procedural Issues" and "Law of Developing Nations" have developed from this research as well as from the incorporation of the central theme in all mainstream courses.

The Centre for Canadian American Studies is affiliated with Windsor's Faculty of Law and provides a research base for scholars and students who wish to pursue interdisciplinary research into the relationship between Canada and the United States.

Windsor's border location is a factor that the Faculty of Law draws on to its advantage. Windsor's Faculty of Law is small but by combining efforts with nearby American institutions such as University of Detroit and Wayne State University, Windsor offers students some unique opportunities. The joint J.D./LL.B. program enables students to obtain a Doctor of Jurisprudence (J.D.) from the University of Detroit Mercy Law School while they are taking their LL.B. from the University of Windsor. Students get both degrees in three years (with one summer spent taking classes) or three and a half years. This gives students the opportunity to be called to the bar in any state in the United States or common law provinces in Canada. Students who are not participating in the joint program can take courses at the University of Detroit and Wayne State University in Detroit on special permission while paying significantly lower Canadian tuition fees.

Another result of the combined efforts of the University of Detroit Mercy, Wayne State University, and the University of Windsor is the Intellectual Property Law Institute (IPLI). The IPLI's primary purpose is to offer a rich curriculum in the field of intellectual property. On an annual basis Patent

Law, Advanced Patent Law, Copyright Law, Entertainment Law, Trademarks and Unfair Competition, and Aspects of International Communications are offered. Other courses will be offered according to demand and availability of instructors.

Another strength of Windsor's Faculty of Law is the hands-on experience students can choose by participating in the Clinical Law Program, the Clerkship Program to the Supreme Court of the Northwest Territories, the Community Legal Aid, and the *Windsor Review of Legal and Social Issues*.

The Clinical Law Program is an optional, full semester credit program, introducing students to lawyering skills in a community clinical setting. Second- and third-year students are given an intensive orientation program and take two courses — Legal Professions, which examines ethics issues in legal education and practice; and Interviewing, Counselling, Negotiation, and Trial Techniques, which introduces students to the development and evaluation of lawyering skills. Students handle files involving social welfare, landlord and tenant disputes, workers' compensation, immigration, and consumer and human rights law under the supervision of staff lawyers. What makes this program different from other clinical programs is that law students work together on files with social work students where social problems are involved, with a goal of providing a more holistic approach to problem resolution.

Students looking for a less intensive way to apply their legal knowledge and serve the community of Windsor can volunteer at the Community Legal Aid (CLA). Volunteers are involved with files concerning landlord and tenant matters, minor criminal offenses, and student problems such as Ontario Students Assistance Program (OSAP) disputes and student appeals.

The Clerkship Program to the Supreme Court of the Northwest Territories annually gives two students the opportunity to Clerk to the Supreme Court for the Northwest Territories. The Clerkship is treated as a supervised research project and the successful students will gain experience in court research and memoranda writing.

The *Windsor Review of Legal and Social Issues* is one way for students looking for editorial experience, a chance to publish articles, comments, or book reviews, and gain applied experience.

Financially, Windsor's Faculty of Law has not suffered from budget restraints. Since the early 1980's, the University's Board of Governors has taken the stand of a balanced budget. Jeff Berryman, Dean, comments: "We only had incremental growth during the period of rapid growth, but now in the depth of the recession our programs have not suffered any cutbacks in terms of staff. We have been able to weather the cuts very well and we have been able to recruit or replace faculty." In the last five years five faculty have been replaced. Seven of the twenty-five faculty members are women, and three are visible minorities at Windsor's Faculty of Law and as a result of the affirmative action and employment equity program in place. The goal is to have fifty percent of the faculty to be women by the year 2000.

WHERE THE PROGRAM COULD IMPROVE

There seems to be some confusion over the concept and the implementation of the Faculty of Law's theme of "Access to Justice." The application of access to a legal education seems to be firmly in place, supported by the research done by the faculty, the *Windsor Yearbook of Access to Justice* (an academic interdisciplinary journal which deals with either access or justice issues), and an admissions policy which admits a mix of students atypical of most law schools.

However, the theme loses clarity when it comes to its implementation. One might expect a law school whose mandate is priority of justice issues to have more than only two courses offered in this area (Access to Justice: Procedural Issues and Law of Developing Nations). One might have expected to see more courses in the areas of human rights and immigration for example. It is also interesting to note that these courses are not given a very high weight, nor are they offered very frequently. In practice, there seems to be more of an emphasis on Canada/U.S. relations.

The recent addition of a twenty-five dollar application fee caused an outcry from the student body. Although twenty-five dollars is one of the lowest application fees required from Canadian law schools, and can be waived in case of hardship, this could be an obstacle to some applicants pursuing a legal education. The students interviewed felt this was a symbolic contradiction to the theme of access to justice.

ON WINDSOR

The University of Windsor's campus is in the middle of a residential area where students can readily find accommodation. Most students share a house with an average rent of $300 for a house shared by three people or $500 for a one-bedroom apartment. The campus is a twenty-minute walk from downtown. The architecture of the campus is a mix of historical buildings and modern ones.

When students were asked about what it was like living in Windsor as a student, it was difficult to get positive comments. One student described

Windsor as "one big sign pointing to Detroit." Like David, the little city of Windsor overwhelmed by the Goliath of Detroit, the town of Windsor is overshadowed by American media. The *Globe and Mail* and the *Toronto Star* are available as well as the *Detroit Press,* the *Financial Post,* the *New York Times,* and the *Wall Street Journal.*

The pollution is so bad that most students commented that they buy bottled water and feel the air quality is poor, especially in the summer when temperatures become very hot. Windsor is further south than northern California; therefore, when you are looking for a house make sure it has air conditioning.

WHAT THE STUDENTS SAY

(Pseudonyms have replaced the following students' names)

The Strengths of the Program

"The cohesiveness of the student body is the biggest strength. The minute you start you get a support network from second- and third-year students. The orientation program is excellent. Most of the people aren't from Windsor so you tend to evolve around the school where you make a lot of friends quickly." Raymond LL.B. '92

"The small size is a strength and there is a sense that you are a part of something. It is not a cut-throat environment." Lisa LL.B. '92

"The first-year legal writing program is a strength. We are given more practice in writing legal memorandums making us fully prepared for legal research work. It is very much a hands-on experience. It gives us a good foundation which leads to good summer jobs and articling jobs as a result." Elizabeth LL.B. '92

"It is interesting to get an American perspective by taking courses at the University of Detroit." Larisa LL.B. '92

"I liked the idea of a central theme of Access to Justice and that they sought out groups through their admissions policy that were not typical of law schools. They are trying to counteract the elitist image." Larisa LL.B. '92

Where the Program Could Improve

". . . Too many of our professors only teach to make enough money to do their research and treat students with contempt. I would like to see the teaching aspect get more weight. We fill out evaluations but they don't seem to mean anything." Tina LL.B. '93

"Windsor has prided itself on the theme of Access to Justice. No one really knows what it means but it sounds good. . . . Not much is done within the school to flesh out what it means and put it into practice. Whether our reputation is deserved in this area or whether it is just a buzzword is unknown." James, articling student

"Sometimes there can be tension between our theme of Access to Justice and a lean, mean, cost-effective machine. The administration just decided on a twenty-five dollar application fee. This barrier seems like a contradiction to their theme of access." Larisa LL.B. '92

"The course selection provides the basic courses, but you might only be able to take one course in an area of interest." Lisa LL.B. '92

"They have a long term plan in place to upgrade the library and it is very much needed." Larisa LL.B. '92

The Controversy

"Fifty percent of the population of lawyers will soon be women and I have no problem with that, but I understand that women will have different problems. I took a class to find out what the issues were. The issues didn't centre around what we could do collectively but what women could do. This divides the student body. There are male colleagues of mine who are aware of the issues and would like to express their viewpoint in support of women but are not allowed to." Leonard LL.B. '92

"There is a slight gender problem. Feminism is perceived as a bad thing and as only radical militant feminism. It is very subtle and low key but it is there. I see it in class when feminist issues are raised. The class seems to perceive it as outside the study of law." Larisa LL.B. '92

On Faculty

"The 'odd ball' professors are really helpful. They don't see themselves as being in a rarefied atmosphere but simply as another person involved in the process." Tina LL.B. '93

"Leigh West teaches Legal Process, Contracts, Judicial Review, and Occupational Health and Safety, and Bill Bogart teaches Civil Procedure, Administrative Law, and seminars on Access to Justice. Both are excellent teachers who teach people both academically and in the broader context. However, we have a lot of deadwood on faculty as well. About one-third of the faculty aren't doing very much and don't care very much about teaching, but they have tenure." James, articling student

"John Wilson, who teaches Property, Native Law, Advocacy, Regulation of

Trade Practices, Securities Regulation, Law and Economics, Advanced Criminal, Civil Procedure, and Commercial is a former practitioner and has a very good lecture style. He is more of a storyteller and keeps your interest. He sets a challenging exam but prepares you well." Elizabeth LL.B. '92

"Brian Mazer teaches Criminal Law, International Law, and Legal Professions. He goes out of his way to be helpful to students." Tina LL.B. '93

Other Comments

"I was accepted at Queen's, Western, and Windsor, but Queen's and Western didn't seem to be that progressive towards minorities whereas Windsor strives towards having twenty percent minority representation." James, articling student

"I don't feel I have to do the things that the twenty-six year olds do to be accepted and I live in residence. If I can come in at fifty years old and be known and accepted, then that says a lot for the school." Tina LL.B. '93

"I wasn't accepted by any other law school in Ontario and I was chosen by Windsor off the waiting list. Now I am third in my class and I have been able to compete with students from the University of Toronto for a great job on Bay Street. I feel I am in just as good a position as students from other law schools. Windsor is thought of highly by recruiters." Raymond LL.B. '92

"Almost fifty per cent of the class comes from Toronto. As a result we have formed the '401 Club' where we share rides back and forth from Toronto. On Friday afternoon you see cars and cars of law students going back to Toronto and coming back Sunday." James, articling student

CIVIL LAW SCHOOLS OF CANADA

Université Laval

■ INQUIRIES

Faculté de droit
Université Laval
Pavillon Charles-De Koninck
Ste.-Foy, Québec
GIK 7P4
(418) 656-3511

ADMISSIONS INFORMATION

■ **APPLICATION DEADLINE DATE FOR ADMISSIONS**

Fall Term:

1 February for students residing outside of Canada
1 March for all other candidates

Winter Term:

1 September for students residing outside of Canada
1 November for all other candidates

■ **REQUIRED TO SUBMIT**

Official copies of the Québec Diplôme d'études collégiales (D.E.C.)
and/or all university academic transcripts

■ **EDUCATION REQUIREMENT**

A Québec D.E.C.

■ **AVERAGE GPA**

not available

- **AVERAGE TEST D'ADMISSION**
  not available

- **RATIO OF APPLICANTS TO REGISTRATIONS**
  9.1 : 1

- **SIZE OF INCOMING CLASS**
  330 (265 admitted in September and 65 in January)

- **CAN YOU DEFER ACCEPTANCE**
  No

- **APPLICATION FEE**
  $15

- **TUITION FEE**

  The 1992-93 tuition fee
  for Canadian students is $50 for one credit
                                             $5 per credit for sundries
                                             $5 per credit for materials

  The 1992-93 tuition fee
  for foreign students is $243 for one credit
                                               $5 per credit for sundries
                                               $5 per credit for materials

CLASS PROFILE

- **AVERAGE AGE OF STUDENTS ENTERING THE PROGRAM**
  not available

- **PERCENTAGE OF THE CLASS WHO ARE WOMEN**
  60%

- **PERCENTAGE OF WOMEN WHO ARE TENURED FACULTY**
  20% of all tenured professors

- **PERCENTAGE OF THE CLASS WITH**

CEGEP	50%
University studies	50%

- **PROFILE OF LL.L. POPULATIONS**

Natives	2% (8 students)

| Visible minorities | n/a |
| Mature Students | n/a |

OTHER RELATED PROGRAMS

A certificate in law is available to those twenty-one and older who would find legal knowledge useful in their jobs, but do not need to be a lawyer. Fifty-seven students are enrolled in the Post-Graduate Notary Diploma program. Two streams of Master of Law programs are offered; one is research-oriented with a thesis requirement and the other is a professional track Master's requiring more course work and an essay. Approximately one hundred students are registered in the Master's of Law programs. A Doctoral program is also offered.

A part-time program is available, allowing students to take as few as one course per term without permission as long as they finish the program in seven years.

ADMISSIONS REQUIREMENTS

Laval's Faculté de droit admits students directly from CEGEP, university, or mature students who do not meet the education requirements. The number of spaces allotted to each category is in proportion to the number of applications, thus giving each group equal opportunity for admission. The test d'admission de droit Civil developed by the Univeristé de Montréal is not used by Laval's Faculté de droit as part of their admissions process. Instead, Laval's Faculté de droit uses an aptitude test they have developed themselves and it is only administered for a few categories that are described below.

The majority of students admitted apply directly after CEGEP and the main criterion determining admission for the CEGEP category is academic performance. The average grade point average (GPA) required for admission is not available because it is contingent on the quality of applicants that apply each term, making it difficult to predict. If an applicant has been out of CEGEP, or any other type of post-secondary institution for more that two years, they will be required to take the test d'admission.

Applicants who have studied at Université Laval are classified in a separate admission category and, depending on the number of credits acquired at the university, the application is evaluated on the basis of either the CEGEP grades or the university grades. The test d'admission is not required.

Students from other Québec universities are classified in another category. Those who acquired less than forty-five university credits are required to pass the test d'admission. The selection criteria is based on the CEGEP and university grades, weighted at sixty percent, and on the results of the test d'admission, weighted at forty percent. For applicants who acquired at least forty-five university credits, the application is evaluated only on the university grades.

A mature student may first be defined as a candidate who is at least twenty-one years old, who did not attend school for two years, and who has not acquired a college or university degree. The application of those candidates is evaluated on the basis of the test d'admission and on their personal and professional experience. Mature students may also be defined as candidates who are at least twenty-one years old, and who acquired a college degree or university credits. Those candidates are classified in one of the following categories: College candidates, Candidates from Université Laval, Candidates from another Québec university, or Candidates from outside Québec. The applications are evaluated according to the specific criteria of each of those categories.

In 1991, an affirmative action policy was put into place whereby up to ten aboriginal students are to be admitted each year. Successful completion of the pre-law preparation course at Université d'Ottawa is required. No test d'admission is required. As support for aboriginal students admitted to the program, the Faculté de droit has hired a support person, Marie-France Chabot, whose area of expertise is methodology. Her role is to help students develop skills and aid them in exam preparation.

CHARACTER OF THE SCHOOL

Laval's Faculté de droit is unlike any other law school in Canada both in its structure and its interactive approach with the rest of the faculties of the university. Other law schools in Canada have a tendency to isolate themselves from the rest of the university by being in a separate building, not allowing, or restricting the number of courses to a maximum of one or two that a student can take outside of the Faculty of Law, and having as a general characteristic, a student body that does not socialize with the rest of the population. Laval follows none of these patterns. Laval's Faculté de droit is housed in the social science building. Taking two courses outside of the Faculté de droit is a *mandatory* part of the law curriculum and students from all faculties are encouraged to attend the concerts and speakers organized by the law student society as part of their festival in first term.

Most of the students attending Laval's Faculté de droit come from the outlying regions of eastern Québec. They do not know anybody when they arrive and fast friendships are quickly formed. There is a sense of camaraderie amongst the students who wish it. For those who want more anonymity and do not want their life to centre on the Faculté de droit, the large size of the school accommodates this as well.

STRENGTHS OF THE PROGRAM

Established in 1854, Laval's Faculté de droit, is one of the older law schools in Canada and serves the eastern region of the province of Québec. Located in the provincial capital of Québec, the law faculty has close ties to the government function. Areas of law such as constitutional law, administrative law, and public law are what Laval's Faculté de droit is best known for. However, with a full-time faculty of fifty-four professors, the faculty can offer a wide range of courses and teaching styles.

Over half of the faculty have a Ph.D. and their backgrounds of study cover a range of countries including France, the United Kingdom, and the United States. Research is emphasized at Laval's Faculté de droit. *Les Cahiers de Droit* is a law review written and run by professors and promotes the development and evolution of legal science in Québec and is published four times a year.

La Revue Juridique des Étudiants et Étudiantes de l'Université Laval (RJEL) is a student run review which promotes student research abilities and editorial talents. Involvement in the *RJEL* is regarded favourably by firms as it gives them an opportunity to familiarize themselves with a student's work before hiring them.

Laval's Faculté de droit's unique feature is the flexible structure of its program. The LL.L. program is a three-year program but students are not promoted by year. The concept of first, second, and third years is replaced by a modular structure based on pre-requisites. Students can choose their courses as they wish, without the restriction of what year a course belongs to, as long as they have the appropriate pre-requisite. The Faculté de droit requires a minimum of fifteen mandatory courses (forty-five credits). Of the remaining fifteen optional courses, three are semi-compulsory in that the student has to choose: one course out of four courses in methodology, one course out of six offered in critical approach to law, and one out of four courses in international law.

Further flexibility is provided by the two points of entry into the program. Students can apply for admission in September or in January. Most September applicants are students applying directly from CEGEP whereas the majority of January applicants are students applying with university backgrounds. The mandatory first-term courses are offered every term, making it possible to always pick up needed pre-requisites. If a student should happen to fail a pre-requisite course, they can repeat it the next term and upon successful completion they can continue on.

Laval's Faculté de droit has two exchange programs that students can apply for. An exchange for one term with the University of Western Ontario provides students with some exposure to the common law legal system. If they wish to pursue it further, they can return to Western after the completion of their civil law degree and get their common law degree in one year. A civil law exchange with Aix-Marseille in France is also available.

WHERE THE PROGRAM COULD IMPROVE

Budget constraints in the last few years have hit the law library particularly hard and the library is the focus of the law school fund raising drive.

The large size of the student body results in large class sizes which make interaction between the students and professors during class difficult. Research is an emphasis at the faculty level but this does not filter down to the level of the students. Almost every student interviewed was concerned that they were not forced to get more experience in research and writing. Only one large paper is required as part of the mandatory requirements.

Due to a recent retirement, the criminal law area needs to be built up. Not many faculty positions have become available in the last few years, but the administration is now starting to actively recruit new young faculty.

ON STE.-FOY

The first buildings of Université Laval's campus were built in the 1950s, creating an architecturally modern campus that is approximately twenty minutes from "old" Québec by bus. Ste.-Foy is a small town that has become a dormitory suburb of Québec. The atmosphere is quiet, peaceful, and safe. Ste.-Foy is the home of Place Laurier, the second largest shopping mall in Canada.

Accommodation is readily available, with a typical one-bedroom apartment costing approximately $325 per month. Limited residence accommodation is available on campus as well.

WHAT THE STUDENTS SAY

(Pseudonyms have replaced the following students' names)

The Strengths of the Program

"Public law in the areas of government, constitutional, and labour law are strong at Laval." Julie LL.L. '93

"Every class has the same weight of three credits and you can take every

course during summer too. There is a lot of flexibility in the program at Laval."
Benoit LL.L. '91, LL.B. '92

"It is a fairly rigorous program in general and I found that the midterms were worthwhile and counted for quite a bit. The half courses force you to be in the books for most of the year. It keeps the pressure on you to be up to date."
John LL.L. '91, LL.B. '92

"There is a good student life with lots of spirit. We are always a big team at the law games [a social event that law schools across Canada participate in] and people participate in sports and all other activities." Melanie LL.L. '93

"Students coming to Laval come from small towns and don't know anyone when they arrive. They are looking to make friends and they are unaffected."
Julie LL.L. '93

"It is a big university and you are on your own. You develop your autonomy and you can figure out how to do things yourself." Melanie LL.L. '93

"Laval has midterm exams instead of one hundred percent finals and this helps you to keep up with your studies. By continually reviewing your material you have a better grasp of the material at hand." Lesley LL.L. '93

"A lot of practitioners are brought in to teach and this is good because you see the practical side of the law. The professors balance this out by giving you the theory." Lesley LL.L. '93

"The law school is part of the social science building and this is a plus because you see different aspects of university life." Lesley LL.L. '93

"Laval used to have most of its students coming from CEGEP but now there is more diversity [eg. mature students]. There are some people in their late twenties, thirties, and forties and the younger students look up to them. There is a kindergarten on campus for the children." Jean LL.L. '93

"There is plenty of choice in terms of courses and there are many interesting classes." Robert, articling student

"There is a lot of support for the people who participate in the competitive moot court competitions. There are good coaches and they lend you whatever books you need. If they don't have them in the library, they will find them."
Robert, articling student

"The athletic facilities are excellent. There is an indoor pool and hockey rink, indoor soccer, track, volleyball, and good change room facilities. It is a big complex with lots of well organized activities." John LL.L. '91, LL.B. '92

Where the Program Could Improve

"It is too big. There are about seventy-five students in the classes and the teachers are open to questions, but they are not open to debate because of the big classes." Melanie LL.L. '93

"The library is a shame. If they do not invest in the library soon there will be too much to catch up on. The budget was cut and the library was hit hard. Most of the United States periodicals were cut and it is almost impossible to do up-to-date research. I don't know how they can have a master's degree with such a poor library." Richard, articling student

"The library is very poor. As soon as you start your research you find important authors missing and you have to borrow them from other schools. It is very ugly and it has poor lighting." Julie LL.L. '93

"I do not think we write enough in the program. I didn't know how to write a brief when I started my articling. We only have to write one paper of about fifty pages and you can choose what course you can do it in so people often pick an easier one. There is an elective research course you can take, and most teachers give you the opportunity to write a paper if you want to, but it should be mandatory." Robert, articling student

"At bar school, many Laval students are known to be good at pleading, but poor at writing." Julie LL.L. '93

"There should be a better system for allocating bursaries that is more motivating. There are only a few available for academic excellence and there is not much information on what they are looking for when you apply." Melanie LL.L. '93

Controversies

"There isn't any tension between men and women at Laval. Common Law schools are experiencing what Laval did ten years ago. The feminist movement was stronger in Québec about fifteen years ago." Benoit LL.L. '91, LL.B. '92

"There are always the linguistic debates but there isn't any anger. The Anglophone students who come from Western fit in well." Robert, articling student

"The only controversy is politics. The majority of people are independents and there are some federalists, but you don't hear much from them. The two groups get into a lot of discussions but it is friendly." Julie LL.L. '93

On Faculty

"I really appreciated the great relationship you can have with professors. They are very accessible and they don't make you feel intimidated. They participate in the social activities." Robert, articling student

"Many professors are authors and they think about what they teach and they know how to analyze. They are not just repeating what is in the textbook but critiquing it." Robert, articling student

"Some professors are lawyers and this is good because you get more of a practical view, but some of the practitioners just come in for one or two classes and it is difficult for them to get their point across. Some teachers teach to themselves and not to the students." Christine LL.L. '92

"Henri Brun teaches a course on the Canadian and Québec charters in the undergraduate program and he also teaches at the master's level. People appreciate his experience. He has pleaded to the supreme court several times and can give you all the different ways of viewing things." Robert, articling student

"Jacques DesLauriers is very popular because he makes hard classes of bankruptcy easier to understand. He has been the recipient of the best teaching award." Christine LL.L. '92

"Daniel Gardner is a young professor who is very up to date and prepares well for his classes. He asks a lot from his students but gives a lot of himself as well. Professor Gardner teaches obligations." Benoit LL.L. '91, LL.B. '92

"Pierre Garon teaches criminal law and showed us that when you practise criminal law you deal with people's lives. He is very human." Julie LL.L. '93

Comments

"You only have fifteen hours of classes a week. It isn't that hard if you like reading. It is important to get involved since you will be working with these people when you are a lawyer." Benoit LL.L. '91, LL.B. '92

"The more studies at the university level you have before you come to law school helps. I did not have this background. I don't regret it but it would have helped. It is a very competitive world and a lot of lawyers are looking for jobs and articling positions." Marie LL.L. '93

"There are next to no visible minorities. At graduation there was one person in a wheelchair, one black person, some Anglophones, and the rest were primarily Francophones." John LL.L. '91, LL.B. '92

"The social status of law is bigger than it should be and students can be influenced by this. You shouldn't feel pressured to go into law. Outside Québec, you have to do undergraduate study first and this is good. It opens your mind to other things and you can understand why law is like it is. You have better judgement. Law alone is very technical. You don't deal with the big issues since you don't have to think why the law is built that way or about the social roots of the law." Julie LL.L. '93

"Ask yourself why you want to be a lawyer because it is not for everyone. Lawyers have a different way of thinking and it is a different way of life. I think you have to have a certain personality to be a lawyer. You have to be a thinker in the sense that you have to analyse the many different sides of a story non-emotionally and think quickly on your feet. You have to be able to sustain a lot of pressure and have self confidence." Lesley LL.L. '93

Université de Montréal

- **INQUIRIES**
  Faculté de droit
  Université de Montréal
  C.P. 6128, Succursale "A"
  Montréal, Québec
  H3C 3J7
  (514) 343-6200

ADMISSIONS INFORMATION

- **APPLICATION DEADLINE DATE FOR ADMISSIONS**
  1 March

- **REQUIRED TO SUBMIT**
  - Official copies of all Québec Diplôme d'études collégiales (D.E.C.) and/or university academic transcripts

- **EDUCATION REQUIREMENT**
  Applicants are required to have completed the Québec (D.E.C.) or a minimum of two years after the secondary level.

- **AVERAGE GPA**
  not available

- **AVERAGE SCORE FOR TEST D'ADMISSION EN DROIT CIVIL**
  not available

- **RATIO OF APPLICANTS TO REGISTRATIONS**
  9.7 : 1

- **SIZE OF INCOMING CLASS**
  335

■ **CAN YOU DEFER ACCEPTANCE**
   No

■ **APPLICATION FEE**
   $15

■ **TUITION FEE**
   The 1992-93 tuition fee is approximately $1,026 (or $513 per semester) for Canadian students.

CLASS PROFILE

■ **AVERAGE AGE OF STUDENTS ENTERING THE PROGRAM**
   not available

■ **PERCENTAGE OF THE CLASS WHO ARE WOMEN**
   approximately 65%

■ **PERCENTAGE OF WOMEN WHO ARE TENURED FACULTY**
   23% (five out of seven positions within the last four years have been filled by women.)

■ **PERCENTAGE OF THE CLASS WITH**
   Statistics are not available but the administration is working towards having a student body where fifty percent have CEGEP backgrounds and fifty percent have university backgrounds.

■ **PROFILE OF LL.L. POPULATIONS**
   information not available

OTHER RELATED PROGRAMS

A specialized diploma in Law is offered (DESS) in administration, civil, and commercial areas of the law, and fifty-three students are registered in the post-graduate notary diploma program. Students can also do their LL.L. degree on a half-time basis. Eighty-six students are registered in the Professional Masters (LL.M.) that does not require a thesis. A Professional Master's is also available with a thesis and the areas of specialty are civil law, commercial law, and administrative law. One hundred and thirty students are registered in the Professional Master's with thesis program. A Doctorate in Law (LL.D.)

leading to research or teaching is also available and twenty-three students are currently enrolled.

ADMISSIONS REQUIREMENTS

Approximately ninety-six percent of the 335 places at the Faculté de droit are filled by applicants applying under the **Regular Category** of admission. Within this applicant pool, forty-seven percent of the places are filled by students applying directly after the completion of their Diplôme d'Études Collégiales (D.E.C.). The main criterion determining admission for applicants with a D.E.C. is the merit of their academic background. Normally students with a D.E.C. are not required to take the test d'admission en droit civil.

The remaining fifty-three percent of the places in the regular category are filled by students who have at least two years of university courses towards their baccalaureate. All applicants who have university backgrounds are required to take the test d'admission en droit civil. This is an aptitude test developed at the Université de Montréal and used by faculties of law at McGill University, Université d'Ottawa, and Université de Sherbrooke. The test d'admission de droit civil is similar to the LSAT, but it is adapted to the French language and culture. When applications for law school are received by the faculty, selective invitations to write the test are sent out to the applicants. The test can be written only once a year in late March or early April. An applicant's academic performance is compared to that of the pool of applicants and modified accordingly. This modified academic score and the score on the admissions test is then put into a formula whereby the academic performance is given a weight of sixty percent and the admissions test is designated a weight of forty percent. An index score is calculated and the scores are ranked from the top down and offers are sent out. In cases where the scores are similar, an applicant's extra-curricular activities and curriculum vitae will be taken into consideration.

Applicants who do not have the college level requirements but are at least twenty-one years old can apply to Faculté de droit under the **Mature Student Category**. Applications in this category are reviewed in a more holistic manner, taking into consideration the admissions test score as well as achievements they have had in the work place or any specific knowledge that they might have that can be compared to an academic curriculum.

All applicants must possess an adequate knowledge of the French language. Those students who did not attend a French university or CEGEP are required to take a French language test to determine their language proficiency.

At present there is no special native student category.

CHARACTER OF THE SCHOOL

In all civil law schools the dropout rate between first and second year is high compared to common law schools and therefore the pressure to perform is intense. This pressure may be felt more at the Faculté de droit than at other civil law schools because of the large student body and metropolitan location of the university.

Each year 335 students enter their first year of law at Faculté de droit, but the majority of students come from Montreal and the surrounding areas. The students tend to seek out students that they already knew at CEGEP, or who have similar backgrounds to theirs, and form groups. Within these groups, and their small sections in first-year, the students form close ties and support each other in their studies. However, interaction and co-operation between groups is less common. In addition to this, the major law firms choose their students in the first term of second year and their close proximity to the law school adds to the pressure and competitive atmosphere.

The large student body allows students to choose between anonymity or involvement. There is a growing number of mature students at the Faculté de droit who have a life outside of the school and are not very involved in the student life. For them, the anonymity of a commuter school is appreciated. For those who want to have a very involved student life, the large population provides many clubs, organizations, and social activities and a good school spirit. Regardless, on the weekends the school empties since most of the younger students live with their parents in the Montréal area and there are few residence facilities available for law students.

There is little racial diversity in the student body but there are students from France and Ontario participating in exchange programs.

STRENGTHS OF THE PROGRAM

Faculté de droit à Montréal is the largest law school in Canada, established 113 years ago. Its large size allows for courses to be offered in almost every field of law including aboriginal and environmental law. Faculté de droit à Montréal has the largest curriculum of international courses in Canada. Part of the student's mandatory curriculum is a six-hour course on computers and the law, where students get hands-on experience in the computer laboratories.

Approximately fifty percent of the curriculum is optional, with only three courses plus a writing course that are mandatory in second and third year. This provides students with opportunities to take advantage of the broad course selection.

The Public Law Research Centre (CRDP) is established at the Faculté de droit à Montréal. Founded in 1962, its mandate is to promote research in public law and, more specifically, in constitutional and administrative law. Present work concentrates primarily on the laws regulating health and communication, law theory, and sociology of law as well as constitutional, administrative, and certain aspects of civil law. The presence of the CRDP may contribute to the theoretical slant of the curriculum, with courses examining the historical and social aspects of the law.

Students have the opportunity to become immersed in an English language environment and explore the common law legal system through an exchange program with Osgoode Hall. Approximately three to ten students per year spend three semesters at Osgoode. Any student from Faculté de droit à Montréal can spend one year at Osgoode after the completion of their civil law degree at Montréal and get their common law degree as well.

Students who want to go farther afield can apply to participate in the exchange program with Université Poitiers in France. In third year students can spend one semester in Poitiers and the credits will count towards their degree from Université de Montréal and students from Poitiers can attend the Faculté de droit à Montréal. Approximately ten to fifteen students participate in the exchange. A law degree is four years in France and students can take a fourth year at Poitiers.

Faculté de droit offers students credit for their involvement in clinical study. Approximately sixty percent of students participate in the clinic where they can be placed in one of a variety of legal environments. The clinical study program is twenty years old.

Students interested in obtaining publishing and editing experience may be interested in becoming involved with the *Editions Themis*, a law review.

For the past five years the Faculté de droit à Montreal has had a woman dean — Madame Hélène Dumont — and it has more women students and faculty than any other law school in Canada. Even at the graduate level, approximately fifty percent of the students are women.

WHERE THE PROGRAM COULD IMPROVE

The large size of the law school and the financial constraints placed on the faculty have provided students with few opportunities to practise their lawyering skills. It is possible for students to go through the entire three years of the program without participating in a moot court exercise. There are relatively few practical courses, given the size of the curriculum, and students who apply to take them are chosen by lottery. Not all students are successful in securing a place. As a result, students may not know whether litigation is something they would be good at or not. The Faculté de droit à Montréal is a traditional law school which emphasises the theoretical aspects of law.

The large size of the law school provides students with the advantages of a broad selection of courses and teaching styles, but the down side is the large class size and the increased competitive spirit.

ON MONTREAL

Université de Montréal's campus is located only five kilometres north of downtown Montréal. Most of the students attending the Faculté de droit live at home, but for those who are from not from Montréal, housing is affordable and available close to campus. The excellent transit system makes it easy to live farther from campus for even more reasonable rents and it is advisable to use the transit since parking on or near campus is a problem.

Living in Montréal during the continued talks on unity exposes students daily to the national debate. The student body is not all of one view, but because the student body is almost completely Francophone there is a common ground of understanding and little political tension.

WHAT THE STUDENTS SAY

(Pseudonyms have replaced the following students' names)

The Strengths of the Program

"Civil law in general is very strong. There are a lot of professors who are authorities in this area." Marie, articling student

"There is a good choice of courses and a lot of professors are practising law at the same time, so they are not just teaching theory." Denise LL.L. '92

"When you are applying for your stage, most firms tell you that they regard Université de Montréal as having a very strong curriculum." Zoe LL.L. '92

"One of the best things is the student life. It is a large school but it can be small if you go to the social activities and get involved. In first year you are divided into four sections of seventy people and each class has its own classroom and you have the same desk all year. You get to know the people in your section very well." Cleo LL.L. '92

"There are so many things you can get involved in like the yearbook, newspaper or other activities where you get to know students from all years." Pamela LL.L. '92

"There is a very good atmosphere at Montréal. The people are younger than in common law schools and they are not married so they are more involved in the school and there are lots of things to do. We are also involved in the community to help those who need it. I think you need to have contacts when you are a lawyer and activities are a good way to meet people." Denise LL.L. '92

"You can get involved in legal aid in second or third year and it is worth one course. Legal Aid serves the entire university community and gives students advice, tells them what their options are, or tells them how to do things; but we can't represent them in court since we haven't passed the bar. This was a good aspect of what I did in my third year because I got to apply what I learned to real people." Caroline, articling student

"In second year I was matched up with another student. We picked a case in an area of law, going through each step and all the paperwork. We presented our case in front of a real judge and competed with another team. This way you get to feel if you want to litigate or not. It's a lot of work and it lasts all year for six credits. It was very interesting. Other students did a research paper of about forty pages on their own under the supervision of a professor. You can also work for a teacher as a research assistant for three credits." Pamela LL.L. '92

Where the Program Could Improve

"In second year the moot court is only open to around seventy students who are picked by lottery, and in third year there is a moot but again but it is limited and successful candidates are chosen by grades. You can go through your three years without being in a moot or doing a final argument." Caroline, articling student

"Not too many students got to present a case like I did. You have to apply and you are selected. There is a lot of talk of cutting this program but I think they should offer more." Pamela LL.L. '92

"It is too big and there is not enough money per student. Not everyone can do a moot and there isn't the same contact with the professors. I am in third year and I still have fifty students in my class." Denise LL.L. '92

"There are too many students and the groups are too big. In the more popular classes you can have groups of eighty to ninety and you can't get through the course material because there are too many questions." Pamela LL.L. '92

"There is a lot of competition, especially in second year, when you are applying to law firms. You have to have good grades to get in, good grades to stay in, and good grades to get hired by good firms or to get into master's programs. There is a lot of competition. I almost gave up after first year." Pamela LL.L. '92

"You feel competitive in the first year of law school since when you start you want to be the best litigator. The major firms choose students in first term of second year." Leon LL.L. '92

"The library is not open very late at night and it closes during the Christmas holidays. When I was working on the Jessup moot competition it was a nightmare since we had to work at the library within the times posted. The administration of the school is not very flexible." Cleo LL.L. '92

"They should try to get students with more mixed backgrounds in terms of race, religion, and social background to get more insight. At Montréal, law school is a series of courses whereas at Osgoode it is more of a process and more of a formation of ideas. You are always asked about your views on aspects and problems of the law. At Montréal you get out of classes and party." Leon, articling student (took part in the exchange program with Osgoode)

"There are not many Japanese, Chinese, or Black students in the faculty of law although there are in the other faculties. Maybe they don't apply." Pamela LL.L. '92

"It would be nice to have a national program. We can't do our common law degree at the Université de Montréal but there is an agreement with Osgoode and Dalhousie where you can get a common law degree in only one more year." Zoe LL.L. '92

"Maybe the program should last four years since there are still so many things I haven't seen. I didn't take classes in bankruptcy and seizure because there was not enough time. It would be nice if we had a national program and a joint M.B.A./LL.L. McGill is the only school in Quebec to offer these two programs." Michel LL.L. '92

Controversies

"In Montréal, feminism is not an issue. For one thing the Dean is a woman and we are not doing law because we are women, we are just doing it. At least sixty percent of the student population are women." Caroline LL.L. '92

"Traditionally, law is regarded as a bourgeoisie education and is not interested in issues. People are more active at McGill. Here the climate is totally apolitical." Cleo LL.L. '92

"Gender issues are dealt with by the teachers. A lot of women teachers incorporate it into their classes. If something is sexist it gets immediate attention and an immediate solution. Sixty-five percent of the class are women so there is no need to be aggressive." Zoe LL.L. '92

"We are politically aware but the questions we focus on are not always the same. There is no anxiety over the separatist issue. Not all Québecers feel the same about it. When Francophones talk to Francophones we are not of the same mind but we can still understand each other since we are of similar backgrounds." Zoe LL.L. '92

"People are very interested in politics. They write about it in the paper and they talk about it in class. They have opinions and are not afraid to share them." Pamela LL.L. '92

On Faculty

"There is a very good relationship with the professors. The professors are very involved with how their students are doing. A few young professors have been hired and they will sit with you at the cafés, and if you don't understand something you can always ask them." Marie, articling student

"Pierre Paul Côte is lively, interesting, loves teaching, and it shows. He likes to be with students and is always available to talk. He teaches corporate law, contracts, and corporate finance." Cleo LL.L. '92

"Christianne Dubreuil is a new teacher who teaches insurance. She practised law before she came to Université de Montréal and she presents a practical point of view." Marie, articling student

"Jean Pineau teaches civil law. He is someone you respect. He knows what he is talking about." Michel LL.L. '92

"Louise-Hélène Richard teaches company law. She is young, dynamic, knowledgeable, and very approachable. She follows her notes and you understand everything." Pamela LL.L. '92

Other Comments

"I found first year hard and it took time for me to learn to adapt. Don't decide if you like law school or not in first year. You have to give it time." Caroline, articling student

"It is good to know English. You will often be working with Anglophones, especially if you want to work in the big firms in downtown Montréal and during the interviews the lawyers would ask you questions in English to determine how well you could speak it." Caroline, articling student

"You need to know English well since a lot of the judgements are in English." Michel LL.L. '92

"Don't just restrict yourself to law. If your focus is just on law it is too narrow. It is better to study something else first. Twenty-three is too young to be a lawyer." Denise LL.L. '92

"If you already have a degree, do not be afraid to participate even if the people are younger than you. If you are from out of province it might be a shock to have nineteen-year-olds studying law but they are serious; give them a chance." Cleo LL.L. '92

Université D'Ottawa/ University of Ottawa *

■ **INQUIRIES**
Faculté de droit
Civil Law Section
Université d'Ottawa
57 Louis Pasteur
Ottawa, Ontario
KIN 6N5
(613) 564-2254

*NOTE: At the Université d'Ottawa/University of Ottawa it is possible to obtain a degree in civil law, which is required for practise in Québec, or common law, which is required for all provinces in Canada except Québec. For information on the common law degree please see the University of Ottawa under the common law section.

ADMISSIONS INFORMATION

■ **APPLICATION DEADLINE DATE FOR ADMISSIONS**
1 March

■ **REQUIRED TO SUBMIT**

General Applicants

- Official copies of all secondary and post-secondary university academic transcripts

Mature and Native applicants

- Supplementary information form
- Résumé
- Two letters of recommendation

■ **EDUCATION REQUIREMENT**

Applicants are required to have completed the Québec "Diplôme d'études collégiales" (D.E.C.) or the equivalent or an undergraduate university degree or the equivalent.

■ **AVERAGE GPA**

not available

■ **TEST D'ADMISSION EN DROIT CIVIL SCORE**

not available

■ **RATIO OF APPLICANTS TO REGISTRATIONS**

6 : 1

■ **SIZE OF INCOMING CLASS**

180

■ **CAN YOU DEFER ACCEPTANCE**

No

■ **APPLICATION FEE**

$15 application fee plus $30 evaluation fee
$20 fee for "Test d'admission en droit civil"

■ **TUITION FEE**

The 1992-93 tuition fee will be $2,082 for Canadian students and $7,138 for non-exempt Foreign students.

CLASS PROFILE

■ **AVERAGE AGE OF STUDENTS ENTERING THE PROGRAM**

21

■ **PERCENTAGE OF THE CLASS WHO ARE WOMEN**

64%

■ **PERCENTAGE OF WOMEN WHO ARE TENURED FACULTY:**

24%

■ **PERCENTAGE OF THE CLASS WITH:**

D.E.C.	61%
D.E.C. plus one or two years of university	12%
a university degree	18%
other	9%

■ **PROFILE OF LL.L. POPULATIONS**

For all three years of the program

Mature Students	17% (31)
Native Students	2% (4)
Minority Students	n/a

OTHER RELATED PROGRAMS

A one-year Certificat en Droit General is offered through the faculty of Civil Law on a part-time basis to be completed in two or three years. It is useful for people wanting a general understanding of the law, but the Certificat program is not designed to prepare students for the practice of law and is entirely distinct from the undergraduate program. Completion of the Certificat program does not give an applicant advanced standing if they decide to apply to the LL.L. program.

At the undergraduate level there is the Programme de licence en droit civil and a programme de droit notarial.

At the Master level, there is the LL.L./Master of Business Administration, Master of Law (Constitutional and Administrative Law, Human Rights, and Comparative Law are privileged fields).

The Master and Ph.D. degrees in law are done jointly with Common Law. An LL.D. Doctoral programme in research is open to those who have already demonstrated a capacity for scholarly research and writing.

The number of students admitted to the part-time program is determined by the section yearly and is available only to students who cannot study full-time for very specific reasons such as single parent responsibilities that does not permit full-time studies or a physical or learning disability that makes full-time studies difficult. It is not structured nor meant to be a program that permits persons to complete a law degree while working full-time. The part-time program must be completed within six years.

ADMISSIONS REQUIREMENTS

Applicants applying to the Civil Law Section of the Faculty of Law apply directly to the Application Centre at Guelph instead of applying to the Faculty of Law at the Université d'Ottawa. A basic requirement of the Civil Law program is proficiency in oral and written French and a good knowledge of

English. Evidence of an applicant's proficiency in French is shown by having attended a French school or by having a good score on the Test d'admission en Droit Civil. Where there is any doubt of proficiency on the part of the Admissions Committee, applicants may be interviewed.

There are three categories of admission for the Civil Law Program at Ottawa: General, Mature, and Native. Approximately eighty percent of the applicant pool are in the General Admissions Category, and within this group there are equal numbers of applicants with a Diplôme d'études Collégiales (D.E.C.) and a university degree. The decision to admit applicants in this group is determined almost completely by the cumulative academic average and the score on the Test d'Admission. These two factors are put in an admissions formula to produce an index score upon which the admissions decision is based.

The Test d'admission is an aptitude test developed by the Université de Montréal as a language and culturally corrected alternate to the LSAT. The Test d'Admission is written once a year and applicants must apply by 1 April to be invited to write it. The test is made up of four parts with the first three parts testing general aptitude and the fourth part testing skills such as analytical thinking and reading comprehension specific to the area of law.

In terms of the calculation of the academic average, each applicant's academic average is looked at in relation to everybody else's and it is translated into the same scoring scale as used by the Test d'Admission (ie. twenty to eighty). To ensure that no one is put at a disadvantage, applicants' academic averages from CEGEPs are compared as a group and, similarly, applicants with academic averages from universities are compared as a group.

The translated academic average is then put into an admissions formula where it is designated a weight of sixty percent and the Test d'Admission score is given a weight of forty percent. The resulting index scores are then ranked from the top down and offers are sent out accordingly.

An admissions formula is not used when reviewing applications from mature and native applicants. Applicants in the Mature Category must be out of school for a minimum of five years with significant work or other achievements which would persuade the committee that they could succeed in the program. Along with academic performance, reference letters, achievements in the work place, and perhaps an interview are part of the criteria used in the decision-making process. Native applicants who are not applying under the general category will take a Programme d'Admissions Predroit en Français in the summer for seven weeks and their admission is usually conditional upon its successful completion. This program was established in the summer of 1990 and is funded by the Ministry of Indian and Northern Affairs.

CHARACTER OF THE SCHOOL

The Université d'Ottawa's Faculty of Law is unique in Canada and maybe the world. The two main legal traditions of Civil and Common law are taught in the same faculty and the same building. Students wishing to study Common Law can choose to study in English or in French, but they do not have to be bilingual. The combination of Common Law in both official languages, and the presence of Civil Law in French, makes the Université d'Ottawa's Faculty of Law distinct.

National unity issues have perhaps heightened the existing tensions between the French Civil Law and English Common Law students. Friendships between the groups are neither natural nor forthcoming. Both groups are housed in the same building to encourage integration but, for most students, interaction is negligible. The development of camaraderie and understanding is time consuming and must be purposefully sought out. Most students have neither the time nor the inclination.

Most of the students in the Civil Law program come from the Montréal area of Québec directly from CEGEPs. They have left behind their circle of friends and family and there is a strong sense of camaraderie among them. For many, it is their first time living away from home and they depend on each other for support through the difficult first year. There is a fair amount of anxiety of students in their first year since the attrition rate has been as high as approximately forty percent (the majority of these are failures and some withdrawals).

STRENGTHS OF THE PROGRAM

The Université d'Ottawa's Faculty of Law, Civil Law Section, is located in a common law province and is the only civil law faculty in Canada outside of the province of Québec. The faculty takes its strength from its geographic situation of being located in the capital of Canada. Public Law is an area of strength with good relationships between the faculty and many departments of the federal and Ontario government.

The Faculty of Law, Civil Law Section, is also actively developing relations with foreign universities and facilitates communications with departments of federal government with these people. The Civil Law Section assisted in the development of Canadian Studies in Argentina. Within the last five years, the faculty has entered into agreements with six or seven universities in South America to begin an exchange of professors, students, and legal material, and to attract foreign students to the Master's and Ph.D. programs.

"Part of our mandate is to accentuate the role of developing these [international] relationships in the future, but we are a faculty of a university and, therefore, our first mission is to give the best training to our students," comments André Braën, Dean of the Faculty of Law, Civil Law Section.

The Université d'Ottawa's Faculty of Law library itself serves the needs of both the common and civil law sections. It is rich in droit canadien et québécois and there are also important collections in Comparative Law, Constitutional Law, Administrative Law, International Law, and Human Rights, which are the fields of concentration for Graduate Studies in the Faculty of Law. The Human Rights Research and Education Centre, established in the Faculty of Law in 1981, has developed the largest public collection in Canada of human rights documents.

In addition to the Université d'Ottawa's Faculty of Law library, students have access to the libraries of the Supreme Court of Canada (the richest and most important of law libraries in Canada), the Department of Justice, other libraries of departments and institutions of the Federal Government, and the National Library of Canada.

WHERE THE PROGRAM COULD IMPROVE

Although the concept of having French and English, Common and Civil Law together to encourage interaction seems rational, in reality it does not achieve its goal to the extent one might think. The Common Law and Civil Law Sections are quite isolated physically — in that they are on different floors — and administratively, in that there are two Deans, two admissions processes and administrations, and two separate student societies. A definite and concerted effort on the part of the student will be required to take advantage of the opportunity that exists.

The last time a new faculty member was hired was in 1989, so little rejuvenation of the established faculty has taken place. The students interviewed expressed concern over the inflexibility of the administration and faculty who, in their opinion, resisted change in terms of evaluation.

Ottawa's institutional economy has had a negative effect on the commercial law area. It is difficult to get practitioners who speak French and practise civil law outside of Québec. (Only common law is practised outside of Québec.)

Each year, four or five students in the Civil Law Section pursue editorial experience by working as assistants with the *Revue Generale de Droit* and *Revue Femmes et Droit*. Also a Legal Information Clinic is operated by students.

ON OTTAWA

The campus of the Université d'Ottawa is situated in the heart of downtown, a ten-minute walk from the Rideau Centre, the Market, and the Rideau Canal. The faculty of law is completely self-contained in Fauteux Hall. Student lockers are in the basement, classes are all held in Fauteux Hall, and the library is on the top two floors of the five-storied building. Overground tunnels give accessibility to cafeterias, some residences, and social science buildings.

One student described the winters in Ottawa as "real winters," cold but fun, with Winterlude, and some students and professors skating to school. In February, the faculty and students get together and organize a Law Show with skits and satire. In the summers, the bike paths are great.

Ottawa has the atmosphere of a small town. "It's a quiet bureaucratic town that goes to sleep after 5 pm — a very relaxed atmosphere to study in," commented one student. If excitement is what you are looking for, the bars in Hull stay open until 3 am. Compared to the cost of living in Montréal, Ottawa is an expensive city to live. A one-bedroom apartment within walking distance may be priced around $400. The vacancy rate in Ottawa is about one percent. There is no problem finding accommodation but it is not a tenant's market. In Hull, the vacancy rate is 4.5 percent and it is cheaper, but the time taken in travelling to and from the campus is a factor. Residence accommodation is also available.

WHAT THE STUDENTS SAY

(Pseudonyms have replaced the following students' names)

The Strengths of the Program

"We are a very small faculty, with a class size of sixty in first year and thirty to forty in second year. We have a good relationship with the professors and they get to know us by name. We all come from Québec and are away from home facing the same predicament. Therefore, we are a very tight-knit group." Sylvie LL.L. '94

"I really appreciate the friendly ambience in class and the atmosphere of a small family. . . . Most of my circle of friends are at the university and we are developing a network that we can use later." Etienné LL.L. '93

"We are a faculty of four hundred people in all three years so it is personalized, but we get the resources of approximately one thousand people because of common law." Etienné LL.L. '93

"There is a good mix between all years of classes. When first-year students come in they are assigned second- or third-year students that they can call on. This has been of some help to some people." Robert LL.L. '92

"Ottawa is very strong in public law and provides you with a general traditional training." Claudette, articling student

"All the library facilities are very good." Angie LL.L. '93

"In second year we had a moot court. The moot can take around seventy people which is a large proportion of the second-year class, so it is easy to get involved." Etienné LL.L. '93

"I am involved in the Pliqnauet (civil law) mooting competition between the civil law universities. It lasts all weekend and it is a really good experience because you get to write a factum and prepare a plea lasting around twenty minutes. We practise three to four times in front of practitioners and faculty. A judge from the Supreme Court helps us with our pleas before the competition." Jeanne-Marie LL.L. '92

"Since we are located in Ottawa, there are lots of jobs available for students as lawyers with the federal government, and if you are doing research you can talk to the ministers who are specialist in their fields." Thérèse LL.L. '92

Where the Program Could Improve

"The administration could be more receptive to the students' demands regarding one hundred percent finals. . . . I would like the administration to be interested in what we have to say. They are not listening to us. Everything that we propose is defeated." Thérèse LL.L. '92

"When we get into second or third year we should be in a position to have an input into what decisions are the most appropriate ones with the administration. There is a big line between administration and students." Robert LL.L. '92

"There is some difficulty finding professors to teach elective classes in corporate commercial law since there are not many practitioners who want to teach in Ottawa." Angie LL.L. '93

"We don't have a lot of teachers that have specialties in areas other than public law, human resources, or commercial law." Jeanne-Marie LL.L. '92

"You come in wanting to change the world but the first obstacle you get is your own faculty who encourage you to get freedom of expression and to take the initiative but want you to do it elsewhere." Jeanne-Marie LL.L. '92

"It is easier to get into the Université d'Ottawa than Université de Montréal, but compared to other schools a lot of people fail in first year. There are approximately 195 students in first year and in second year this drops to about 110." Claudette, articling student

"I wanted to have access to classes in other faculties but this wasn't possible."
Claudette, articling student
"There should be more emphasis on research and writing skills; for example,
I don't know how to update an article. I did it maybe once four years ago."
Claudette, articling student

Controversies

"In civil law we don't see the feminist or economic point of view. In our
courses they teach the basic law." Angie LL.L. '93
"I have noticed the difference between the two faculties [common and civil
law]. Common law students are more likely to protest. We are not like sheep,
but I am just kind of sick of the constitutional issues and others. I just want
to focus on my studies." Robert LL.L. '92
"There is no unity between common law and civil law sections. It is only a
factor when we go outside the faculty." Thérèse LL.L. '92
"We have an update program for aboriginal peoples and throughout their
degree they can have tutors. There is some controversy over this because some
people say why do it for them and not others." Jeanne Marie LL.L. '92

On Faculty

"We may not have some of the big name faculty like Université de Montréal
but they give you both sides of the issue. If they write the book in the area,
they are going to give you their perspective. The younger faculty are more
dynamic and can relate more to student problems because their law degree
wasn't that long ago for them." Thérèse LL.L. '92
"Yvon Duplessis teaches environmental law and discourse. He has conviction
and believes in what he teaches." Albert, articling student
"Denis Nadeau was one of the best teachers I have ever had. He was an
excellent communicator although his exams were very tough. He taught
labour law and administrative law." Claudette, articling student
"Benôit Pelletier is a good professor. He has worked in the federal government and teaches labour law." Jeanne-Marie LL.L. '92

Other Comments

"Personally, I believe that people should be a little older before they come to
law school. It's a problem with maturity. When you come in out of CEGEP and
you are only nineteen, you are not mature enough. Law school isn't hard —
it is just the adjustment to being away from home and the stress of law school."
Sylvie LL.L. '94
"A lot of lawyers consider Ottawa a lesser school since it is easier to get in

and, therefore, they think it is easier to graduate, but this is not true. It is a really tough school. I think the reputation of Ottawa is getting better because Ottawa students are getting good jobs." Robert LL.L. '92

"First year is a frustrating, hellish experience. In second year they overload you because of the moot and in third year you have the same work load, but you are used to is so we are a bit more relaxed." Thérèse LL.L. '92

"We don't have a lot of courses on Women and the Law or Aboriginal courses, but we know the basic law and if you want to specialize you can do it in the field. If you get too specific you might not find a job." Thérèse LL.L. '92

"I always saw law as a tool rather than an end in itself. In first year I found it boring, but you shouldn't get depressed since this isn't really what it's all about. In second and third year you have more choices and when you graduate you can do what you want." Claudette, articling student

"We had sexist teachers but the women don't say anything. They don't see the difficulties they will have to confront in the work force." Albert, articling student

"It's not difficult. You don't have to work every night, but you have to learn how to study and select what is important to study and what is not." Albert, articling student

Université de Sherbrooke

- **INQUIRIES**
  Bureau du registraire
  Université de Sherbrooke
  Sherbrooke, Québec
  J1K 2R1
  (819) 821-7514

ADMISSIONS INFORMATION

- **APPLICATION DEADLINE DATE FOR ADMISSIONS**
  1 March

- **REQUIRED TO SUBMIT**
  - Academic transcripts
  - Personal statements
  - Résumés
  - Reference letters
  - Tests d'aptitude aux études en droit score for applicants who have taken university courses and to mature applicants

- **EDUCATION REQUIREMENT**
  Diploma of Collégial Studies (D.E.C.) or equivalent

- **AVERAGE GPA**
  not available

- **TEST D'ADMISSION EN DROIT CIVIL SCORE**
  not available

- **RATIO OF APPLICANTS TO REGISTRATIONS**
  9.6 : 1

- **SIZE OF INCOMING CLASS**
  260

- **CAN YOU DEFER ACCEPTANCE**
  No

- **APPLICATION FEE**
  $15

- **TUITION FEE**
  The 1991-92 tuition fee is $585/term for Canadian students (Foreign students are not eligible for admission).

CLASS PROFILE

- **AVERAGE AGE OF STUDENTS ENTERING THE PROGRAM**
  22

- **PERCENTAGE OF THE CLASS WHO ARE WOMEN**
  61%

- **PERCENTAGE OF WOMEN WHO ARE TENURED FACULTY**
  1%

- **PERCENTAGE OF THE CLASS WITH:**

Completed CEGEP	70%
at least one year of University	20%

- **PROFILE OF LL.L. POPULATIONS**

Aboriginal native students	0%
Visible minority students	0%
Mature students	10%
Half-time students	1%

OTHER RELATED PROGRAMS

Master of Law in health law and a half-time program

ADMISSIONS REQUIREMENTS

There are three categories of applicants at Sherbrooke's Faculté de droit: applicants from CEGEPs, applicants with at least one year of a university education, and mature applicants. At present there is no special category for Native applicants, but it is being considered.

Approximately seventy percent of all applicants are in the category applying directly from CEGEPS, and in this category, the decision to admit is determined solely on the basis of the academic course average. Applicants within this group do not have to take the Test d'admission en droit civil, but this is currently under review and it is likely that it will be required for September 1994.

Applicants who have a **minimum of one year towards a university degree** are required to write the Test d'admission en droit civil and to have a minimum of seventy percent overall average in their university course work. A formula is used in the admissions process whereby the academic average and test scores are given a weight of fifty percent each. The results are rank ordered and applicants are offered admission from the top down until the allocated places are filled.

In the mature student category, **mature applicants** are defined as individuals who have worked for at least five consecutive years without attending an academic institution. Approximately ten percent of applicants fall in this category. Mature students are required to write the Test d'admission en droit civil as part of the admissions requirements. An average score would be in the seventy-fifth percentile and scores below the fiftieth percentile are rejected. Half to three-quarters of applicants who fall between these two values are granted interviews.

The admissions committee applies the category that is most favourable to the applicant. For example, if the applicant did poorly in university but well in CEGEP, the committee would only use the CEGEP average when making a decision. If a student has a master's degree, it is considered as part of the overall university average.

CHARACTER OF THE SCHOOL

Sherbrooke's Faculté de droit is a traditional faculty that prides itself on its practical approach to the teaching of law. The atmosphere is similar to that of a CEGEP; it has a very structured curriculum, giving students few opportunities to choose electives, and a highly regimented scheduling of classes, where students take all their classes in one room and sit at the same desk all year.

The student body is a very spirited and fun loving group. Very few students come from Sherbrooke itself. Most of the students come from the Montréal area, leaving behind their friends and family usually for the first time. When they arrive, everyone is on an equal footing since no one knows anyone else and they form close friendships. Every year students from law schools across

Canada participate in a week of social activities called the "Law Games." This began as an English law school tradition until approximately four years ago when the Francophone law schools were invited. Since that time Sherbrooke has won first prize for the law faculty with the most spirit.

STRENGTHS OF THE PROGRAM

The strength of Sherbrooke's Faculté de droit comes from the emphasis it places on providing students with a good basis in the fundamental and professional aspects of law. All courses in first and second year are compulsory, leaving third year to be filled primarily with electives. All students attending Sherbrooke's Faculté de droit have a large group of courses in common, covering the basic areas of the law.

"We instill a legal culture in our students," comments Normand Ratti, President of the Faculté de droit. Students can participate in simulated trials and competitions that are held by the faculty for the best simulated criminal law trial, civil law trial, and international law trial.

Sherbrooke's Faculté de droit does not run its own legal aid clinic, but students have the opportunity to work in the legal aid system of Québec where there is a close relationship between the faculty of law and the clinics, judges, and social centres. Thirty-five to forty students participate in the legal aid system each year.

The school spirit within the Faculté de droit is very strong, as is the relationship between the students and the professors. The student-faculty ratio is very good and the class sizes are relatively small. The incoming class of 260 are divided into small groups so that class sizes in first and second year do not exceed sixty students. In third-year classes, there might be thirty-five students in a class.

Students who wish to become familiar with the common law system outside Québec have the opportunity to participate in the summer exchange program at Dalhousie University in Halifax. Specialized concentrations in Notorial Law and Health Law are also available.

WHERE THE PROGRAM COULD IMPROVE

The emphasis on the practical and fundamental aspects of law is so strong at Sherbrooke's Faculté de droit that there is little attention paid to the more theoretical aspects of law. There are few courses offered that study law in a social or comparative context, and because of the few electives available in the program there is little opportunity to take these courses. The faculty have been more involved with teaching in the past, but a stronger emphasis has been placed on research recently. The administration has identified this as an area that could be improved and, as a result, the requirements for faculty promotion have had a stronger research component added.

Faculty are involved in *Le Revue de Droit de Université de Sherbrooke* but students participation is limited to proof-reading only.

Sherbrooke's Faculté de droit is a young faculty and the people who founded the program are still actively involved. In fact, most of the faculty are either part of the original founding group or are graduates of Sherbrooke's Faculté de droit. This has perhaps narrowed the outlook and direction of the law faculty.

Financially, the faculty is coping but is still under considerable restraint and therefore is limited in any new initiatives. During the years 1980-86 the faculty had a fifteen million dollar deficit that used up one-eighth of their budget in 1985. Presently the deficit has been reduced to five million, allowing money to be injected back into the faculty. However, there are still insufficient funds for growth.

ON SHERBROOKE

Université de Sherbrooke's campus is situated on top of a hill with a beautiful view of the countryside. The university is about a fifteen- to twenty-minute bus ride from downtown, and the bus system is excellent. Around the university accommodation is available and reasonable.

Sherbrooke is a quiet city surrounded by countryside, removed from the hectic pace of Montréal which is only an hour and a half away. Cross-country-skiers will appreciate the availability of ski trails within a five minute drive, and for downhill skiers, the hills can be seen from the Faculté de droit. Mt. Orford is only a twenty-minute drive and Vermont is close by as well. The atmosphere of the town is friendly, and approximately thirty to forty percent of the population is Anglophone.

WHAT THE STUDENTS SAY

(Pseudonyms have replaced the following students' names)

The Strengths of the Program

"Sherbrooke takes a very practical approach with little theory. They try to teach you as much about the present sense of law as possible. For example, you start with article number one of the civil code and proceed on from there. The program is oriented towards the written law, not the theory." Albert LL.L. '92

"Sherbrooke has a general program with the first two years mandatory and four out of the ten courses in third year being compulsory. We have no choice but to have a general field of law. The curriculum has now changed to allow some optional courses in second year. Even so, a general program is good because if you don't know what your field is you will never know if you like it or not. I never would have taken insurance law, but I had to because it was compulsory. I found that I loved it and that is the area that I will practise in." Catherine LL.L. '92

"Everyday the classes are structured the same. You have three hours of classes, five days a week, either from 8:30-11:30 am or 1-4 pm for thirteen weeks. The next term you switch so that if you went in the morning you now go in the afternoon. The sameness gives stability for young people coming out of CEGEP." Cynthia LL.L. '92

"There are no snobs at Sherbrooke. Professors are not put on a pedestal and there are no gangs of students from upper or lower town." Gill LL.L. '94

"Sherbrooke is very small and non-competitive and people help each other. Most students are young and they aren't there because they always wanted to be a lawyer, but because they just thought they would try it. It is not very competitive at all." Albert LL.L. '92

"We have a good library and a very good clinical legal activities program where you can work in different settings from working for someone from legal aid to working in a consumer goods environment." Gill LL.L. '94

Where the Program Could Improve

"Sherbrooke is known to be a very technical school. Some people say law school should prepare you intellectually. You should know the principles so you can approach problems, but Sherbrooke's curriculum seems to be designed with a view to preparing students to write the bar. People often congratulate themselves for the high pass rate that Sherbrooke has on the bar exams but in effect, Sherbrooke is modelled on the curriculum of bar school. . . . You learn by rote but it is the principles that should be learned in school. If you are given a problem you should know how to go about solving it." Jean-Yves LL.L. '92

"There is a lack of writing courses. There is only one writing course in first year. Research and writing is very important for a lawyer but you are not prepared for that. The program doesn't efficiently emphasize writing and research. You could go through the whole degree without writing a paper." Jean-Yves LL.L. '92

"Students seem more concerned about preparing for exams than exploring interesting issues in the law. ... There is no feminism and law course or native law course." Jean-Yves LL.L. '92

"They accept so many students and they try to weed them out. The first day of classes they tell you to look to your left and look to your right; one of these people won't be here next year. We went from sixty in first semester to forty in second semester." Albert LL.L. '92

"There are no large law firms in Sherbrooke and therefore there are no big name practitioners that they can call in." Albert LL.L. '92

"The relationship between the administration and the students is not good. You never know when or how they make their decisions. The university should be made for students and they should have more say than just having one place on the administrative board." Frank LL.L. '92

"The administration should be more friendly. They stick so much to the rules that they forget to be teachers. The secretaries are very helpful and nice though." Cynthia LL.L. '92

"Out of 750 students, including the bar, there is only one black student, two Egyptians, and two Vietnamese students including myself." Cynthia LL.L. '92

"It is a traditional school and they don't want to move too fast. It's too bad since the young teachers have good ideas. The established professors feel they have a good formula and don't want to mess around with it." Charles LL.L. '92

"The professors teach theory during the year but the exams are practical. There should be more individual work and assignments during the year instead of one hundred percent finals. We should be applying all the rules of law together like in a paper concerning a case and be noted on this." Catherine LL.L. '92

Controversies

"The law book co-operative is an issue. Law books are so expensive that the students have tried to set up a co-operative, but the law faculty and the book store have an agreement that there will be no other bookstore on campus. This shows how conservative they are. It is much easier to support the book store than explore alternatives." Gill LL.L. '94

"Controversy doesn't exist here. The students are the least controversial I have ever seen. They don't complain very much at all." Charles LL.L. '92

"We don't really talk about politics. There are Liberals and Parti Québécois but we know what we believe in and at the same time we respect each other. At the university most people know two, or sometimes three languages, so language is not usually an issue. If someone is going to take your language away from you that's one thing, but if someone is talking in front of you in English then that is OK." Frank LL.L. '92

On Faculty

"The professors are extremely accessible and very well organized to the point of almost spoon feeding you. You get the impression that they care about you. It is not a snotty or obnoxious atmosphere." Jean-Yves LL.L. '92

"Robert Kouri wins the teaching award every year and is unanimously appreciated. His specialty is medical law and he is a prolific writer. Professor Kouri combines pedagogic skills with knowledge in this area." Jean-Yves LL.L. '92

"Suzanne Nootens teaches health law and droit de personne. She was a medical doctor in Europe before she came to Sherbrooke. Even though I wasn't interested in that topic, you could see that she took the time to go beyond the material we covered. She had a vision and could consider other things." Gill LL.L. '94

Other Comments

"In first year you have four sections of about seventy people. . . . In second year you have three sections of about seventy people. In my year, fourteen people had left by Christmas time." Valerie LL.L. '94

"Start studying from day one and work regularly but also keep time for yourself. If you become too much a part of the process you can become narrow-minded and your sense of self becomes your grades. Keep your ideals even though at times you feel you have no impact on your life and you are being told what to do and how to do it." Gill LL.L. '94

"First grow up. It is awful going to law school too young. You can learn it but you don't understand it. You are too young at eighteen. Another degree is not necessary academically, but in terms of maturity it is. You have to be open-minded and have read a bit. Understand the basics of politics and the history of Canada." Frank LL.L. '92

"Getting a degree first before going to law school is important. It gives you confidence. In the first year you get a thirty percent midterm and a lot of students fail this badly. This can be shattering, but if you already had a degree you would be more confident that you could do it. Also, having a degree helps structure your mind. When someone is lecturing you would know what is important and what isn't." Cynthia LL.L. '92

"You really work hard and you don't make a lot of money. It is a vocation. Don't do it for the money, do it because you want to help people." Charles LL.L. '92

Unique Characteristics of Law Schools

- **Calgary**'s Faculty of Law is the youngest English language common law school in Canada and it modeled itself after another young law school, Windsor. The founding dean of Calgary's Faculty of Law, John McLaren, was one of the early deans at Windsor's Law School. As a result, they have a common bond — an emphasis on access to a legal education.

- **Université Laval** teaches civil law and is the only law school in Canada where you can enter the program in January and progress by course prerequisite instead of by year.

- **McGill University** is the only university in Canada to offer a National Program where students can obtain a civil law degree required to practise law in the Province of Québec, and a common law degree, required to practise law in the rest of the provinces, in four years at the school. Graduates of this program can practise law anywhere in Canada.

- **Moncton**'s École de droit, founded in 1978, is the youngest Faculty of Law in Canada and the smallest. Moncton's Faculté de droit was the first law school to offer students the opportunity to study common law in French and it remains the only French university in Canada to offer the joint Common Law and Master in Business Administration program in French.

- **Faculté de droit à Montréal** teaches civil law and is the largest law school in Canada, established 113 years ago.

- **Osgoode Hall Law School** is the largest common law school in Canada and offers four intensive programs in Advanced Business Law, Criminal Law, Immigration and Refugee Law, and Poverty Law at Parkdale Community Legal Services.

- The **University of Ottawa/Université d'Ottawa**'s Faculty of Law is unique in Canada and maybe the world. The two main legal traditions of Civil and Common law are taught in the same faculty and the same building. Within the Common Law Section, applicants can choose to study in English and in French, but they do not have to be bilingual.

- The **University of Toronto**'s Faculty of Law is among the most highly selective law schools in North America and has the highest standards in Canada, based on a combination of undergraduate academic record and LSAT score.

- **University of Victoria**'s Faculty of Law is the only law faculty in Canada to offer a Co-operative Law Program.
- **University of Windsor** is the only university that has a program where you can become qualified to practise in Canada and the U.S. with a combined LL.B/J.D.

LAW SCHOOLS WITH HALF-TIME PROGRAMS

- University of Alberta
- University of British Columbia
- Dalhousie University
- University of Manitoba
- Université de Montréal
- Queen's University
- University of Saskatchewan
- Université de Sherbrooke
- University of Toronto
- University of Ottawa, Common Law Section
- University of Windsor
- University of Victoria

LAW SCHOOLS WITH EXCHANGE PROGRAMS

- Université Laval has an exchange with the University of Western Ontario for civil law students wanting some exposure to common law. Students can also exchange with Aix-Marseille in France.
- Université de Montréal has an exchange with Osgoode Hall Law School for civil law students wanting some exposure to common law. Students can also exchange with Poitiers Université in France.
- Osgoode Hall Law School has exchanges with the Faculty of Law, University of Kobe, Japan, or the Southwest Institute of Political Science and Law, Chongqing, China.
- Univerité de Sherbrooke offers a summer exchange program, for civil law students wanting some exposure to common law, at Dalhousie University in Halifax.

- University of Victoria offers an exchange program with Chulalongkorn University in Bangkok, Thailand, or other acceptable foreign institutions for one term in second or third year.
- University of Windsor students can spend a semester studying law in London, England, through the London Law Program of the University of Detroit, Mercy's Law School.

LAW SCHOOLS WHICH OFFER BOTH CIVIL AND COMMON LAW DEGREES

- Université d'Ottawa/University of Ottawa
- McGill University

LAW SCHOOLS WITH WOMEN DEANS

- University of Alberta, Acting Dean, Ann McLellan
- University of British Columbia, Dean Lynn Smith
- University of Calgary, Acting Dean Sheilah Martin
- Université de Montréal, Dean Hélène Dumont (1992 last year)
- University of Victoria, Dean Maureen Maloney

RECENT WINNERS IN MOOTING COMPETITIONS

Gale Cup Moot

1992	First Place:	Dalhousie University
	Second Place:	University of Calgary
	Third Place:	Osgoode Hall Law School
1991	First Place:	University of British Columbia
	Second Place:	Dalhousie University
	Third Place:	University of New Brunswick
1990	First Place:	University of Saskatchewan
	Second Place:	University of Victoria
	Third Place:	University of British Columbia

Jessup International Moot

1992	First Place:	University of Calgary
	Second Place:	McGill University
	Third Place:	Université Laval
1991	First Place:	University of Saskatchewan
	Second Place:	University of Toronto
	Third Place:	University of Calgary
1990	First Place:	University of Calgary
	Second Place:	University of Toronto
	Third Place:	Université d'Ottawa — Droit Civil

Laskin Moot

THE 1992 LASKIN MOOT

TEAMS:

First Place:	University of Ottawa — Common Law
Second Place:	Université de Montréal
Third Place:	Université Laval

FACTUMS

First Place:	McGill University
Second Place:	University of Ottawa — Common Law
Third Place:	Université Laval

ORALISTS

First Place:	R. Khana (University of Windsor)
Second Place:	B. Brun (University of Western Ontario)
	M. Baz (Université Laval)
	E. Zeitz (University of Saskatchewan)
	M. Pelletier (University of Western Ontario)
Third Place:	I. Roy (Université d'Ottawa — Droit Civil)

JUDGES DISCRETIONARY PRIZE
University of Western Ontario

THE 1991 LASKIN MOOT

TEAMS:

First Place:	University of Toronto
Second Place:	McGill University
Third Place:	Queen's University

FACTUMS

First Place: Dalhousie University
Second Place: McGill University
Third Place: Osgoode Hall Law School
                  University of Ottawa — Common Law

ORALISTS

First Place: C. Hyde (University of Ottawa — Common Law)
Second Place: D. Derstine (University of Toronto)
                  S. Sutherland (University of British Columbia)

JUDGES DISCRETIONARY PRIZE

M. Bryant (Osgoode Hall Law School)
J. Gurofsky (Western University of Ontario)

THE 1990 LASKIN MOOT

TEAMS:

First Place: Université de Ottawa — Droit Civil
Second Place: University of Toronto
Third Place: Osgoode Hall Law School

FACTUMS

First Place: University of Toronto
Second Place: University of British Columbia
                  Dalhousie University
Third Place: McGill University

ORALISTS

First Place: C. Vary (Université d'Ottawa — Droit Civil)
Second Place: T. Bulmer (University of Alberta)
Third Place: S. Landry (Université Laval)

JUDGES DISCRETIONARY PRIZE

University of Windsor

Comparative Statistics of Canadian Law Schools

The following common law information is taken from the *Summary of Committee for Law Admissions, Statistics Services and Innovations (Classi) Statistics — 1991* prepared by Brent Cotter, President of CLASSI, and Brian Mazer, Professor of Law, in November 1991.

GENERAL COMMENTS

1. The 1991 increase in the number of applications and applicants across the whole system was not as great an increase as in 1990, or as substantial as the increases in 1988 and 1989. It is, nevertheless, the largest number of applications in our history. CLASSI does not possess the information to determine conclusively whether the increase in the total number of applications represents an increase in the total number of applicants or whether applicants are making applications to more schools (applicants commonly make multiple applications to law schools). However, based upon some fairly reliable indicators, such as the number of people writing the LSAT and the relatively steady acceptance rate with respect to law schools' offers, it appears that the increases are predominantly a function of increases in applicants.

2. As well, it is the general impression of admissions personnel that the quality of the applicants is as good as it has ever been in our history, and probably a good deal better than ever. This is supported by the quantitative data (LSAT scores and academic records) on the qualifications of admitted applicants at virtually all of the law schools and the growing diversity of our student population.

3. Early indications (such as the numbers of registrants for the LSAT and the much greater than anticipated attendance at the 1991 Law Fair in Vancouver) suggest that applications to Canada's common law schools will be at similar or slightly higher levels in 1992.

4. Interest in legal education continues at record levels in common law Canada. This increased interest has not been matched by any expansion in

access to legal education. There has not been any significant increase in the number of places available to qualified applicants since the opening of three law schools in the late 1970s and 1980. Indeed, some local initiatives of limited duration intended to moderately increase the size of some law schools' first-year classes have now ended (as intended), causing the number of law school places in some regions to have declined. We can anticipate continued high demand for legal education in the next few years.

APPLICANTS AND APPLICATIONS

1. The total number of completed applications received by common law schools in 1991 was 30,400, a 4.6% increase from the 29,074 applications received in 1990. This is consistent with the general upward trend in the number of applications that has existed since 1985 when the collection of comprehensive statistics for all common law schools began. In 1985, a total of 19,045 applications were received by common law schools. The applications received in 1991 represent a 59.6% increase from those in 1985.

2. Applications from "special status" applicants (school-defined categories which include all minority applicants, mature applicants and others) increased to 4,520 in 1991 from 4,282 in 1990, an increase of 4.1%. Special status applicants have increased 223.5% from the 1,850 applications received in 1985. Applications from special status applicants presently represent 14.8% of the total pool of applications.

3. Applications from aboriginal Canadians increased to 335 from 311 in 1990 and 225 in 1989. This is an increase of 7.7% in the last year and a 48.9% increase since 1989. Since 1985 there has been an increase of 153.8% in the number of applications from aboriginal applicants. Even with this increase since 1985, however, applications from aboriginal persons represent only 1.1% of the total application pool.

4. Applications from women now represent 44.3% or 13,469, compared with 44.13% (or 12,921) in 1990. Applications from women in 1985 totalled 7,021 or 38.5% of the total pool of applications.

5. The number of applications to law schools in Ontario increased only 1.3% while the increase in the rest of the country was approximately 8.9%.

FIRST-YEAR PLACES AND THE FIRST-YEAR CLASS

6. There were approximately 2,261 places available in Canada's common law schools in 1991, compared with 2,245 places available in 1990. This is an increase of .2%. There has been an increase of 3.6%, or a total of 79 places, over approximately 2,204 places available in 1985.

7. The number of "special status" students enroled in the law schools increased to 383 (16.81% of all first-year students) from 319 (14.05%) in 1990. These numbers are substantially higher than the 254 (11.5%) special students enrolled in 1985.

8. The number of aboriginal students enroled in first-year law increased to 84 in 1991 from 60 in 1990 and 50 in 1989. This is an increase of 40.0% in the last year and an increase of 350.0% over the 24 aboriginal students enrolled in 1985. Nevertheless, native students represent only 3.68% of our first-year law student population.

9. There are 1,112 women enrolled in first-year law at Canada's common law schools in 1991. Women represent 48.79% of the total first-year class. This is the highest number and percentage of women ever enrolled in first-year law at Canada's common law schools. It is substantially higher than the 1,043 women registered in first-year law in 1990 (45.93%) and the 1,084 (47.61%) in 1989. It also reverses the only decline in the last few decades in the number of women enrolled in first-year law (1990). By comparison, in 1985, a total of 888 first-year students (40.3% of the first-year class) were women. In 1991 seven of fifteen common law schools have a first-year class with more women than men.

10. The first-year class in 1991 has a median age of 25.57 and a mean age of 25.4, compared with a median and mean age of 24.43 and 25.62, respectively, in 1990.

ONTARIO COMMON LAW SCHOOLS – COMPARATIVE STATISTICS

	ADMISSIONS CRITERIA					CLASS PROFILE				FINANCIAL	
	Deadline Date	Education Requirements	G.P.A. Average	LSAT Average Percentile	Entrance Formula	Apply Accept Ratio	Size of Incoming Class	Age Average	Women in Class	Tuition (92/93)	Application Fee
Osgoode	February 1 / May 1 for Native Appl.	2 Yrs. beyond Senior Matriculation	3.6 Range 3.2 – 4.2	83rd Range 44 – 99	Yes LSAT=1Yr. University	11:1	330	23	47%	$2,457	$40
Ottawa English	February 1	2 Full Yrs. Undergrad Studies	80%	80th Range None	None	22:1	120	26	53%	$2,124 *	Apply $15 Evaluate
Ottawa French	February 1	2 Full Yrs. Studies	80%	Not Required None	None	3:1	60	24	57%	$2,124 *	$30
Queen's	February 1	2 Full Yrs. Undergrad Studies	72% – 92% Range	81st Range 44 – 99	None	20:1	160	26	46%	$2,324 * (91/92)	$30
Toronto	February 1	3 Full Yrs. Undergrad Studies	83% Range 78% – 94.5%	93rd Range 80 – 100	None	13:1	179	25	51%	$2,230 *	$40
Western	February 1	2 Full Yrs. Undergrad Studies	80% Range 75% – 91%	89th Range 43 – 97	Yes GPA=80% LSAT=20%	18:1	155	25	46%	$2,272 *	$30
Windsor	February 1	2 Full Yrs. Undergrad Studies	N/A	N/A	None	17:1	145	27	52%	$2,277	$25

Source: These figures based on the class of 1991–1992 statistics gathered by CLASSI (Committee for Law Admissions, Statistics Services and Innovations)

* Includes student interest fee

For more detailed information please refer to the chapters on the individual law schools.

Marking System Scale Conversions

Percentage	Letter Grade	Nine Point	Four Point
90-100	A+	9	4.3
85-89	A	8	4.0
80-84	A-	7	3.7
75-79	B+	6	3.3
70-74	B	5	3.0
65-69	B-	4	2.7
60-64	C+	3	2.3
55-59	C	2	2.0
50-54	C- (or D)	1	1.7

WESTERN COMMON LAW SCHOOLS – COMPARATIVE STATISTICS

	ADMISSIONS CRITERIA						CLASS PROFILE			FINANCIAL	
	Deadline Date	Education Requirements	G.P.A. Average	LSAT Average Percentile	Entrance Formula	Apply Accept Ratio	Size of Incoming Class	Age Average	Women in Class	Tuition (92/93)	Application Fee
Alberta	February 1	2 Full Yrs. Undergrad Studies	3.8 Range 3.4 – 4.2	80th	Yes GPA = 67% LSAT = 33%	8:1	180	26	42%	$2,100*	$50
UBC	February 1	3 Full Yrs. Undergrad Studies	3.6 Range 2.7 – 4.3	83rd Range 37-99	Yes GPA = 50% LSAT = 50%	9:1	240	26	48%	$2,732*	$40 BC App. $50 Out of Prov. App.
Calgary	February 1	2 Full Yrs. Undergrad Studies	3.3 Range 1.8 – 4.0	76th Range 15 – 100	None	17:1	68	28	65%	$2,500 (approx.)	$45
Manitoba	March 1	2 Full Yrs. Undergrad Studies	3.7 Range	85th Range 49 – 99	Yes GPA = 40% LSAT = 60%	11:1	97	25	40%	$2,650	$40
Saskatchewan	Early Jan.15 Regular March 15	2 Full Yrs. Undergrad with 12 Humanity credits	3.4 Range	74th Range 47 – 99	Yes GPA = 50% LSAT = 50%	10:1	110	25	50%	$2,500 (approx.)	$35
Victoria	March 31	3 Full Yrs. Undergrad Studies	3.6 Range 3.2 – 4.2	88th Range 63 – 99	Yes GPA = 70% LSAT = 30%	18:1	100	26	53%	$2,521	$40

Source: These figures based on the class of 1991-1992 statistics gathered by CLASS! (Committee for Law Admissions, Statistics Services and Innovations)

* Includes student interest fee

For more detailed information please refer to the chapters on the individual law schools.

Marking System Scale Conversions

Percentage	Letter Grade	Nine Point	Four Point
90-100	A+	9	4.3
85-89	A	8	4.0
80-84	A-	7	3.7
75-79	B+	6	3.3
70-74	B	5	3.0
65-69	B-	4	2.7
60-64	C+	3	2.3
55-59	C	2	2.0
50-54	C-(or D)	1	1.7

EASTERN COMMON LAW SCHOOLS – COMPARATIVE STATISTICS

| | ADMISSIONS CRITERIA | | | | | CLASS PROFILE | | | FINANCIAL | |
	Deadline Date	Education Requirements	G.P.A. Average	LSAT Average Percentile	Entrance Formula	Apply Accept Ratio	Size of Incoming Class	Age Average	Women in Class	Tuition (92/93)	Application Fee
Dalhousie	February 28	Within 1 Year of degree completion	3.3 Range	81st	Yes GPA = 60% LSAT = 40%	14:1	156	25	48%	$3,063	$25
McGill	February 1	2 Full Years Undergrad Studies	80% Range	87th	None	20:1	50*	25	49%	$1,916	$40
Moncton French Common Law	Apr.30(92/93) Mar.1(93/94)	Within 1 Year of degree completion	3.2 Range	not required require French proficiency test	None	5:1	49	26	51%	$2,050	$50
UNB	March 31	3 Full Years Undergrad Studies	3.6 Range 2.8 - 4.2	N/A	Yes GPA = 60% LSAT = 40%	16:1	80	24	51%	$2,350	$25

Source: These figures based on the class of 1991–1992 statistics gathered by CLASSI (Committee for Law Admissions, Statistics Services and Innovations)

* 75% of all students are enrolled in the National 4 Year Program which confers both civil and common law degrees.

For more detailed information please refer to the chapters on the individual law schools.

Marking System Scale Conversions

Percentage	Letter Grade	Nine Point	Four Point
90–100	A+	9	4.3
85–89	A	8	4.0
80–84	A–	7	3.7
75–79	B+	6	3.3
70–74	B	5	3.0
65–69	B–	4	2.7
60–64	C+	3	2.3
55–59	C	2	2.0
50–54	C–(or D)	1	1.7

CIVIL LAW SCHOOLS – COMPARATIVE STATISTICS

	ADMISSIONS CRITERIA					CLASS PROFILE				FINANCIAL	
	Deadline Date	Education Requirements	G.P.A. Average	Admissions Test	Entrance Formula	Apply Accept Ratio	Size of Incoming Class	Age Average	Women in Class	Tuition (92/93)	Application Fee
Laval	Fall/Winter March 1 September 1	DEC or 2 Full Years Undergrad Studies	N/A	Laval test d'admission	N/A	9:1	256 (Sept) 65 (Jan) 330	N/A	N/A	$1,762	N/A
McGill	February 1	DEC	CEGEP 87% University 79% Range 67-86%	LSAT 87th or U. de Montréal test d'admission	None	6:1	90-95%*	23	57%	$1,916	$40
Montréal	March 1	DEC or 2 Full Years Undergrad Studies	N/A	U. de Montréal test d'admission	N/A	10:1	335	N/A	65%	$1,026 2 semesters	$15
Ottawa	March 1	DEC or Undergrad Degree Equivalent	N/A	U. de Montréal test d'admission	Yes GPA = 60% Test = 40%	6:1	180	21	64%	$2,082 2 semesters	$15 appl. fee $30 eval. fee $20 test fee
Sherbrooke	March 1	DEC or Equivalent	N/A	U. de Montréal test d'admission	Yes GPA = 50% Test = 50%	10:1	260	22	61%	$1,170 (91/92) 2 semesters	$15

For more detailed information please refer to the chapters on the individual law schools.

* 75% of all students are enrolled in the National 4 Year Program which confers both civil and common law degrees.

Source: These figures based on statistics from the class of 1991/92.

University	Diploma Programs			Undergraduate Programs				LLB Programs Combined with Graduate Programs									Graduate Programs		
	Legislative Drafting	Certificat en droit General	Law (DESS)	Postgraduate in Law	LLB Co-op	Programme de Droit Notarial	BA, BSc, or B.Com/LLB	MA–Phil./LLB	MBA/LLB	M.Env.Sc./LLB	M.L.S./LLB	J.D./LLB	MPA/LLB	MPM/LLB	MSW/LLB	PhD/LLB	Master of Law MLM	Doctorate	PhD Legal Philosophy
Alberta				◆					◆					◆			◆	◆	
UBC									◆								◆	◆	
Calgary																	◆		
Dalhousie									◆		◆		◆				◆	◆	
Laval				◆													◆	◆	
Manitoba																			
McGill									◆				◆		◆		◆	◆	
Moncton						◆			◆										
Montréal			◆			◆			◆				◆		◆		◆	◆	
UNB							◆*										◆		
Osgoode									◆	◆							◆	◆	
Ottawa	◆	◆							◆								◆	◆	
Queen's								◆							◆		◆		
Saskatchewan							◆										◆	◆	
Sherbrooke																	◆		
Toronto									◆								◆	◆	◆
Victoria					◆								◆						◆
Western								◆	◆										
Windsor									◆			◆							

* Only for students enrolled in these undergrad programs at UNB and St. Thomas University.

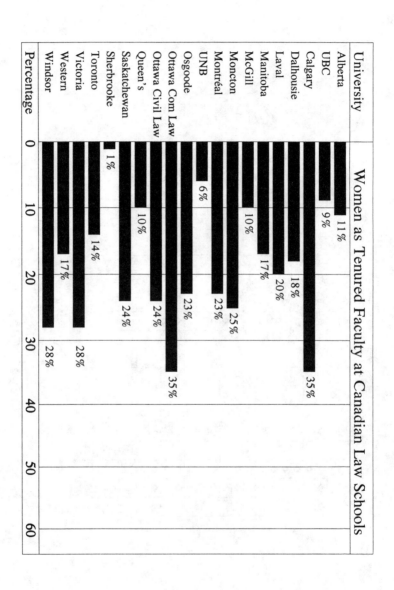

Women as Tenured Faculty at Canadian Law Schools

University	Percentage
Alberta	11%
UBC	9%
Calgary	35%
Dalhousie	18%
Laval	20%
Manitoba	17%
McGill	10%
Moncton	25%
Montréal	23%
UNB	6%
Osgoode	23%
Ottawa Com Law	35%
Ottawa Civil Law	24%
Queen's	10%
Saskatchewan	24%
Sherbrooke	1%
Toronto	14%
Victoria	28%
Western	17%
Windsor	28%

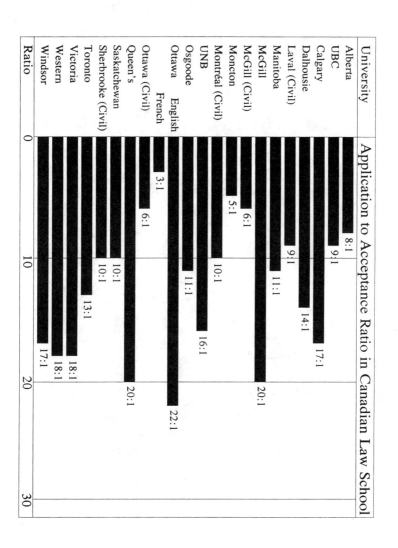

University	Application to Acceptance Ratio in Canadian Law School
Alberta	8:1
UBC	9:1
Calgary	9:1
Dalhousie	14:1
Laval (Civil)	17:1
Manitoba	11:1
McGill	6:1
McGill (Civil)	5:1
Moncton	
Montréal (Civil)	10:1
UNB	16:1
Osgoode	20:1
Ottawa	11:1
Ottawa English	22:1
Ottawa (Civil) French	3:1
Queen's	6:1
Saskatchewan	20:1
Sherbrooke (Civil)	10:1
Toronto	10:1
Victoria	13:1
Western	18:1
Windsor	18:1
	17:1

Ratio: 0 10 20 30

Location of Universities
That Offer a Law Degree

Legend For Map of Canada

1. University of Alberta
2. University of British Columbia
3. University of Calgary
4. Dalhousie University
5. Université Laval
6. McGill University
7. University of Manitoba
8. Université de Moncton
9. Université de Montréal
10. University of New Brunswick

11. Osgoode Hall Law School
12. University of Ottawa/Université d'Ottawa
13. Queen's University
14. University of Saskatchewan
15. Université de Sherbrooke
16. University of Toronto
17. University of Victoria
18. University of Western Ontario
19. University of Windsor

Addresses for Law Schools in Canada

Law Admissions
4th Floor, Law Centre
University of Alberta
Edmonton, Alberta
T6G 2H5
(403) 492-3067

Administration
Faculty of Law
University of British Columbia
1822 East Mall
Vancouver, B.C.
V6T 1Z1
(604) 822-6303

Admissions Office
Faculty of Law
University of Calgary
Calgary, Alberta
T2N 1N4
(403) 220-7222

Dalhousie Law School
Weldon Law Building
6061 University Avenue
Halifax, N.S.
B3H 4H9
(902) 494-2068

Faculté de droit
Université Laval
Pavillon Charles-De Koninck
Ste.-Foy, Québec
G1K 7P4
(418) 656-3036

Faculty of Law
The University of Manitoba
Robson Hall
Winnipeg, Manitoba
R3T 2N2
(204) 474-9773

Admissions and Placement Officer
Faculty of Law
McGill University
3644 Peel Street
Montreal, Québec
H3A 1W9
(514) 398-6602

École de droit
Université de Moncton
Moncton, N.B.
E1A 3E9
(506) 858-4564

Faculté de droit
Université de Montréal
C.P. 6128, Succursale "A"
Montréal, Québec
H3C 3J7
(514) 343-6200

Admissions Office
Faculty of Law
University of New Brunswick
P.O. Box 4400
Fredericton, N.B.
E3B 5A3
(506) 453-4693

The Admissions Officer
Osgoode Hall Law School
York University
4700 Keele Street
North York, Ontario
M3J 1P3
(416) 736-5040

Chair of the Admissions Committee
Faculty of Law
Common Law Section
University of Ottawa
57 Louis Pasteur
Ottawa, Ontario
KIN 6N5
(613) 564-4060

Faculté de droit
Civil Law Section
Université d'Ottawa
57 Louis Pasteur
Ottawa, Ontario
KIN 6N5
(613) 564-2254

Registrar
Faculty of Law
Macdonald Hall
Queen's University
Kingston, Ontario
K7L 3N6
(613) 545-2220

Admissions Committee
College of Law
University of Saskatchewan
Saskatoon, Saskatchewan
S7N 0W0
(306) 966-5874

Bureau du Registraire
Université de Sherbrooke
Sherbrooke, Québec
J1K 2R1
(819) 821-7514

Admissions Office
Faculty of Law
University of Toronto
78 Queen's Park
Toronto, Ontario
M5S 2C5
(416) 978-3716

Admissions
Faculty of Law
University of Victoria
P.O. Box 2400
Victoria, British Columbia
v8w 3H7
(604) 721-8151

Student Affairs Officer
Faculty of Law
The University of Western Ontario
London, Ontario
N6A 3K7
(519) 679-2111 ext. 8425

Admissions Office
Faculty of Law
University of Windsor
Windsor, Ontario
N9B 3P4
(519) 253-4232 extension 2925